W9-ADP-908

Greek tragedies have often been staged in the modern theater to comment on contemporary life. In an original, lively exploration of the modern performance and reinterpretation of ancient Greek drama, *Ancient Sun, Modern Light* by Marianne McDonald examines Greek tragedies by Aeschylus, Sophocles, and Euripides as performed under the direction of Suzuki Tadashi, Peter Sellars, Tony Harrison, Heiner Müller, and Thomas Murphy.

Ancient Greek plays are timeless because of their adaptability. Precise reworkings of these dramas make them extremely responsive to modern demands. Sellars, for example, directed Sophocles' *Ajax* to illustrate the corrupted power of the Pentagon. Müller's version of *Medea* made the connection between Jason's abuse of Medea and our own ecological abuse of the planet. The enduring appeal of Greek tragedy is its celebration of the redemptive power of individual human suffering, McDonald concludes.

Ancient Sun, Modern Light is supplemented by fascinating interviews conducted with Harrison about *The Trackers* (based on

(continued on back flap)

ANCIENT SUN, MODERN LIGHT

Greek Drama
on the Modern Stage

MARIANNE McDONALD

Columbia University Press
New York

WINGATE UNIVERSITY LIBRARY

COLUMBIA UNIVERSITY PRESS

NEW YORK   OXFORD

Copyright © 1992 Columbia University Press
All rights reserved

Library of Congress Cataloging-in-Publication Data

McDonald, Marianne.
  Ancient sun, modern light : Greek drama on the modern stage /
Marianne McDonald.
     p.   cm.
  Includes bibliographical references and index.
  ISBN 0–231–07654–1 (alk. paper)
  1. Greek drama—Presentation, Modern.   2. Greek drama—History and
criticism.   3. Theater—Production and direction.   I. Title.
PA3238.M37   1992
882'.0109—dc20   91–20995
                                                                          CIP

Casebound editions of Columbia University Press books are Smyth-sewn
and printed on permanent and durable acid-free paper

                                                                            ∞

Book design by Teresa Bonner
Printed in the United States of America

c 10 9 8 7 6 5 4 3 2 1

p 10 9 8 7 6 5 4 3 2 1

*To all those who have the courage to reshape the world
through their texts
To all those who have the courage to play
To all those who are free and who fight to preserve
the freedom of others*

CONTENTS

Illustrations follow p. 84

ACKNOWLEDGMENTS

M̲y ᴀᴘᴏʟᴏɢɪᴇs for the many who have helped me whom I may have omitted here. In some cases I have included thanks in the individual chapters. There are many nameless, yet I wish I could acknowledge my gratitude for the word or phrase which helped formulate an idea. I wish to thank those who have helped shape this manuscript and honored me with their time and friendship, expertise and suggestions: Professor Athan Anagnostopoulos, for the transcription and translation of the interview with Theodoros Terzopoulos, Professor George Anagnostopoulos, Doctor Dominick Addario, Professor Page duBois, Professor William Fitzgerald, Karla Holasek, Professor George Huxley, Doctor Adrian Jaffer, Professor Bernard Knox, Professor David Konstan, Professor Ed Lee, Professor Reinhard Lettau, Albert Liu, Professor Thomas MacCary, Bridget McDonald, Professor Miyoshi Masao, Wanda Roach, Professor Thomas Rosenmeyer, Professor Edward Said, Ikuko Saito, Professor Kate Stimpson, Professors Avrum and Mary Stroll, Professor Aiko Tada, Melia Tatakis, Professor Franco Tonelli, Professor Zeno Vendler, Roswitha Goeppert Woolley. Special thanks to Tony Harrison, Thomas

Murphy, Peter Sellars, Tadashi Suzuki, and Theodoros Terzopoulos for their talks and interviews, elucidating remarks and patience. Thanks also to the photographers who added the light of their illustrations, especially Micha Langer and Vicki Hallam. Thanks also to the editors and staff at Columbia University Press, especially Jennifer Crewe, Joan McQuary, Roy Thomas, and Leslie Bialler.

ANCIENT SUN, MODERN LIGHT

PROLOGUE

MY PRIMARY aim in presenting some modern adaptations of ancient Greek tragedies in this nondramatic format is to investigate how these classics are still alive and relevant to contemporary issues. What is it that makes these classics still exciting to us today?

Though I have been trained as a classical scholar and have spent most of my professional life in traditional philological studies, I have not been drawn to academic or conventional productions; rather I have sought out those creative writers and directors who have reinterpreted the classical texts for modern audiences. At the outset, then, important issues of theory and practice are raised, and I shall here attempt to deal with those issues before addressing individual productions in detail. We must therefore at least look at what "the classics" are, and I will begin to suggest ways in which they can be adapted. This could mean no less than a "philosophy of the relevant": how can the aesthetic, social, political, and religious dimensions of a work of art be shifted from one culture to another without losing its identity as a work of art?

The creative artists I am interested in have acknowledged this transference: for example, this is not Euripides' *Medea*, but Heiner Müller's *Medeamaterial*, and so forth. Nevertheless, Euripides is behind it all, and behind him is the myth. Indeed, I find it helpful to compare my selected modern artists' relation to their ancient sources to the ancient artists' relation to myth: there is no "Medea text" as such; it has been dissolved in the process of adaptation. As Claude Lévi-Strauss suggested, every literary adaptation of a myth becomes part of the myth. So Euripides, though he has formed our conception of the suffering of Medea, is not like a link in a chain, but rather like a catalyst in a solution: certain particles of the myth are precipitated out, but the others remain suspended. All this is available to our selected modern artists.

Today questions that ten or fifteen years ago were of interest only to academics revising their curricula of study have become more common, especially through the popular publications of critics such as Allan Bloom, E. D. Hirsch and John Silber, and through various political statements by such as those by former Secretary of Education William J. Bennett.[1] What exactly makes up our common cultural heritage? Should we privilege certain Western texts, establishing them as a canon of required reading, or attempt to supplement that canon with readings drawn from non-Western cultures and, within the West, with textual representation for minorities and women? Throughout this century, the notion of what precisely constitutes "the classics" has more and more become a political issue.

In Britain, even between the wars, and ever more vociferously now, knowledge of Greek and Latin came to be considered a mark of privilege and upper-class education first at Eton, Harrow, or Westminster, then at Oxford or Cambridge. So now such knowledge is disparaged for that very reason. Whereas throughout the eighteenth and nineteenth centuries speeches in both houses of Parliament were modeled after Thucydides and Cicero (and often contained frequent untranslated quotations from them and other historians and philosophers of Greece and Rome), such a reference today would be considered "political"; it might suggest that certain things do not change and that we can possibly learn from the past. Indeed, detractors would say that what must be changed is in fact the so-called wisdom received from the past: hierarchies, systems of authority, even the very notion of "history."

Somehow, also, the Western classics are charged with practicing a variation of Orientalism, a "disease" diagnosed by Edward Said, who exposes the Eurocentric view of the Orient: "The Orient was, therefore, not Europe's interlocutor, but its silent other."[2] Recall how Euripides depicted Helen's Phrygian slave in his *Orestes:* he spoke bad Greek; he was *barbaros*. In other words, therefore, the classics *can* be construed as alien infringements of local boundaries, as "weapons" of cultural imperialism used to supplant native literature.

In the United States, because many of the radical students who attempted to take over the universities in the 1960s have now in fact done so as deans, department heads, and "grievance officers," policies of hiring and firing faculty and revising curricula have been radically revised. Although young scholars in traditional disciplines such as textual criticism and source studies still get tenure at major universities, there is tremendous pressure on them to become "politically correct." They are expected to espouse the causes of feminism and gay liberation, not to mention righting the balance of representation for blacks, Hispanics, Asians, Native Americans, and other ethnic groups. No more drastic reordering of priorities can be imagined, and yet it has been quickly accomplished: scholars of previous generations were historically oriented in the sense that they tried to preserve the past; now scholars are actively reinterpreting the past to make it acceptable to the present and to assure that the future will not in the least resemble it. In literary studies this can take the form of defacing monuments: Shakespeare is abused for Prospero's mistreatment of Caliban; Aeschylus' *Oresteia* is seen as a vehicle for the "Politics of Misogyny" (to use Froma Zeitlin's phrase).[3]

What effect has this had on the study of Greek and Roman antiquity? Notoriously, things come late to the classics; it was well into the 1960s when the New Criticism of the 30s was first applied to classical texts. But the classics have never been the private property of classics departments. Further, if the classics were required additions to all curricula, one wonders if we would be more, or less, intolerant and imperialistic than we are?

T. S. Eliot and Frank Kermode have told us that the classic par excellence is the *Aeneid*, not the *Iliad* or the *Odyssey*. What continues to grip Virgil's readers is his complete integration of sex and politics in all their violent forms, what he calls *furor* and *pietas*. The *Aeneid* can easily be read as a protofascist tract justifying the channeling of erotic violence into the service of the state. What saves Virgil is his constant correction of his own Augustan themes: Is the future of Rome a false dream? Was not Italy a serene, pastoral landscape before Aeneas arrived? Why must Turnus die?

It seems to me that while the classics have been used in the modern period in various elitist programs—social, political, academic—their true essence is not in the projection of authority and dominion, but rather in their *humanitas*. This is nowhere more evident than in Greek tragedy. Jean Anouilh had to make the character of Antigone unattractive in his adaptation of Sophocles' play in order to get it produced during the German occupation of Paris, but it still became a rallying point for the French Resistance. Before that, Hegel had disparaged Antigone's resistance to the state, and productions of *Antigone* were blacklisted by the Greek colonels after their coup in 1967. Hegel disparages Antigone's resistance to the state. Martha Nussbaum in *The Fragility of Goodness,* her study of the philosophical argument of Greek tragedy, was faulted by Richard Wollheim for failing to take into account the psychology of heroes. Though political and philosophical uses have been made of Greek tragedy, surely its constant appeal is rather its celebration of the redemptive power of individual human suffering. I am convinced that this aspect, in our generation, is what has attracted our greatest creative artists to Greek tragedy.

Now I must admit to certain complexities in the process of adaptation. First, we do not live in a heroic age, and much of the suffering depicted in these modern adaptations generally seems more generic than individual. Second, we know that the Greeks did not tolerate sex and violence on stage in their tragic festivals, which were civic and religious rituals; yet many of the modern adaptations accost us with every conceivable atrocity. What has happened and why?

Very briefly, I would like to define Greek idealism and suggest the ways in which each of my modern adapters has dealt with it. I shall proceed quite simply, by comparing Plato's concept of *methexis* and Aristotle's distinction between *dynamis* and *energeia*. In the mature dialogues of Plato, after he has developed his theory of the forms, he insists that particulars only "participate" in universals.

The universal has absolute existence separate and apart from any example thereof: there is a Form "tableness" in which a particular table only partakes. Aristotle challenged this, maintaining that universals exist only in particulars. His model for the relationship was taken from the natural world: each plant and each animal has an innate "potential," *dynamis*, which can reach "fulfillment," *energeia*, in its maturity. If we apply this distinction to Greek heroism, which is the fullest expression of Greek idealism and the particular concern of Greek tragedy, we see these projections. The individual hero, Antigone, or Ajax, or Hercules, according to the Platonic model, can only approach but can never completely achieve the Form of Heroism; according to the Aristotelian model, however, heroism is simply the fulfillment, and nothing more, of the individual hero's capacity to be heroic.

From our perspective there might not seem to be so great a difference between Plato's and Aristotle's notions of the hero, and that is because we do not look at the world as they both did, in terms of tendencies toward perfection; we are not idealists. We see each individual as unique, complete, in and of his or possibly her own self; if we think of this person somewhat generic on more specific terms as American, a teacher of Greek, gray-haired, we are categorizing her but not seeing her in relation to the ideal of her type. In other words, we tend to level, whereas the Greeks sought to elevate. The dramatists I am going to discuss call our attention to particular phenomena—war, rape, murder—but they never suggest that there is anything behind or beyond that phenomenon. If anything, their adaptations gain their power through a kind of stylized theatrical repetition, seldom through a naturalistic chronological development, and never through transcendence. There is, however, always a resonance with the Greek originals from which these modern versions have come.

At the same time, however, the dramatists in my study show us a faceless universe. One might have thought that focusing on the particulars would make us think of those particulars as somehow unique, but these artists do not aim for that. Hecuba in Suzuki's *Trojan Women* is not specifically Hecuba, but rather "the Bereaved Mother"; the quirkiness of Euripides' original is lost. But, lest I begin to sound like one of those classical scholars who think we are all deprived because we do not live in fifth-century Athens, I must hasten to explain that I think these modern adapters of ancient tragedy do what they do very well. We cannot put ourselves back in the theater of Dionysus in 415 B.C. and experience *The Trojan Women* as Euripides' first audience did. I think these modern adapters do what dramatists should do—that is to depict the world in which we live. The world they depict is fragmented; they litter their stages with the debris of modern life. Their sufferers are not remarkable for any unique characteristics; how can suffering be special after Hiroshima?

The proposition logically presents itself that there is a new generation of artists adapting ancient tragedy and they should be compared with the previous generation; Anouilh, Jean-Paul Sartre, Jean Giraudoux created fine drama out of Aeschylus, Sophocles, and Euripides. I think it useful to consider them as "modernists" and my group—Suzuki Tadashi, Peter Sellars, Heiner Müller, Tony Harrison, and Thomas Murphy—as "postmodernists." For the previous generation the ancient tragedies were still patterns; they held them up and drew their drama out of the friction created with their own.[4] The current generation sees no patterns, no sense to the suffering. They can only show us scene after scene of the same suffering. The difference, then, is that modernists could still make collages out of the fragments of the past, but we cannot; for us everything is just bits and pieces.

The classics are works that have survived. The ancient Greek classics—particularly the tragedies, which are my focus—have been filtered through time. From about one hundred twenty-three plays by Sophocles we have seven, the same for Aeschylus (although he may have written only about ninety), and nineteen by Euripides, who also seems to have written fewer than Sophocles, and perhaps just a few more than Aeschylus. Ten of Euripides' and the seven by each of the other main playwrights of Greek antiquity survive largely because of a Roman canon: they were taught in schools as the best by these authors. The other nine of Euripides' plays were found in an alphabetical treasure trove, a fourteenth-century manuscript discovered by chance. This manuscript was probably a copy of one out of eight or nine of the original codices that contained all of his works. Only in his case do we have a random selection of ancient Greek drama.

In addition to theory, and in some cases in spite of it, one must consider the dramatic presentation itself. One should also allow for "play" at the crux of a good play: playful accidents can be more evocative than words. Euripides is condemned by Aristotle for plays like *The Trojan Women* which merely exploit the pathetic, leading to Aristotle's calling Euripides the most tragic of the tragedians, not intending this as much of a compliment. Nietzsche also thinks Euripides debased Dionysus' art; Euripides makes it too Apollonian, too rational, and even introduces the lower classes on the stage and, worst of all, employs their "vulgar" language. Aristotle and Nietzsche also agree on the reprehensible temerity of Euripides in making a woman intelligent.

The Trojan Women has been called the most powerful antiwar drama ever written. Sartre has a version called *Les Troyennes*, in which he claims, "The gods are killed with the men, and that common death is the lesson of the tragedy."[5] Michael Cacoyannis performed *The Trojan Women* on Broadway, and made it into a film. Suzuki chose to use it in a Japanese setting depicting the agony following Hiroshima; a Japanese woman identifies with Hecuba and reenacts the play as her present catharsis. Tony Harrison in *Common Chorus* has women perform Euripides' *Trojan Women* for the soldiers at the nuclear installation at Greenham Common in England. Performances in this case have shown that this play has survived the criticism of the past and provides the new criticism of the present. As Harrison says in his *Lysistrata*, "So don't say it's just a bunch of ancient Greeks / It's their tears that will be flowing down your cheeks."

Harrison uses one of his final images to voice a note of hope, contrary to Sartre's interpretation of *Trojan Women* as ending in "total nihilism." Hecuba proceeds to her "day" of slavery, and day is a source of light. To say a person still looked on the light in Homer meant that he was still alive. Light might also be equivalent to the *anagnorisis* in tragedy; to see the light may be the tragic perception that can lead to catharsis and a new commitment to life. It is the alternation of light and dark that makes perception possible, and affirmation can be defined by negation. Friedrich Hölderlin expressed this well, in his epigram to Sophocles: "Manche versuchen umsonst, das Freudigste freudig zu sagen; hier spricht endlich es mir, hier in der Trauer sich aus'' (Many have tried in vain to express the height of happiness in terms of happiness, but finally here I have found it expressed, here in tragedy).

It is difficult to abstract just what quality makes a play survive, or creates a powerful impact on an audience, such that it is revived again and again, satisfying similar yet ever fresh needs. In the case of the *Trojan Women*, suffering, defeat, loss, and death are the themes and these are certainly constants in the history of human-kind. But it is not enough to show the occurrence of tragic mile-stones, one must also provide commentary, particularly in the inter-action of the protagonists—their emotional commentary. Acting and staging are important incarnations of a text that moves. Emo-tional reaction, however, cannot be the sole method of judgment, unless we accept T. S. Eliot's claim that "every precise emotion tends towards intellectual formulation," as he earlier claimed of Sophocles and Shakespeare, "All great poetry gives the illusion of a view of life."[6]

In judging a play, perhaps we should emulate the Platonic model of the soul as a chariot with driver (the rational: informed judgment) and horses (the irrational: emotions and appetites). Both elements must come into play in the decision of an expert.

Aristotle said that ancient tragedy was more philosophical than history because it spoke in generalities whereas history spoke of particulars. Sophocles was said to speak of men as they ought to be, and Euripides of men as they were, so Sophocles might be considered the poet of the ideal; but Euripides, showing a dramatic exactitude comparable to historical exactitude, was the one who dealt with particulars. He has been called the first psychologist. Generalities may be more clearly retained in modern representations; a particular is more easily lost. We can see the parallel between Hecuba's sorrow and any person's sorrow following a war, but we do not thrill as the ancients did to the appearance of a god in a magic chariot, and the latter is frequently omitted in modern performances. So also the clasping of knees in a traditional suppliant's appeal does not have the same resonance for a modern audience as it did in the fifth century B.C.

The potential purpose of a drama somehow plays a role. The success of that purpose may determine a classic. But there are also many examples of failures in this sense: the *Trojan Women* did nothing to alter the brutality of the Peloponnesian War. But still playing the classics can be a way of expressing discontent with a regime that would censor the performance of a modern play. *Antigone* is one that has been so used. Andrzej Wajda, for instance, has a version with the chorus dressed in miners' helmets, and they represent Solidarity as much as Antigone in their cries for freedom. This version was performed in Delphi in June 1989, so that June's omen has become today's reality. Sometimes a classic provides a "safe" means for criticizing a present regime, and as Peter Weiss says explicitly in his *Marat/Sade*, "After all, we are only talking about the past."

There is a debate about whether drama is to please or to educate; many plays have an ideological thrust. Power can be achieved by identification or alienation, sometimes both. We see how Bertolt Brecht used his *Verfremdungseffekt* to educate, but also to shock a person out of complacency. Sophocles does this with his heroes, who each have an alienating component, if just from their obvious isolation; Ajax and Oedipus come immediately to mind.

Euripides instead forces us to identify with the victims. His plot also will show his characters not alienated, but overconnected, as Agamemnon is to Iphigenia, or Orestes to Electra. Iphigenia is sacrificed by Agamemnon in what resembles a marriage ritual, the sham pretext by which she is lured to Aulis; but the only marriage is to her father's lust for power and to the army's lust for victory. So also Orestes' incestuous relation to his sister, suggested by Euripides, is visually enacted by Suzuki, and is a correlation to his murdering his mother as a kind of rape, the ultimate supplantation of the father. Both Cacoyannis in his film *Iphigenia* (Greece 1977), and Suzuki in his *Clytemnestra*, visually suggest sexual intertwinings in addition to the other themes.

There are many criteria, and as many critics. Perhaps the artistic judgment that enters into determining a classic is based on something like a mean, much as virtue is defined by Aristotle as a mean. Contrary to mathematics, Aristotle sees ethics as an inexact science, and those who best determine the main principles are an educated elite. So also one might envision something comparable for art critics and art creators. This elite, or intellectual, artistic hegemony should be open to anyone with a bit of talent who is willing to take the time to be educated, and the principles would vary with the circumstance. Since Gödel and Heisenberg, we see that even our knowledge of the universe is incomplete and indeterminable, and Wittgenstein showed this for language, which he considered the last philosophical frontier. We must avoid essentialism while skirting chaos. That is why the Aristotelian mean in this case may provide the nonconstricting answer, being neither trivial nor too exact.

I would also argue that criticism should not be strangled by its own rhetoric. We should not simply write or speak in our limited areas of specialization, thus ensuring an audience that is limited or excluded, but instead we should broaden our discourse. As I favor tampering with the classics, I favor breaking out of our categories; we should even commit the ultimate sin and try to communicate in a clear way, so that what we say can be understood by the nonspecialist.

At a conference on Heiner Müller's works in Berlin the participants were classified as *Denker* ("thinker": scholar, critic, and dramaturg) or *Arbeiter* ("worker": actor, director, artist, composer), and I felt properly insulted since I was a mere *Denker*. This classification was a warning about panels: which ones would be boring but to be tolerated (one *had* to invite *some* scholars) and which would be interesting—those given by people who described what they were "doing" rather than merely "thinking." And then there was the actor's own delivery and interpretation to be considered. At a conference, how can you compete with a sensitively delivered speech? Antony will always outshine Brutus. At a conference on ancient drama at Delphi, I gave a joint paper with an actor, Barrie Rutter, who played Papposilenus in *The Trackers;* he delivered lines from Tony Harrison's reworking of Sophocles, *Ichneutai* (*The Trackers of Oxyrhynchus*) in Leeds dialect. So that is one way to cope at a conference. I feel one should see territories as organically overflowing rather than staked out. At conferences we must eschew esoteric language and abandon all hierarchies: critics should learn from directors and directors from actors.

So also in print I would argue for communication over scholarly self-indulgence—and no jargon. This involves some risk, because a clear position opens you to clear attack. But that seems so much more interesting than for everyone to assume safe, fashionable stances backed by massive bibliographies and stable professional positions. Brendan Kinnelly has spoken of these posturings as ". . . thoughts like old coats wrapped round a freezing mind . . . fashions in clothes and writing almost cause me to scream in the street."[7]

The *Arbeiter* must join the *Denker*, and art I believe cannot be isolated from its historical and political context. The place of the interpreter may be to translate some of the messages with reference to original and present plateaus locating them on a contour map for an audience that may not have full access to original and present notations.

Although this can be dangerous and can lead to some constricting canon, perhaps each country should evolve its own elite, educating those interested on their own various campuses and in their own developing theaters, and eventually having them determine their own classics. In many cases this has already been done, or is in the process of formation. Also, the words "elite" and "canon" now seem to be nasty ones in our postmodern vocabulary—but whenever a theatrical season is determined, an elite has chosen its canon. We simply have to recognize what happens when such choices are made.

In the case of ancient classics we have the added problem of a dead language. Language and culture are barriers that are crossed with difficulty; however, the attempt to share should be made. Hooray, to Jonathan Miller, who, Jim Carmody says, "has been willing to visit the past as a foreign country and to reject the notion of classic text as an instance of a generic dramatic 'universality.' "[8] We need particular translations and performances for particular works. Classical drama should be like a foreign land, understood, respected and admired for its particularity. We should remember Hugo of St. Victor: "The man who finds his homeland sweet is still a tender beginner; he to whom every soil is as his native one is already strong; but he is perfect to whom the entire world is as a foreign land."

Time we have seen as the touchstone of a classic, and history provides the salt to season the production. With every classic we have at least two historical and cultural contexts—the past in which the drama was written, and the present in which it is being performed. Each must inform the other.

Our time particularly appreciates Greek drama, and George Steiner in speaking of the various classics that have survived, noted that instead of Shakespeare, "It is, on the contrary, Oedipus and Electra, Antigone and the Eumenides, who have been given incessant voice in twentieth-century high theatre and poetry."[9] He ventures to explain this "eternal return": "it is myth and its commitment to transcendence which generate, which compel, the dynamics of recursion, of repetition (that 'asking again') across time."[10]

These myths allow us to see our own inner demons, and now these demons can lead us to irrevocable decisions. We can direct these inner "demonic forces" outward toward the enemy, without realizing that the enemy could very well be ourselves. This century's technology enables the human race for the first time to commit suicide in the guise of murder. So perhaps Greek tragedy speaks to us most eloquently when it asks us to look death in the face. In modern times this death has become collective, but perhaps a personal choice may still have some effect on avoiding the final apocalyptic catharsis.

Theater is one of the last repositories of thought. Television with its sitcoms, soaps and video games is one of the more insidious drugs infiltrating the world. We see also that even war can be represented as an elaborate video game; we concentrate on "hits" rather than losses or human deaths. We are losing the ability to think and reason, enslaved instead by the image that demands no response on our part besides the simple act of perception. We should restore danger to television and encourage the performance of plays that demand a response on our part. We must also encourage the performance of plays in theaters and make them more financially accessible to all people. Local productions should be a part of every grade school, high school, or university. The heritage of the classics should not be given only to the elite, but allowed to enter the dialectic of a wide public that represents the diversity of our country.

I consider the productions of the plays discussed in this book successful, and I shall now make a few suggestions about why they succeed. We all know (although "we all know" is a dangerous statement) why some productions fail; A Kabuki Macbeth, for instance, which was performed in La Jolla in 1989, was an example, I think, of destroying the good elements in both Kabuki and Macbeth. The physical training of the former was missing, as was the language of the latter, and in the process only a ludicrous reduction was accomplished.

Another clear failure in my opinion was a performance I saw in

1989 in Delphi of *Philoctetes* put on by an Italian company. There was only one character, mainly in a cave, "conversing" with a television set. This essentially eliminated tragic conflict. I tend to think that tragedy necessarily involves human conflict, and without the physical presence of Neoptolemus or Odysseus this tragedy is reduced to solipsistic musings. This tired message that we are victims of the media displaced the real medium of tragedy.

Is this truly a new tragic conflict operating in a modern setting? What might it mean to posit that conflict only occurs as a passive activity before the television where an agon exists not as one force polemically aligned against another, but as a passive technology, influencing without a will a passive receptor equally lacking a will? Or is this simply irony and no longer tragedy? Is it a form of the postmodern pastiche replacing parody, as Fredric Jameson has suggested, since the judgment or referent underlying parody is no longer present?[11]

Conflict and questioning are vital to ancient tragedy; man must ask questions even if it leads to his own destruction (as it did in Oedipus' case), because without the questions he is a puppet, not a man. Plato said the unexamined life is not worth living, and Julien Benda bemoans that modern intellectuals no longer ask questions, but have instead become the spokespeople of regimes.[12] Good drama asks questions. It does not matter if these questions are unanswerable, at least they must be asked.

Aeschylus shows god questioning god, Sophocles shows man questioning god, and finally Euripides shows man questioning himself. Modern reworkings of classics question the present in terms of the past, and new insights can be gained that are not only essential for understanding but for the survival of the human race.

The productions of plays I consider successful and which are the subject of my investigation all ask questions, or show conflict. The first are three plays directed by Suzuki Tadashi, *The Trojan Women* and *The Bacchae* (based on Euripides' plays), and *Clytemnestra* (based on *The Oresteia* by Aeschylus, *Electra* by Sophocles, and *Electra* and *Orestes* by Euripides); then Sophocles' *Ajax*, directed by Peter Sellars, translated and transformed by Robert Auletta; then Tony Harrison's *The Trackers* (based on Sophocles' *Ichneutai*); Heiner Müller's *Verkommenes Ufer Medeamaterial Landschaft mit*

Argonauten (somewhat derived from Euripides' *Medea*); and finally Thomas Murphy's *The Sanctuary Lamp*, with its allusions to Aeschylus' *Oresteia*.

Suzuki translates much of the ancient texts into Japanese, but with additions and variations he does create something new. Sellars' *Ajax* is close to the original, but also new by provocative means of staging and textual expansion. Harrison's *The Trackers* is closer to Sophocles' play than his *Medea*, but both provide original poetry and novel productions. Müller translates only to deconstruct: a word here, a word there, sails at us in verbal assault. Murphy read *The Oresteia* and remembers some of the themes; the text of his play has the feel of a classic remembered.

Successful revivals of classics often connect with issues that are vital to a modern audience. They can range from literal translations and imitations of what one supposes the originals to have been like to the most avant-garde versions that fragment the classical themes, using them simply as an alphabet. Just as Aristotle's moral man must make a judgment, so the critic and audience has to use a mean, and prior experience, to determine whether the revival or re-creation is a success. I do not believe that value judgments are null and void because "truth" is problematic. Certain constructs, perceptions, and intuitions have more validity than others. Recall Boswell's claim that everyone knew that what Bishop Berkeley thought about the nonexistence of matter was false, but he could not refute it. Johnson's response was to kick a stone saying, "I refute it *thus!*" Likewise, by our daily choices we all refute the postmodern philosophic pastiche that denies objective values.

I shall now simply give an overview of what I will be treating in more detail in each chapter. Suzuki's three plays are each studies of power and its abuse in public and private contexts. He takes elements from Noh and Kabuki, recent Japanese history, coupled with a rigorous physical training for his actors, and revives the Greek classics, injecting the life of these Western signifiers into his own theatrical and historical tradition.

In *The Trojan Women* we see the devastation that America has visited on Japan (if only the aftermath of Hiroshima). A survivor imagines herself as Hecuba and relives the ancient tragedy in terms of her present situation. The Japanese god Jizo is as impotent for shaping events as the ancient gods Poseidon and Athena were arbitrary. As usual, men are swatted for the gods' sport, or as Euripides and Suzuki might see it, women for the sport of men.

In *Clytemnestra* we have a particularly Noh-oriented drama dealing with a wife and mother who succeeds in destroying a husband and son, a nightmare of the *amae* society. We remember Doi Takeo's book, *The Anatomy of Dependence* [*amae*], describing the destructive dialectic of dependence as it is particularly manifested in Japan.[13] Orestes is eventually slain by Clytemnestra, who has returned as a ghost and impales Orestes while he is in an incestuous embrace with his sister. Clytemnestra is typical of the ghosts in Noh drama, returning in a jealous rage and exacting from the living the revenge they could not exact in life. This nightmare fantasy is an obvious corollary to the place of women in Japan; it represents vengeance for suppression. Like women in fifth-century Athens, Japanese women are for the most part relegated to the domestic sphere. The husbands work in the outside world and given their usual late hours and numerous workdays, they return home on a long-term basis only when they retire. Suzuki's *Clytemnestra* shows what could be waiting for them at home.

In *The Bacchae* we see Japan in the form of Dionysus exacting vengeance on America in the guise of Pentheus. The irrational dismembers the rational, just as the Japanese cartels are dismembering American industry (as America earlier dismembered Japan after the war). The magical ritualistic enslaving of Pentheus is a gruesome expansion by Suzuki of Euripides' text. Dionysus leads Pentheus off to his death in a ritualistic dance, in which he is shown as little more than a puppet. Suzuki's incorporation of elements from Bunraku, (the Japanese puppet theater), provides additional ominous symbolic commentary.

The presentation by La Jolla Playhouse of Sophocles' *Ajax*, via Auletta's translation from Sophocles, with Peter Sellars directing, is an excellent example of a play being successfully placed in a modern context (it takes place in front of the Pentagon, after a recent skirmish in Latin America). It shows how the military abuses its powers and seeks absolute control through its manipulation of sources of information. This adaptation/translation retains much of the ancient text, although reworked in places and translated into idiomatic English. Additions to the text, the new setting and the innovative casting all add up to a modern political commentary of which Noam

Chomsky would have been proud. What happens here illustrates the manufactured public consent that pervasively operates through well-controlled media.

Sellars' *Ajax* deals with the theme of communication and of words as power. He shows the military trying to suppress facts to shore up their own position. His own production is a defiant act directed against this control, and in a talk he gave in Vienna (reprinted in this volume) he said that art is the last refuge for truth: people now only listen as they indulge in their recreation.

Both Sellars and Suzuki have characters played by people of different races. Sellars even has a black Athena in *Ajax*, which choice he claims is serendipitous. Although this might have been by chance, the result leads to edged political commentary, and particularly apt since the appearance of Martin Bernal's book *Black Athena*, which shows the great debt European culture, based on Greek culture, owes to Africa and the Middle East.[14]

Suzuki, on the other hand, uses the different races to express certain conflicts and confrontations. Clytemnestra and Tyndareus are played by Japanese and they convey ancient times versus the modern as represented by Orestes, who is played by an American Caucasian. In the *Bacchae*, Bacchus is played by Shiraishi Kayoko and Pentheus by Thomas Hewitt and there seems to be an obvious confrontation between Japan and America, East versus West. These are two examples of the use of racial and cultural differences, an issue raised at a conference on "The Classics in Contemporary Theater" at the University of California, San Diego (February 1990). "Minorities" can be used at random or as additional signifiers. "Minorities" obviously also differ as to locale. In some places it is amusing to have the few token white Europeans. In Japan they are generally the villains and in martial art movies are often quite knowledgeable about jujitsu or karate (the Japanese hero, on the other hand, generally knows judo).

Settings for new productions may differ from the very modern (the Pentagon in Sellars' *Ajax*) to the very ancient (Tony Harrison's setting for *The Trackers* was in Delphi's stadium). So also settings can be religious (Thomas Murphy's Orestian Delphi becomes a Catholic church in *The Sanctuary Lamp*) or secular (Müller's trash heap with World War II memorabilia for *Medeamaterial*). Harrison follows ancient tradition by using masks in his *Oresteia*, saying that the mask forces a person to look on horror and the eyes cannot close; so also the audience sees tragedy and is forced to come to terms with matters usually avoided, particularly those involving death. Harrison uses the ancient mask to force moderns to face their present tragedy: the ancient tragedy is itself a mask.

Harrison says a mask allows one to face truth. A play necessarily involves some artificiality,, but the play can also function as a mirror of reality. The only way to face Medusa, the Gorgon, without turning to stone is by looking via a reflection, and good drama in this case is an active mirror: it does make us look! One is protected (the theme is old) but one must see (these things happen now). Plato recognized the danger of plays, and we should cultivate this danger. We should prefer Gorgias, who claimed that he who lies is the most just, and he who is deceived is the most wise.[15] The playwright is a clever liar who allows us to approach truth through the mirror of his play.

After Suzuki and Sellars, I will be treating two of Tony Harrison's plays. He sounds an antiwar theme in all his works, but in *The Trackers* and *Medea, A Sex War Opera*, the war is generalized to one of culture and the sexes respectively. There is again the question of power and who has it, who abuses it, and how. In the first play, art is the prize and Apollo would keep it for himself. But his satyrs rebel, and precious papyri are burned (or used for needs more immediate than reading). The lyre cedes to the ghetto blaster, and past yields to present which involves sharing or destruction. The question is raised whether art is viable when people are starving. The result is obvious; what is not offered freely will be taken, or destroyed. Papyri will be used for survival, not perusal; they will be burned for heat, or layered for blankets.

The Trackers shows the otherness of the past and of art, particularly the elitism of specialized education. There is horror at the abuses (such as those told of in the fable of Marsyas, who dared to take up Athena's flute and challenge Apollo; he was flayed for his insolence). He represents all who have challenged the possession of art by the gods, or by society's elite. But the play also conveys regret concerning the neglect of education, a lack that will prevent our return to a past whose language we cannot speak and whose mentality we cannot understand since we do not know its context.

Harrison's *Medea* involves the terrorizing of each sex by the other, advocating another look at the "other." Once again, while coexistence with celebration of otherness is advocated, mutual obliteration is shown. Both plays end in isolation, noncommunication, and destruction.

Heiner Müller's *Verkommenes Ufer Medeamaterial Landschaft mit Argonauten* shows a world violated by man as Medea was violated by Jason. Theodoros Terzopoulos takes the pieces of Müller's fragmented vision and assembles a mosaic of ritualistic repetition; he exorcises despair by merging the wartime experiences of Germany in World War II and its aftermath, and in modern Greece, during and following this war. He uses the body movements of ritual dancers from Thrace as Suzuki uses the ritualized movements from Noh drama to express the agony of the postwar victim. Terzopoulos via Müller also uses the unconscious as a weapon to destroy rationality and to express the logic of the body, as if it were the atavistic memory of man. Whereas Harrison suggests alternatives, Müller's landscape is one of total devastation, and the present is simply the garbage pile of the past, with humanity about to be added to the heap.

Thomas Murphy uses Ireland as his tool for dissecting the present. He investigates man's role in relation to his fellow man and god, or perhaps man and his image of god. *The Sanctuary Lamp* achieves a catharsis of guilt through the enacted play which is influenced by both Aeschylus and the Catholic Church. A legal trial (such as depicted at the end of the *Eumenides*) and a formal confession (as found in the Catholic Church) are replaced by communal drinking and conversation—still the preferred mode of confession in Ireland today. The play ends with the hope of a new day, and some of dawn's warmth is generated by the heart of man.

The two major traditions that have shaped the West are the Judeo-Christian and the Hellenic. The former is oriented more toward God, while the latter is oriented more toward man; the former toward the law, and the latter towards negotiation. Murphy merges the two, but clearly opts for man. He would agree with Heracles, who told Theseus that the man who would choose wealth and power over friends is mad. Human interaction, as expressed by the Greek term *philia*, is what Euripides offers as a counter to the chaotic universe that he perceived he lived in, and what the gods in a whimsical moment might have provided. Murphy in *The Sanctuary*

Lamp shows the lamp lit and tended by man. The playwright carries on this light and fire in his revival of the ancient revelations.

I think it is clear that I do not regard the classics as imperialistic weapons. A classic may arise in any country and enter the realm of immortal signifiers; it is up to us how we choose to use it. The ancient Greek dramatists had special messages that deserve resending by moderns. The ultimate test will be further survival. People listen if they are affected. The classics also provide a frisson of recognition and puzzle pieces to be rearranged by those familiar with their past. Each country has its own classics to inform its present, but I concentrate on the Greeks whose influence has ranged not only throughout the world but time.

Frank Kermode ended his study of "the classic" by saying, "So the image of the imperial classic, beyond time, beyond vernacular corruption and change, had perhaps, after all, a measure of authenticity; all we need do is bring it down to earth." And our earth now is diverse. We are urged in this postmodern age to refine our sensitivities to difference and to increase our tolerance of incommensurability. I would argue that the classics have now become "other," and that we should celebrate the difference of the model.[16]

and signaled a theatrical revolution; he introduced a new approach to theatrical production and acting. He also presented Western theater to Japan in a unique way. We shall first look at Suzuki's career and place him historically in the context of both Japanese and international drama. Then we shall look at his method and finally at the dramatic presentations themselves.

Until the Meiji revolution in 1868, Japan was essentially cut off from the Western world. The Tokugawa period (1603–1867) was known as a period of national isolation. In the Meiji period (1868–1912), and continuing throughout the Taisho (1912–1926) and Showa (1927 to the present), there was a turn outward and a new interest in Western cultural development.

One can say that Western theater was first introduced in Japan with the translations of Shakespeare in 1871. There were several performances of Shakespeare in Japanese: for instance, in 1885 a performance of *The Merchant of Venice* in Kabuki style, and a performance of *Julius Caesar* in 1901 by the *Shin-pa* or "New School." Of course, the older Japanese forms such as Bugaku, Noh, Kyogen, Bunraku, and Kabuki continued while these experiments in Western drama were being made.[1]

Even newer schools were Tsubouchi's *Bungei Kyokai* and Osanai Kaoru's *Tsukiji Sho-Gekijo*, and they represented the "New Drama" (*Shin-geki*). These groups had even closer ties with the West, taking less and less from the traditional Japanese dramatic forms. Professor Takahashi Yasunari (Tokyo University) has pointed out that besides a somewhat slavish imitation of Western dramatic presentations, namely a realistic rendering of the text, what was thought to be the philosophy was also conveyed (i.e. "the belief in the rational psychological motivation of all human behaviors, and also the underlying assumption that the ultimate standard of reality is logical explicability").[2] This Eastern perception of the Western mind, as revealed in Western drama, is fascinating: it was that which seemed so radically different from their own worldview that they focused on.

At first, there were literal representations. Osanai, the founder of the *Shin-geki* school, gave performances of Chekhov and Ibsen as he had observed them on their native stages. His disciple Senda Koreya led the "Actors' Studio," *Hai-yu-za*, in presentations of Brecht; a *Shin-geki* joint production of Chekhov's *The Cherry Orchard* took place in 1945 after the war.

This originally leftist-oriented theater became the new ortho-
doxy. It was supposed to represent the "people's" views, and yet, in
fact, it was an intellectually elitist theater. It ignored the traditional
popular forms of theater, such as Bunraku, Kabuki, Rakugo, and
Manzai, and also gave priority to simple renditions of the text, in
the belief that the truth of drama was mainly in the word rather
than the method of performance.

The Little Theater movement in the late 1960s criticized this
Shin-geki approach. One of these groups was headed by Kara Juro
and was called the *Jokyo Gekijo*. It was also called *aka-tento* because
of the red tent in which performances were held; another group, led
by Sato Makoto, was called *kuro-tento*, "black tent." Suzuki was
the most original and dynamic of this new movement and founded
the *Waseda Sho-Gekijo* in 1966.

Suzuki's first productions were *The Little Match Girl* by Betsuyaku
Minoru, *A Girl's Mask* by Kara Juro, and *On the Dramatic
Passions* (Part I) by Suzuki himself. This last tells of a mentally
deranged woman who is kept in her room by her family; she dreams
that she is the heroine of several Kabuki and Shin-pa plays. She
takes the roles and projects the image, as Takahashi says, of "unre-
quited passions and savage resentments."[3] This play certainly leads
to his later treatment of classical plays: *The Trojan Women, The
Bacchae*, and *Clytemnestra*. In each case, individual fantasies are
acted out according to classical roles; Suzuki wrote these parts specifically for Shiraishi Kayoko, the magnificently talented actress who
embodies Suzuki's whole theatrical mission.

Here we should see that Suzuki has reintroduced the actor as the
theatrical priority. He has often been compared to Jerzy Grotowski,
who with his "Theater of the Poor" not only represented themes of
the people, but demanded rigorous training and devoted performances from his actors. For instance, Grotowski was known to
demand that an actor fall from a rather dangerous height if he
wished to convey "falling from a height."

The training Suzuki requires demands complete commitment from
his actors; it aims at making drama truly dramatic and involving by
establishing a common psychological resonance: they "bond" together. Acting is also to begin with physical exercise, and the actor
is to develop his body as well as his method of delivery.

Suzuki has reintroduced Bunraku, Kabuki, and Noh, the traditional forms of Japanese theater, into his drama. He also incorporates theories from the martial arts. Even popular songs find their way into his plays. Perhaps Kabuki and the songs represent the theater of the people, but the Noh drama and martial arts are elitist forms. Both Kabuki and Noh are considered traditional, however, since they flourished in the Tokugawa period. One might say that the opening to the West was a form of popularization, certainly introducing democratic ideas that in many ways are still foreign to Japanese culture. Suzuki has somehow made a successful synthesis of uniquely Western and uniquely Eastern forms of art, ranging from the most elitist to the most popular, in some cases even vulgar (e.g., Marlboro wastebaskets on the set of *Clytemnestra*).

It has been said that Shiraishi, Suzuki's main actress, is the reincarnation of Okuni, who founded Kabuki in the seventeenth century. In any case she brings a dynamic, almost supernatural intensity to the stage, and this involves the audience in a close physical sharing of the action. One can compare the religious basis of the Greek drama.

Japanese costumes, traditional stage movements and movements from the martial arts, and the dimension of fantasy are all peculiarly Japanese elements in this new style. Suzuki has said that his *Trojan Women* may owe more to Kabuki, but his *Clytemnestra* more to Noh (the latter shows Clytemnestra returning as a ghost to kill the two children who were instrumental in her own death).

Ghosts are much more important in Noh and other Eastern dramatic traditions than in Western drama; Shakespeare is an exception in this respect, as in many others. Perhaps it is because of the ghosts of Banquo, Hamlet's father, and Caesar that the Japanese were first drawn to him. We might compare Akira Kurosawa's *Throne of Blood* (Japan, 1957), with its introduction of a ghostlike figure who spins as she tells the future to Macbeth. This ghost and the misty forest, in which the major protagonists seem lost for hours, add an especially eerie element that one also finds in Noh drama and many of Suzuki's treatments.

Both Kurosawa and Suzuki have presented us with their interpretations of *King Lear*, the former in the movie *Ran* (Japan-France, 1985) and the latter in a production that was first mounted in 1984. Suzuki's *Lear* suggests that all the action is taking place in Lear's mind. The line between reality and hallucination is blurred.

Suzuki gave this performance along with Chekhov's *The Three Sisters*, which he treats as a form of comedy. The sisters sit on a couch with parasols, and two male figures keep popping up from vases next to them. There is a scene where they sit on cushions and food is brought in. There is also a masturbation scene to illustrate the solipsistic world of the sisters. Suzuki makes dramatic innovations as they contribute to his dramatic conception.

There are other interpretations of Western drama in Japan, and, of course, Western productions using Japanese talent. In Greece there was a performance from the La Mama Theater of New York of *The Myth of Oedipus* in 1985. Tanaka Min was the choreographer and chief actor/performer in this dance drama. *Medea* has been put on by Ninagawa Yukio, who is known for his Kabuki interpretations, in 1987. This had an all-male cast (in the Kabuki tradition) and generally received good reviews for its acting. Ninagawa also performed *Macbeth* in England in 1988, with samurai costumes and in Japanese.

In 1970 Suzuki performed *On the Dramatic Passions* (Part II) and reaffirmed the emphasis he placed on the priority of acting, besides combining the dramatic effect of original staging and arrangement of actors. As is often the case, international acclaim preceded national recognition. Suzuki was invited to the Theatre des Nations in Paris by Jean-Louis Barrault in 1972. In 1973 he performed *On the Dramatic Passions* at the Nancy Festival and in the Theatre Recamier in Paris. He was also invited to the Mickery Theatre in Amsterdam. His first performance of *The Trojan Women* was in Tokyo in 1974.

Grotowski joined Suzuki's list of admirers and invited him to the Theatre des Nations in Warsaw to give a performance of *On the Dramatic Passions* in 1975. This year also saw a new original production by Suzuki, one he wrote and directed, entitled *Night and Clock*. In 1976 Suzuki closed the Tokyo theater and founded the Toga theater in Togamura, a mountain village around 600 kilometers from Tokyo, in Toyama prefecture. The motto that appears on the brochure describing his work refers to the open-air theater and says in Japanese, "The world is not only Japan; Japan is not only Tokyo; at this Togamura we meet the world." The picture of the open-air theater, which was built in the Greek tradition by Isozaki Arata, shows only the top of the theater from the perspective of the viewer looking from below toward the sky. Thus again, by suggestion and arrangement, Suzuki conveys the idea, so prevalent in Zen and traditional Japanese art, that from the microcosm one has access to the macrocosm.

Dogen (1200–1253), a Zen master, has expressed this idea of containing the large in the small: "Our attainment of enlightenment is something like the reflection of the moon in water. The moon does not get wet, nor is the water cleft apart. Though the light of the moon is vast and immense, it finds a home in water only a foot long and an inch wide. The whole moon and the whole sky find room enough in a single dewdrop, a single drop of water. And just as the moon does not cleave the water apart, so enlightenment does not tear man apart. Just as a dewdrop or drop of water offers no resistance to the moon in heaven, so man offers no obstacle to the full penetration of enlightenment."[4] Suzuki's theater in Togamura is an image of Japanese art, and during the international festival that takes place there every summer, this image reflects the whole world and the history of art.

In addition to the open-air theater, there is an enclosed theater which is built along more traditional Japanese lines. Suzuki based his conception of it on a replica of a Noh stage, which he made in Paris, with mirrors in back and an aluminum floor. He retained the aluminum floor, painted a dark sepia that looks black. It lies atop a wooden structure and the rest of the stage is wooden; floor and columns with opening *shoji* (sliding wood and paper doors) are in the back.

All is painted black and the stage is lit by low-intensity lamps, suggesting the original illumination of Noh stages by candlelight or lanterns. There is also a philosophical component to this low lighting. Noh drama often showed the emergence of a divinity or ghost from the darkness, as it were the primeval womb of the world. This sense of oneness with the world was also the experience of Greek drama for its original audience.

The theater incorporates elements of the original structure, an old farmhouse. The seats consist of stairs, thus resembling the ancient Greek theater. The stage retains the A-frame structure of the roof and some of the old living quarters of the farmhouse.

The group's international performances continued in 1977, with Suzuki's *Trojan Women* played at the Theatre d'Orsay in Paris at the invitation of Jean-Louis Barrault. In 1977, *The Bacchae* was first performed in Tokyo and then in 1981 in Milwaukee, Toga, and Tokyo in a bilingual version. In 1982 the Japan Performing Arts Center and the Toga Festival were born, and henceforth Suzuki productions would be given each summer along with those of foreign companies arriving to present drama, dance, and other performing arts.

The year 1983 saw new productions of both Japanese and Western works. *Chusankai* was written and directed by Suzuki in Tokyo. *Clytemnestra* was done for the first time in Toga, at the festival, and *The Tragedy* (*The Fall of the House of Atreus*) was written and directed by Suzuki and performed at the Imperial Theater in Tokyo. In 1984, *The Trojan Women* appeared at the Olympics Art Festival.

Each summer since 1982 a core group of Japanese and American actors are joined by people from other countries to take part in the International Actors Training Program, an activity of Suzuki's Japan Performing Arts Center. Suzuki holds classes teaching his acting method to students from all over the world. He has also given training in Milwaukee, Los Angeles, and San Diego besides other places in the United States. He has taught at Julliard and the University of Wisconsin-Milwaukee since 1980.

The Olympics Art Festival held in Los Angeles in 1984 allowed one to compare the Suzuki treatment with other avant-garde interpretations of traditional theater, such as the Theatre de Soleil, which combined elements from classical Indian, Japanese, and Italian (commedia dell'arte) interpretations of drama in performing Shakespeare (*Henry IV*, Part 1, *Twelfth Night*, and *Richard II*). These performances were given in French, as Suzuki's was in Japanese. Kevin Kelly, writing for the *Boston Globe*, said that whereas the French troupe claimed that "the universal language of gesture" would make everything accessible even to those not able to speak French, their performance of Shakespeare simply lacked something as a result. This was not the case with Suzuki, however, who "has so concentrated his approach to *The Trojan Women* that there's truly no language barrier at all. The play exists as a purely visceral, yet intellectual, impression, with the sound of its Japanese dialogue a mysterious, declamatory music behind the horrors."[5]

One might even claim that the experience is much like one going to an opera where one does not know the language. In fact, supertitles might not be out of place. One critic said, "For us to hear the play in Japanese is to look at the language through a *shoji* screen. All that's left is a play of shadows. But nothing more is needed."[6] Suzuki provides a synopsis that even includes some of the text, and this, plus a certain knowledge of Euripides, prepares anyone for a thoroughly moving experience. One is tempted to say "entertaining," but Suzuki goes beyond entertainment. He fulfills that function, of course, which is essential to any drama, but he involves the senses to such a degree that one's enjoyment is linked to a profoundly empathetic experience. The line between audience and actors is blurred and the theater is an organic whole: there is no real division between seating space and stage.

This is comparable to the tea ceremony, which incorporates so much of Zen. Once again, through a limited medium one attempts access to the universe. There is a person who serves the tea and one who receives it, but both are so linked in the ritual that lines blur between them and they share and interchange the active and passive roles. This is much the same as in the martial arts. The opponent (and the word for opponent in Japanese, *aite*, also means "partner") should be regarded as an extension of oneself, and thus one eliminates fear through a perception of unity. Fear in this context becomes irrelevant.

Critics at the Olympics Art Festival all agreed that the interpretation of Greek tragedy was best done by Suzuki. Minos Volonakis presented a rather pedestrian performance of *Oedipus Rex* with a young popular actor taking the lead. The declamatory style that is so popular now in Greece simply bored the audience. The artificiality of the delivery was not linked with significant gestures or movement, and the actors seemed from time to time lost on their makeshift stage which imitated Epidaurus's stone circular structure. The acting and staging was as inferior a reproduction of Greek tragedy as the artificial stage was of Epidaurus.

Steven Berkoff also gave his version of Aeschylus' *Agamemnon* at this festival. This did not have the verbal pyrotechnics of his *Greek*, a reworking of the Oedipus legend in which Oedipus, having suffered through to wisdom, ends up happily married to his mother. In *Agamemnon* Berkoff stopped short where he should have been more daring, and was daring where the point was irrelevant or unnecessary (e.g., a Negro chorus was used to convey the racist cliché that blacks are more "primitive" than whites—and the program even stated this intent).

One article claimed of Suzuki's *Trojan Women* that "the same play took the L.A. Olympic Theater Festival by storm in 1984. Suzuki has dazzled Western audiences with the 'strange and cruel beauty' of his adaptations of Greek tragedies and Shakespearean plays, even though they were in Japanese. By drawing on Noh and Kabuki traditions, Suzuki seeks to recapture the energy of primitive theater, which has been lost, he believes, in the modern technological world."[7]

Suzuki's drama also provides political commentary. In his *Trojan Women* one can see the suffering of women at the hands of exploitative men, with specific reference to World War II and American atrocities such as Hiroshima. Suzuki has said, "War's still a fresh memory for us, and a reality that we're threatened with today. In this play I wanted to show how women pay, terribly, for wars that men create." Kevin Kelly quotes Suzuki as criticizing "Japan's present prosperity . . . built on the misery of the poor."[8] Suzuki deals with the question of how freedom is destroyed by people exploiting technology, who use other people as things.

All the international performances in the Greek and Toga festivals are performed in their native languages. When the director Theodoros Terzopoulos was asked if the performances at Delphi might be translated into Greek or English, he shook his head and smiled, seeming to think the question naive. "After all, the point of inviting these different groups is that they'll perform in their own languages and dialects, with the intention and belief that native theater can only heighten our understanding of human potential and fate."

What is the Suzuki method and how does it convey the truth of tragedy? Suzuki himself has written about his method in an article called "Culture Is the Body." He explains that a "cultured society" means for him "one where the perceptive and expressive abilities of the human body are used to the full" (p. 6). He points out that a civilized society is not necessarily a cultured one. A civilized society expands the capabilities of the human body (e.g., with a microscope or telescope one has expanded vision). But at the same time there is a fragmentation; we also can develop a dependence on this technology and sometimes the original human function becomes impaired through disuse. The role of consumer in many cases has replaced that of producer. Vonnegut says, "Movies are prosthetic extensions for people who cannot read and have no imagination." A play makes us a more active participant than a movie does, and Suzuki's goal is to engage us completely. The actors use the human body totally; so too we are urged to respond emotionally, even religiously.

Suzuki speaks of the Noh theater. Artisans made the costumes and masks, carpenters the stage. The stage was often lit by candles. Gods do not fly on stage in elaborate *machinae*. As Suzuki says, "Noh theater is pervaded by the spirit of creating something out of human skill and effort . . . it is a creation of animal-energy" (p. 6).

He feels that along with the technological expansion of the modern stage, there has been a comparable reduction of human capabilities. Acting does not seem to have its previous importance if one can achieve a similar effect by lighting or scenic pyrotechnics. Suzuki then is like Aristotle, who considered spectacle the least important aspect of drama.

What Suzuki says he is trying to do is "to bring together the physical functions once dismembered; to regain the perceptive and expressive abilities and powers of the human body." How does he do this? First of all, as we have noted, his stage does not rely on technological gimmicks. He uses the ancient Greek theater, or a modified Noh theater. Both lighting and sound effects are kept to a minimum. The emphasis is on the actors: their delivery, their movement, their gestures, the way they go from place to place and where and how they stand. The costumes are often the traditional ones of Kabuki or Noh drama (without the masks however), and the props are also simple ones, usually handmade. Occasionally, counterpoint is provided (in *Clytemnestra,* a wastebasket with the Marlboro cigarette logo is introduced to suggest that the modern has invaded the ancient).

The actors' training is rigorous. Theirs is a dormitory life, and the actors are responsible for preparing their own food and keeping their own quarters in order. They take part in exercises that are devised to allow them to regain the use and knowledge of their bodies. Suzuki has stomping exercises, for instance, which not only allow one to regain contact with the earth (a reminder of mortality and at the same time an essential "grounding" for any movement). An actor must learn to keep the upper half of his body motionless as he stomps. Swaying shows that he is not in control. He has to "feel" the connection between the lower and the upper halves of his body. The pelvic area must be the ultimate source of expression. This is certainly what is also done in the martial arts; Kabuki and Noh training are similar. The *hara* or "gut" is where *ki* or "strength," which can be projected, originates. A common criticism of a bad *karate-ka* (martial arts' performer) is that his strength is in his arms or shoulders. Suzuki believes that the feet are important because they receive the energy of the earth.

Suzuki alternates vigorous stomping with collapse on the floor and a slow rise in response to music, which alternates between the percussive and dynamic and the slow and graceful. This is an exercise in contrasts; the poles define each other. Proper breathing is also emphasized.

Suzuki talks of vectors, one leading toward the sky and the other to the earth; they meet "in the pelvic region, and the energy derived from this tends to radiate horizontally" (p. 7). The feet are to be the source of strength for the upper body as it extends itself. Sliding steps (*suri-ashi*) and stomping (*ashi-byoshi*) achieve this connection with the ground. These movements are used in the martial arts as well as in the traditional Japanese theater. As one moves in karate, for instance, one is told to imagine that the surface of the foot is not to leave the ground more than a paper's thickness. This grounding is necessary for strength in either attack or defense, and breathing is important because it can either help or hinder movement.

Suzuki quotes Origuchi Shinobu, an anthropologist and author of "Six Lectures on the History of Traditional Japanese Performing Art," who says that stomping regularly occurred in traditional dramatic presentations and symbolized the treading down of evil spirits under the ground. Ancient Japanese dance used to have this purifying function. Origuchi also speaks of the "opening Ritual of the Heavenly Stone Wall in the Japanese Creation Myth as the origin of the Sacred Dance [*Kagura*])" (p.7). A goddess, Ameno-Uzumeno-Mikoto, danced while stomping on and striking the bottom of an overturned wooden tub with a stick. He says further, "Perhaps the tub symbolized the earth. The goddess stomped on it and struck it with a stick while making loud noises, actions supposed to wake up and bring out the soul or spirit that was believed to be under the tub, whether sleeping or hiding, in order to send it to the unseen sacred body of the god nearby" (p.7). Suzuki notes that this function is as much to acquire energy as possibly to exorcise. He sees the "evil" spirit entering the body of the exorcist, and thus one overpowers the spirit by acquiring it.

Choral dance in Greece also had a religious function, and again the spirits were divided into those of the air and those of the earth. The offerings to the upper gods were white, whereas black was for the chthonic deities. Dance and contact with the earth would establish up communication. We remember also the stories of Carlos Castaneda, describing the spiritual activities of the Yaqui Indians in Mexico. Dance was one way of entering the separate reality of the world of spirits.

Suzuki speaks of stomping as being necessary not only to understanding the connection to the earth and the interconnection of the body so that it can function as an integrated whole; it also was traditional in Japanese theatrical forms that had their origin in the dance. Suzuki speaks further in terms of creating a "fictional" space, one that "might also be called a ritualistic space, where we can achieve a personal metamorphosis" (p.7). To understand what this means visually and emotionally, one needs only to see Shiraishi act.

Suzuki says that the ancient Japanese stages were built over graves or places where spirits were thought to reside. Noh theaters followed this tradition in part by hollowing out the ground beneath the stage or building the stage over an overturned pot. These devices added resonance to the stage, of course; in addition they possibly had some spiritual connection whereby those spirits added their energy to the performance.

It is the lower body that maintains contact with the earth, and the earth is a primeval source of stability. As Suzuki says, "Perhaps it is not the upper half but the lower half of our body through which the physical sensibility common to all races is consciously expressed; to be more specific, the feet. The feet are the last remaining part of the human body which has kept, literally, in touch with the earth, the very supporting base of all human activities" (p.7). Recall the story in Greek mythology of the giant Antaeus, the son of Poseidon and Earth, who derived his strength in his wrestling matches by contact with his mother, Earth.

The training area in Toga is the stage. A hush accompanies the master's entrance. The term "master," *sensei* in Japanese, is applied to professors, teachers, and doctors, those professionals who have mastered an art and are engaged in passing it on. In Japan this person is treated with the highest respect. Suzuki wears this title well, and his students respond instantaneously to his least suggestions. Often people he has trained run the classes, but Suzuki Sensei observes and comments.

One exercise consists of the actors moving in response to the beat of a sword, or *bo* stick, which is struck against some resilient surface that emits a sharp percussive sound. The actors will freeze at one beat, then resume action with the next. Again this is an exercise in contrasts, all of it directed toward gaining total control of the body.

Exercises and "dance" sequences are followed by rehearsals that in some ways are extensions of the exercise. Entrances and exits, for example, apply the techniques and body control used in practice. The upper body is often still in contrast to the lower body, and the face is expressionless. During a rehearsal of *The Bacchae* when the actor playing Pentheus shouted, "Take him away!" he accompanied the words with a large sweep of his arms, pointing and gesturing imperiously to his guards to remove Dionysus. Suzuki interrupted the rehearsal and said that there should be no gesturing; in fact the lower body should be the source of strength and communication. Nothing need be visible, but nonverbally the actor was to convey though his body's *ki*, or projected strength, what he meant in his words. In Suzuki's method, the whole body should speak even if one is mute.

Many American actors, those trained in Method acting for instance, feel that subtle nuances are lost by the restriction of upper body movements and facial expressions. They have considered the exercises rather mechanical, and somehow particularly Japanese. Some claim, as many a beginning student of the martial arts has done, that Japanese bodies are simply different, that they can scuttle easily and assume positions close to the floor since they usually have short legs. This is, of course, nonsense. I simply think that the Japanese actors and practitioners of karate try harder and practice more than many of their American counterparts. Gradually the beginners learn, or perhaps relearn, the connection between the lower and upper body, one that they certainly had when they were very young. As a result, their performances gain in strength and power.

Proper breathing and the use of the voice are also important in the Suzuki method. The voice must also be grounded in the body, often coming from the gut. In Kabuki and Noh, lines are chanted and delivered with a proficiency that would tax any operatic virtuoso. Shiraishi incorporates these techniques in her repertoire: her performance is electrical in intensity. The scream she cries as Hecuba when her grandchild is killed is felt by each member of the audience as one's own scream.

Shiraishi also has an incredible range to her voice that she has perfected in this Suzuki method. She changes from male to female in *The Bacchae*, playing both Dionysus and Agave, and from an old woman to a young one as she plays Hecuba and Cassandra in *The Trojan Women*. The ease and competence with which she uses her voice as a powerful instrument has enthralled audiences all over the world. Faber describes her voice in these terms: "deep and overwhelming but not musical. It is harsh and guttural, not from her throat or chest, but from caves that crawl with demons—a Delphic oracle who does not speak but is spoken through" (p.18).

This is what Suzuki hoped to achieve. Noh theater can show us a human being transform into a god before our eyes. Kurosawa made use of this technique in *Kagemusha* (Japan, 1980); in this film a commoner is used as a double for the lord Shingen. The same actor plays both roles, but mainly through acting he literally "becomes" either the commoner or the lord. Suzuki makes a fine art out of this tradition. Actors in the West do not seem to have developed this technique.

The summer International Actors Training Program has much in common with martial arts' summer training camps, and, of course, training for Kabuki and Noh. There are enormous physical and spiritual demands made: it is as if one had entered a monastery, or temple, as well as a school. Complete commitment is required, but the results are worth it. So also, as one learns to use the human body as a whole, one learns how to use time. Time becomes the servant rather than the tyrant of the will. It is another tool to enhance one's proficiency.

Suzuki has produced three plays based on Greek tragedy: *The Trojan Women*, *Clytemnestra* and *The Bacchae*. The *Trojan Women* of Euripides is not often regarded as a dramatic masterpiece. There is no plot development per se, just one disaster following another.

H. D. F. Kitto sees the play's unity as residing in the figure of Hecuba, who acts as a symbol of the "sufferings of the defeated."[9]

This play depicts suffering in such a way that many would say that this is Euripides' most powerful play. Aristotle, who awards the palm to plot, would probably not have praised it, but since he called Euripides the most tragic of the poets, Aristotle may well have had this play in mind when he arrived at that judgment. Euripides derived dramatic power from the sufferings of victims rather than the exploits of heroes. Cacoyannis certainly shared Euripides' vision and in his film version added a brief prologue saying that Euripides intended his play to be a "timeless indictment of the horror and futility of all wars." Cacoyannis quotes Edith Hamilton in his preface to *The Bacchae* as saying that *The Trojan Women* "is the greatest piece of antiwar literature there is in the world."[10]

Suzuki also recognizes the dramatic power of this play, and gives this explanation for its continuing impact: "I do not think any other work has so successfully expressed one aspect of universal man. Nor is this just because war itself remains a present reality for us. The fundamental drama of our time is anxiety in the face of impending disaster."[11]

Suzuki uses Euripides' play as an instrument for interpreting, understanding, and most of all experiencing modern events. He says, "I intended to express the disastrous fate of women caused by war, which was initiated by men, and the complete powerlessness of religion to aid the women or the war itself" (p.2). His text, which includes a Japanese translation of many passages from Euripides' play, is by Ooka Makoto and Matsudaira Chiaki. A popular song concludes the play.

A short synopsis of Euripides' play at this point may help us understand what Suzuki is doing in his reworking. The Trojan War lies behind both *The Trojan Women* and *Clytemnestra*. This war has been fought to restore Helen to Menelaus; she had been kidnapped by Paris, son of King Priam and Queen Hecuba of Troy. *The Trojan Women* shows us the sufferings of the women captured after the Trojan War. They are to be divided as spoils among the Greeks. Hecuba is given to Odysseus, Cassandra to Agamemnon, and Andromache to Neoptolemus, the son of Achilles who slew her husband. Helen is to be returned to Menelaus. Polyxena, Hecuba's daughter, is slain at Achilles' tomb as a war offering to his shade.

Her death is revealed to Hecuba by Andromache, whose own young son is sentenced to death. The boy is thrown from the battlements of Troy as Helen goes freely back to her home with her husband. Although Menelaus gives vague assurances she will die, all of us who know the myth, as the Greeks did themselves, know that Helen will live and prosper. Astyanax, Andromache's son, is buried by his grandmother Hecuba against the backdrop of Troy in flames.

Suzuki's version of Euripides' play begins "in the ruins of a cemetery devastated by war just after World War II." The music is intended to suggest mourning for the dead. The god Jizo, a patron god of children, enters followed by three men dressed in black who in the program notes were said to incarnate the fear of death. They are also evocative of the traditional Kurombo, or the stage assistant dressed in black as a convention of invisibility.

Seven men and women scuttle onto the stage, each carrying various items with them (they suggest refugees). Three guards enter dressed as samurai bandits. They appropriately goosestep onto the stage. A fat belly distinguishes one of them, and he thereby contrasts markedly with the refugees. These guards consistently swagger and communicate nonverbally their status as victors relishing their victory and abusing their power. An old woman (Shiraishi) enters, one who has lost her husband, sons, and daughters; she carries her household belongings in a cloth sack.

When the play is performed indoors one sees a stage shrouded in gauzy hangings, conveying the ambiguity of the human soul every bit as much as the mists and webs created by tree branches that Kurosawa used in *Throne of Blood*. The lighting and the music are as symbolic and suggestive as the staging, costumes, and acting. Spatial and temporal connections are constantly being made, linking and contrasting East and West, past and present.

A bamboo flute introduces the scene where the old woman first invokes the dead, as in fact many a poet invoked the Muses. She prays that the spirits return to earth and inspire her, as she says, "You, who would be as fruit of a sweetness to ring through our mouths!" She even speaks of the songs that they would sing. We remember the spirits underneath the ancient theaters, and the Suzuki method that summons them. Thus West merges with East, Muse with ghost.

The first ghost that comes to inspire this old woman is Hecuba, the Queen of Troy, who has just lost her husband and sons and daughters. Their sufferings are identical. She begins with Hecuba's first words in Euripides' play, now in Japanese.

Hecuba talks to Talthybios and he tells what the victors have decided. Cassandra is to share the conqueror's bed, she who had dedicated her virginity to Apollo. Apollo is as ineffective in saving Cassandra as Jizo is the children. Shiraishi transforms herself into the mad Cassandra. Her gestures, which had been broad and slow, now change to a shorter radius and are executed more quickly. Her voice is higher . . . it is clear that she has made the transition from an old woman to a young girl. Cassandra tells how the Trojans will be the ultimate victors: her "marriage" to Agamemnon will only bring him death.

The next scene is with Andromache. Andromache tells her mother-in-law how her fame and reputation have brought disaster on her, now that she must go as concubine to the son of Achilles, the man who murdered her husband, and at whose tomb Polyxena, another daughter of Hecuba's, has just been sacrificed. Andromache is told of the decision to kill her little boy, then she is dragged off and raped. The child (a white muslin doll with long arms and splayed fingers), is "slain" by the soldiers, its arm cut off, and hurled at the grandmother for burial.

Again it is modern times and an old woman is with a young woman in rags, suggesting a parallel with the woman who was just raped; and indeed it is Hecuba and Andromache in the present aftermath of the war. We hear the Toryanse, a children's song. The woman prays for her dead children to enter paradise. The god Jizo looks on impassively.

We seem to return to ancient times, but they are mixed with the present. Hecuba binds the mutilated arm of her grandchild and proceeds to lament his death as the chorus offer gifts, everyday Japanese items they have brought in sacks (from Troy? Hiroshima?). Her words are the same as they are in Euripides' text, saying that lamentation is for the living, not the dead. Hecuba says, "Ah, me. Earth takes you, child; our tears of sorrow cry aloud, our mother." Again there is reference to the earth as giver and receiver of life.

Suddenly sirens blare out and a batten of red and blue searchlights are aimed at the audience; announcements of war disasters are heard and the modern intrudes upon the ancient once again. This effect is not performed when the play is given outdoors. When it is done outdoors, two people, a man and a woman, wander onto the rear of the stage. They turn their backs to the audience and face the lake. They are carrying umbrellas. In either case there is the jarring juxtaposition of modern and ancient, East and West.

Soon a dialogue ensues between Hecuba and Menelaus. Hecuba pleads for Helen's death. She warns Menelaus of giving into his desire for Helen, saying, "She looks enchantment, and where she looks homes are set on fire; she captures cities as she captures the eyes of men. We have had experience, you and I. We know the truth." Menelaus lashes out in anger, and he and his men slay everyone on stage. A bamboo flute is heard and the woman comes back to the present. The dead arise and leave the stage along with the soldiers and the three men dressed in black.

Suzuki says that this indicates the end of the evocation of Euripides' tragedy, but more of his text is to follow, now in a new frame. The old woman unties the sack she is carrying and refers to each of the items as she unpacks them. These are common household items, again a mixture of Japan and the West—a teapot and "Priam's shoe," for instance. The old woman throws an empty can and asks, "Did you see? Did you hear? The crash of the citadel?" and continues with Euripides' verses that refer to the destruction of the city of Troy. She recites both Hecuba's lines and those of the chorus.

Andromache, now a modern woman, approaches Hecuba and offers her some flowers. She speaks of the loss of her husband to the war. She hurls the bouquet of flowers at Jizo who doubles over in seeming agony at the blow. The old woman collapses, and this has been interpreted as her death. We hear a contemporary song, in both Japanese and English. Both the music and the words are strident in their banality. The text tells of a woman forsaken by her lover. Although abandoned, she concludes by singing, "I want you to love me tonight." The modern woman contrasts with the older one; both mourn their losses but the younger one seems to capitulate to the woman who has taken her place in her lover's arms, the endless substitute. The words "I want you to love me tonight," appear to be floating signifiers, and love like the Marlboro wastebaskets, seems to be a new disposable commodity.

Suzuki has said that there are also truths in popular songs. The import of this song is not only an obvious intrusion of the modern, in perhaps a cheapened commercial context, but in addition there is a universal meaning expressed. Lost or thwarted love will always be a subject for poetry and art in general: the classical theme survives in popular song. The contrast is between a woman's abandonment versus the loss that comes through death, after a life of shared experiences. One can argue about comparative values, but the pain is still there in both cases.

Jonathan Saville and others have faulted Suzuki for being too eclectic. Some things seem included without obvious significance and sometimes their inclusion is jarring (e.g. the inevitable umbrella). In Zen practice, if a person dozed off a monk often obliged him by waking him with a sharp blow. Perhaps Suzuki strives to do the same thing in order to hold our attention. Some of the value is serendipitous.

Many have also criticized Suzuki's mixture of the vulgar and the popular, the modern with the ancient, mass culture with the elite, yet this makes him an ideal paradigm for modern Japan. He is mourning and celebrating a loss of innocence. Japan has truly been violated by the "other." The indictment of war is also clear, particularly war's effect on the women who are left alone and condemned to live. The ghosts are inevitably the ones who are better off in Suzuki's productions.

Suzuki clearly draws the parallel between Troy as a victim of the Greeks and Japan as America's victim. The degradation of Japan by America during and following World War II is not simply in its obvious physical manifestations, but also in the insidious imposition of American culture (or lack thereof). With the addition of modern technology, there seems a new vulgar element not previously present in the ancient conquest. Defeat now imposes and celebrates this high-tech cultural pastiche. The slaves of ancient victors were degraded by their captors, but their minds remained still free. Hecuba and Cassandra speak still of the glory of war in that the sufferings of the Trojans would become immortalized in art, as we have seen happen in the epics by Homer and the plays of Aeschylus, Sophocles, and Euripides. But Suzuki's play does not end with a poem like Ooka's, which he has used to begin the play. Rather, as the sirens did before, we have a banal popular song blaring out, advocating the proliferation of love, again and again and again. We do not hear a live singer, but a recorded voice. Is this the American legacy? Vulgarity and bland technological homogeneity along with conquest? The destruction of art and taste (particularly "native" art and taste) along with the usurpation of freedom?

This may be the American legacy, but it has nevertheless found a welcome audience. So where does complicity begin and end? How did we begin with an atom bomb and end with a stand-up comic? Suzuki at least confronts us with the fatal—or possibly even fruitful—mixture. What seems on face value to be deadly for humans and culture, may be a source of new creativity—Suzuki's art is an example.

And what about the two figures who turn their backs on the audience to look out over the lake as they hold their umbrellas? They are certainly a stage division, cutting off the lake in one sense, but in another opening it up, if we share their perspective in our imagination. Do the umbrellas represent an attempt at protection, a sorry shield from the elements or from fate that pathetically leaves us as powerless as the gods seem to be in the face of real disaster? Are these mute figures moderns who turn their backs on antiquity and its lessons . . . namely the play unfolding behind them? Or are these moderns reinforced by the action, implying that we are all molded by the past whether we will it or not? Then again, perhaps this is merely a touch of the absurd, like Beckett's trash cans, or Ionesco's rhinoceros.

Sometimes a director just has a sense of something being appropriate. It is tempting when doing classical plays to draw modern allusions. Des McAnuff made the court in *As You Like It* into a Nazi headquarters and the forest of Arden into a Warhol pop art locale with large hearts carved into the trees. Suzuki also draws a parallel between the Nazis, Tokugawan bandits, and the Americans, but he alludes to the universal, the oppression that follows "victory."

The gods in Euripides were a clear source of the irrational. They were not simply passive, but actively hostile. The beginning of Euripides' play shows Poseidon plotting with Athena to punish the Greeks. He asks her, "Why do you jump from one feeling to another, now hating too much, now loving too much whomever you will?" (*Tr.* 67–68). These gods are as arbitrary, or more arbitrary, than man, but they are effective.

Suzuki's god does nothing. He collapses at the end after being struck by flowers (an image we remember from Cocteau). Does this show his grief or guilt at his impotence? In this respect he does resemble the anthropomorphic Greek gods. Or does it show his ultimate death . . . a symbolic demonstration of his ineffectiveness? Do the gods die if they are not worshipped? In this case, a woman throws the flowers, and the beauty that flourishes becomes a deadly weapon, and its offspring a fatal gift.

In Greek tragedy violence was not shown onstage. Generally, a messenger's speech tells of befallen disasters, and Euripides is a master at recreating verbally the horror of murder. Cacoyannis in his *Trojan Women* (Spain, 1971) shows us Astyanax being pushed from the parapet at Troy. Suzuki shows us a doll being put to the sword, so he combines both treatments—explicitness with euphemism. We see the violence, but we are not subjected to actual blood.

Suzuki is effective in forcing us to accept ritualized action. The stylized movements of the chorus, the absurd props and the dead rising after they have been slain before our eyes, are all conventions that we enter into. They somehow make the reality more vivid. One doesn't think, "This is a doll, so how can I possibly share the emotions of the mother or grandmother who are mourning the loss of a child as represented by this doll." Instead we accept the symbol and experience not only the immediate sorrow of these mourners, but join the mourning for any child lost in a comparable holocaust, a result of war-madness and the fear that comes when reason fails (*Tr.* 1165–66). When the rape of Andromache is added, we see what is implied by the abduction of all the women from Troy. Suzuki involves us in witnessing the violent act.

Suzuki's art stresses the visual and the emotional over the verbal and intellectual, in contrast to what we know is Euripides' forte; we have heard of the spectacular performances of Aeschylus' plays, but Euripides' pyrotechnics are more often in his words. The acting technique itself is based on the nonverbal, and again Suzuki has derived much of this from traditional Japanese theater, religion, and the martial arts. Energy is harnessed and released in emotive explosions. In the end, feeling and effect override our awareness of the visual; the visual is minimized according to Western theatrical standards, but the effect is somehow more powerful.

Shiraishi's acting technique must be seen to be understood. She is as active as the god Jizo is immobile, and this is also symbolic of their respective roles. This is a tragedy of an old woman and Hecuba, not of the gods and fate. Human suffering is at its core. If there is any glory, it is that of a human facing disaster. Cassandra speaks of the glory of the dead and how they will be commemorated, but Euripides shows the glory of the living, the ones who must continue once disaster has struck. But Suzuki takes even this away when the modern Hecuba dies, and we are simply left with her tragedy.

These are universal themes. Hecuba eloquently articulates one: "And yet had God not bowed us down, not laid us low in dust, none would have sung of us or told our wrongs in stories men will listen to forever." [12] Contrary to what Homer thought, we now find new heroes in Suzuki and Euripides, and they are often heroines: the persons to be appreciated are the ones left to mourn and live in disaster's aftermath.

Where does Suzuki depart from Euripides? They possibly differ most clearly in the function that death and tragedy serve. Both artists understood, as Cacoyannis pointed out, "the cycle of human experience being one of recurring disaster, tragedy finds little scope for long-term optimism whichever way it looks." [13] But Euripides' heroines find some resource inside themselves, some hope that gives them the courage to survive. As Hecuba tells Andromache, "Death is not the same as life, in the former there is nothing, in the latter, there is hope" (*Tr.* 532–33). Euripides "reverses the tables against the power of hopelessness to extinguish the spirit of man." [14]

Suzuki's *Bacchae* also carries on the theme of the oppressor versus the oppressed. There is much debate about what Euripides meant: is Dionysus to be loved or hated, or is that irrelevant if we consider Dionysus to be a natural force? Where is valid blame to be placed? Pentheus, or rather Dionysus? Suzuki has eliminated some of the ambiguity and seems to be leaning toward the side of Dionysus. He sees Pentheus as a tyrant who, as he suppresses natural urges in himself, also tries to suppress them in his subjects. Yet these strictured emotions are bound to erupt in both man and the state, leading to psychosis for one and revolution for the other, and the result is frenzied outbursts and death. Art once again is the magic wand, and provides in this instance not so much a commemoration of suffering as a possible means for escape.

Suzuki shows a cycle of oppression, revolution, and oppression reimposed. The tyrant does not escape his people, nor do they him, much as the victors and the victims in the *Trojan Women* share a strange interdependence. Indeed, could one exist without the other? This is true Hegelian dialectic, and an enactment of Marxist prophecy.

We see, however, a fundamental change here. In Euripides' play, Pentheus is a tyrant who misuses his power, who at the same time is representative of a human victimized by a god, a god who outdoes even humans in the scope of his passions. In Suzuki's version, Pentheus wins and we have no sympathy for him.

Suzuki's *Clytemnestra* also adds to the idea of a cycle. Again the oppressor (Clytemnestra) is slain, only to return at the end to slay those who slew her. Suzuki offers a scene where "citizens" consume the parts of the murdered victims and become nauseated. In part Suzuki is depicting the trivialization of violence that seems to have entered modern times. The media usually use violence as a common aspect of entertainment. Sterilized terms abound, so that now "peace initiative" can mean a new deployment of troops. We seem to have incorporated violence into everyday life, and if we don't understand what is happening, the nausea may ultimately prove fatal.

Cacoyannis in his three films based on Greek tragedy, *Electra* (Greece, 1961), *The Trojan Women* (1971) and *Iphigenia* (1977), has also investigated the effects of war on society in general and the individual in particular. The mass tragedy we witness in the *Trojan Women*, Suzuki has narrowed to the personal tragedy of two women, or perhaps four (two in the past and two in the present), with the chorus being caught up in the fate of the principals. Now, in the story of the house of Atreus, one enters into a personal history of murder followed by murder; the public sphere has now become private. Iphigenia is symbolically sacrificed and represents all the youths who will be murdered at Troy and all the children who are to suffer innocently in every war (compare Suzuki's ironic use of the Toryanse, a children's song, just before the brutal murder of Astyanax in his *Trojan Women*).

Once again there is a cycle of violence, this time in a family. A Freudian nightmare becomes real, but with ironic twists. Instead of murdering the father and having the mother for himself, the son has the mother only by killing her, after she has eliminated the father herself. She then returns as a ghost to kill the son in turn—his worst fear, and perhaps secret desire, comes true. Orestes imitates Oedipus and pays for it. Death here seems like a sexual merging:

the son violates the mother and she returns the violation and they are united in death. The father is absent; mother merges with her two children. The dream of having one's mother to oneself becomes a catastrophic nightmare.

At the end of *The Oresteia*, Aeschylus shows a type of reconciliation between the gods governing vengeance (the furies), and those who advocate a man-made justice, as represented by the law courts. Suzuki continues the story with the furies reemerging from man's subconscious. His Clytemnestra gets her vengeance through the human heart: she haunts the mind, and kills the guilty with his own inner demons.

In looking generally at Suzuki's work, do we find any hope in his interpretations? Hecuba dies and Pentheus and Clytemnestra return to kill. Perhaps we are meant to see death in an Eastern perspective. The writer Mishima Yukio certainly seemed to use death as a means for freedom; as Yamanouchi Hisaaki said of him, "Now he had acquired physical strength, by means of which he could extinguish his own body so that his soul could live."[15] Mishima resembles Nikos Kazantzakis, whose tomb says, "I hope for nothing; I desire nothing; I am free." Suzuki sees ghosts and spirits as inspirational sources: they are invoked by his performers. The dead continually return to haunt or inspire. Also there seems to be a more passive acceptance by Suzuki's heroes and heroines; the ones that fight and struggle come to even greater disaster. In Suzuki's presentations, one is continuously aware of the eternal, and of the powerlessness of the individual to fight cosmic forces. There is a sense of futility that makes the sufferings even more pathetic than in Euripides.

What Suzuki has also done for us is to juxtapose East and West, past and present, as actors and actresses flow in and out of the drama, and we flow in and out of time. Disaster is one turn of the wheel of Dharma. The spirits of past and present can teach and inspire us. They can also kill us. The ritual apprehension of these spirits gives a life to Suzuki's performances that engages the audience in a total way. The performance itself becomes a source of life besides a vision of death (or perhaps because it is a vision of death). Audience unites with actor: the stage provides a window to the world and life—a window into ourselves. One leaves the theater as one leaves a church or temple; one has the feeling that one has seen and felt god, particularly god as man/woman, demon and deity. This is what Peter Brook calls the "Holy Theater."[16]

Suzuki Tadashi's *Clytemnestra:*
Social Crisis
and a Son's Nightmare

The Door of Death I open found
And the Worm weaving in the Ground.
Thou'rt my Mother from the Womb
Wife, Sister, Daughter to the Tomb
Weaving to Dreams the Sexual strife
And weeping over the Web of Life.

> William Blake, "For the Sexes:
> The Gates of Paradise"

SUZUKI TADASHI has merged Greek tragedy with traditional Japanese drama to provide commentary on what he sees as a
modern social crisis: the breakdown of the family and the rejection
of traditional values. In Suzuki's prologue and epilogue to his *Clytemnestra*, humans are depicted as puppets, suggesting that free will
is an illusion. Again we find Suzuki making use of a traditional
Japanese art form, the Bunraku puppet theater, to make a new and
different point.

Suzuki has used six plays to create his own version of the tragedy
—namely, the three that comprise Aeschylus' trilogy, *The Oresteia*
(*Agamemnon, Choephoroi,* and *Eumenides*), Sophocles' *Electra,* and
Euripides' *Electra* and *Orestes.* Allusions are made to the basic story
told in the *Oresteia.* Agamemnon is the king of Mycenae (Argos)
and military leader of the Greeks in their expedition against Troy.

A version of this paper appeared in *Views of Clytemnestra, Ancient and Modern,*
ed. Sally MacEwen, *Studies in Comparative Literature,* vol. 9 (Lewiston, N.Y.:
Edwin Mellen Press, 1990), pp. 65-83.

Agamemnon sacrifices his daughter Iphigenia at the beginning of the war to ensure victory, following an oracle. Victorious in the war, he returns home, bringing as his prisoner and concubine Cassandra, the daughter of Priam, king of Troy. Meanwhile, unknown to him, Clytemnestra has taken a lover in his absence, his mortal enemy Aegisthus. The sacrifice of Iphigenia, bringing home a concubine, and an old family curse, all contribute to Agamemnon's being murdered by his wife Clytemnestra. His son Orestes, who fled at the time that his father was slain, is ordered by Apollo to take vengeance. He does this in league with his sister Electra, who has remained in the palace. Orestes is driven mad by his mother's furies, but in a trial conducted at Athens he is acquitted by Athena's vote; she sides with Apollo.

In Suzuki's *Clytemnestra* most of the action takes place in Orestes' mind; however, eventually Orestes' mother returns as a ghost to kill him as he commits incest with his sister Electra. Social imperatives have become internalized. Perhaps this is the ultimate defeat of Japan by the West: the shame society has become a guilt society.[1]

Using critical tools provided by sociology, anthropology, and psychology, I would like to suggest that the mythology of the past is used here to convey psychological truths about the present, describing a society in which chaos is symbolically represented by the role of the deadly mother. I would further like to suggest that the drama itself, as performed by Suzuki, in the midst of our own era's psychological and sociological breakdown, is an existential act of defiance and creation. The ancient Greek myth, which had humans at its center, now reappears as a text of defiance aimed at reclaiming humanism from technology: we are not robots after all.

Suzuki's plays are not so much translated copies as creative transformations that become new originals. One is tempted to call them Japanese, because of Suzuki's adroit use of traditional Japanese forms, but they are neither Japanese nor Greek, rather Suzuki has forged an amalgam of the two. Two traditions, culturally specific, have become an international, universal statement. The particulars are combined in such a way that a common understanding results; the human elements are liberated.

As we saw in the first chapter, all three of Suzuki's reworkings of the Greeks are presented as internal fantasy. Suzuki said of the

Clytemnestra: "I have intended to present an internal view of contemporary man who is becoming more and more isolated because he cannot help but live in a spiritually chaotic state. I have shown this by examining the disintegration of the family, which is considered as the fundamental constituent of society. I suppose that my growing sense of crisis about man's being, which increasingly exists in spiritual isolation, forced me to make this attempt to create a newly dramatized adaptation of the house of Atreus in the Greek Tragedies."[2]

As Agamemnon perverts the relation of father to child by sacrificing Iphigenia, so Clytemnestra perverts the relation of wife to husband, committing adultery and murder; then Orestes violates the son-mother tie by killing his mother. Suzuki takes this a stage further by having the mother kill her son. The *philos* has become *echthros,* the duty-bound relative an enemy, and an ancient myth illustrates Sartre's claim that hell is "the other" ("l'Enfer, c'est les Autres"; *No Exit,* scene 5). Except now the "other" is where one least expects it—in the heart of the family.

How does Suzuki present Clytemnestra? None of the ancient plays upon which he based his work, was called *Clytemnestra,* but Suzuki's choice of title shows us his emphasis on this powerful female figure. His eclectic selection blurs the ancient representations and the result is an Aeschylean Clytemnestra, endowed with the supernatural, vengeful power common to abused females in Noh drama; she confronts the neurotic Euripidean Orestes and, of course, she wins. We see none of the "matricide and good spirits" that Gilbert Murray, following Friedrich Schlegel's interpretation, said characterized the Sophoclean version.[3]

A short summary of Suzuki's version will provide the groundwork for my discussion. Orestes enters the stage with puppetlike motions. The play begins with Apollo seated on a throne on the right and Athena on the left; they are dressed in traditional Japanese costumes. Orestes and Electra are dressed in modern clothes: he is in a T-shirt and shorts, and she wears a slip, items that not only increase our sense of their vulnerability, but also emphasize the contrast between ancient and modern (both the traditional and its rejection).

The first scene is in the present and shows Orestes consumed by guilt after having killed his mother. He assumes a fetal position and imagines the furies who appear at the end of this scene. Next we see Apollo and the furies as two opposed sides of Orestes' conscience. In scene three we return to reality; Electra drags the body of Aegisthus on stage and castrates him during a vituperative monologue. Then we return to mental conjurations: Clytemnestra enters, dragging the bodies of Agamemnon and Cassandra, and defends herself to the citizens. The citizens are dressed in modern clothes and are served by maids; they are served pieces of the dead bodies and become nauseated.

In the next scene Orestes, urged on by Electra, kills his mother, in spite of his mother's emotional appeal. When Clytemnestra sees she has failed, she anticipates Orestes' attack and tries to kill him with a sword. Orestes fends her off and stabs her repeatedly as he stands over her body; the sexual overtones are obvious. A trial follows, with Athena presiding.

Orestes returns to his past (and in some productions plays Agamemnon, his own father, just after he has returned from Troy; in other productions a different actor assumes this role). Agamemnon talks with Clytemnestra, who invites him to walk on a crimson carpet (a symbolic river of blood, recalling and anticipating the deaths associated with the house of Atreus).

Suddenly we are back in the present. Tyndareos, Clytemnestra's father, dressed as a Japanese bourgeois from the last century, returns to accuse Orestes and Electra. He leaves saying that he will ask the citizens to put them to death.

At the beginning of the final scene, we hear a symbolically appropriate popular song, "The River of Fate." Electra tries to kill herself. Orestes prevents her and as they review the hopelessness of their situation, they embrace more and more ardently in a clearly incestuous act. Clytemnestra enters slowly, her shadow projected against the backdrop of a tall tree in the Toga presentation (and against Parnassus when the play is performed in Delphi). We hear a grotesque soundtrack from Noh, slowed down to make it unrecognizable. Clytemnestra stabs her children as they are locked in their incestuous embrace. An epilogue shows all but the gods leaving the stage with puppetlike movements. The gods topple from their thrones: man is a puppet and god is dead.

There have been many critical methods applied recently to the myth of Clytemnestra. Philip Slater has interpreted the story of

Orestes as one "of sex antagonism and mother-son conflict."[4] He suggests that Clytemnestra, the Erinyes, and Electra all represent aspects of the mother: Clytemnestra as "unloving, father-killing"; the Erinyes as "vindictive, devouring, castrating"; and in Electra's case, "the protective and nurturant but also manipulating mother, who uses the child for her own ends."[5] In Suzuki's representation Electra is more sinister. She actually castrates Aegisthus and emotionally castrates Orestes, seeming to absorb him in the sexual act while Clytemnestra delivers the final blow. Suzuki may be conveying the modern Japanese male's fear of a hostile mother, since the way the Japanese boy is usually raised parallels the way a fifth-century Greek boy was raised, by a mother who rules the house in the father's absence.

Slater points out that the Greek male of fifth-century Athens was raised almost exclusively by a mother who had been isolated by the father and deprived not only of the father's company, but of any effective political or economic power.[6] This is paralleled by the position of women in modern Japan. Such a mother is bound to be ambivalent to the male: she showers love on her child as a substitute for the father, but also uses the boy as a scapegoat. The son in turn idealizes and resents the father as he sees him according to his mother's representation.

Melanie Klein and others who have focused on the early period of child development suggest certain expansions of Freudian theory.[7] The early period is said to show a child totally identifying with the mother as a narcissistic extension of self, a stage called "symbiosis." Normal individuation consists in the recognition of the self as independent from the mother, what Lacan called "le stade du miroir," where one derives one's being from a reflection in objects.[8] The mother must be symbolically "killed" so that the child may live; this "matricide" is an existential act to achieve "a personality that realizes itself only in suicide" and "a consciousness of the other that can be satisfied only by Hegelian murder."[9] Guilt normally follows. So also can the child fantasize the mother/other taking vengeance.

Terry Eagleton describes the aftermath of the symbiotic stage in minatory terms: "This merging of identities is not quite as blissful as it might sound, according to the Freudian theorist Melanie Klein: at a very early age the infant will harbour murderously aggressive instincts towards its mother's body, entertain fantasies of tearing it to bits and suffer paranoid delusions that this body will in turn destroy it."[10] Suzuki has activated these "paranoid delusions" most of us share unconsciously, so in his version of the ancient drama we are witnessing a primal nightmare.

Anthropologists, psychologists, and sociologists have noted the strong role of the mother in the Japanese culture. The modern psychologist Doi Takeo has written a book called *The Anatomy of Dependence,* which characterizes Japanese society as one based on a structure of dependence that begins with an all-indulgent mother and an absent father (there is even a chapter called "the Fatherless Society.")[11] Nakane Chie has noted that a wife is more a mother than a wife to her husband, and that in fact "the core of the Japanese family, ancient and modern, is the parent-child relationship, not that between husband and wife."[12]

Okonogi Keigo speaks of the *Ajase* complex, named after the Japanese myth about a son who first imprisons his father for having abused his mother, then tries to kill the mother because of her efforts to keep the father alive while he is in prison (she feeds the father honey which he licks off her naked body). The son, feeling guilty for wanting to kill his mother, breaks out in a noxious skin disease. His mother tends him, and he feels even more guilty, but eventually there is reparation.[13]

This is a symbolic representation of the child's being over-whelmed by the mother, a woman who in fact acts as a mother even to her husband. We see the child expressing hostility which is followed by guilt, particularly in the case of mother-directed hostility. In modern Japan, Suzuki among others has spoken of the increase of children's violence toward parents and also of the self-directed violence of suicide.

We have noted that the conditions of modern Japan are similar to those of fifth-century Athens: the father is essentially absent and the mother uses the children to compensate her frustrations. Mothers in both these cultures exercise power in the *oikos* (the house and family, private society run by women) which they were deprived of exercising in the *polis* (the city and public society run by men). According to Okonogi, the modern Japanese can substitute mother-identification by means of the group: merging with the group replaces merging with the mother.[14]

The importance of the mother in modern Japanese society is

reflected in the fact that a genre of film is devoted to her: the *haha-mono*, "mother film." An example of this is Kinoshita Keisuke's *A Japanese Tragedy*, made in 1953; its theme "was the fall of the Japanese family-system and its mutual-obligation structure."[15] Suzuki claimed that he intended to show this type of "fall" in *Clytemnestra*. It would seem he combined this depiction of a mother in a disintegrating family structure with the popular ghost story found in the modern Japanese film, besides earlier in Noh drama. In these films "the traditional Japanese ghost [is] usually female, with a heavily scarred face, blood running from the mouth, no legs, and long disheveled hair . . . [who] returns . . . to redress old wrongs. All have a single purpose—revenge."[16] Clytemnestra's pale white face, coupled with her long disheveled hair, legs hidden as she glides across the stage in her long robe, well fits this description when she returns at the end for vengeance in what seems to be typical Japanese style. The way Suzuki slides the signified is culturally specific: he replaces the usual female ghost taking vengeance on her lover by a mother taking vengeance on her son, following a murder that has replicated the sexual act. Oedipus thus merges with Orestes and Jocasta with Clytemnestra.

Suzuki has symbolically represented those psychological and so-ciological trends observable in modern Japan that have parallels in the ancient Greek model of patriarchy. The mother takes her re-venge and is all-encompassing; Orestes is overwhelmed by his con-flicting drives. He kills his mother in a frenzied act, conflating a drive to reachieve symbiosis with vengeance for its frustration. After her death he has an incestuous relation with his sister Electra whom he uses as a mother substitute; in modern Japan the sister often functions as a second mother.[17] He is finally destroyed by his con-flicting feelings: the nourishing mother has become murderess, Cly-temnestra has become Medea.

Anthropology as well as psychology can provide us benefits as a critical tool. For instance, Helene Foley notes that we can distinguish "good" from "bad" women in classical drama according to the way in which they align themselves with culture.[18] Although women have been traditionally associated with nature, and men with cul-ture, women are considered "good" insofar as they follow the cul-turally beneficial pattern of ceding to patriarchy and its mandates.[19] As Foley notes, however, the women/nature, men/culture distinction is often a blunt critical tool, a fact apparent in studying Clytem-nestra.[20] This character blurs the distinction by exhibiting male characteristics as she violates the cultural imperatives (in Aeschylus' *Oresteia* she is characterized as "androboulos," (*Ag.*11: "one who thinks like a man").[21]

Froma Zeitlin has seen the *Oresteia* as an affirmation of male dominance in the *polis* and a clear victory for patriarchy. Olympian gods (embodying male supremacy) win over chthonic gods (associated with female supremacy), and the *polis* is victorious over the *oikos.*[22]

Whereas the victory of culture over nature is clear in the *Oresteia*, the victory of patriarchy over the Eumenides is not so clear, at least not as clear as Zeitlin suggests. The result of the vote about Orestes' guilt is a tie. Thomas Rosenmeyer quotes Peter Green to show the uneasy resolution depicted at the end of the *Oresteia:*

> The [the furies] sat demurely while a
> civic committee put fancy costumes on them,
> changed their name (that old crypto-magical
> standby so dear to all rationalists) and
> offered them a niche under the Acropolis.
> Then, the moment it was dark, they winged
> their way back to the place from which
> it had taken aeons to remove them
> —the inner recesses of the human mind—
> and there they have remained ever since,
> defying all efforts to remove them.[23]

We remember also the Athenian wife lurking resentfully in the house, her only place of power.

Melanie Klein well emphasizes the ambiguity in the ending of the *Oresteia* when she says, "I would conclude that the opposing votes show that the self is not easily united, that destructive impulses drive one way, love and the capacity for reparation and compassion in other ways. Internal peace is not easily established."[24] She also recognized the unconscious element in the presence of the Erinyes, since "nobody but Orestes can see the furies" (p. 284). The Erinyes represent "excessive feelings of guilt" (p. 286). Suzuki shows us a most excessive manifestation of guilt in having Orestes' mother herself return to exact vengeance for her murder.

Klein has the concept of the good and bad mother, a vision every child shares: a mother on whom he/she depends for needs and whom he/she hates and resents for that same dependency. In the *Oresteia*, Athena represents the good mother and Clytemnestra the bad mother, although she "was not always a bad mother: she fed her son as a baby and her mourning for her daughter Iphigenia might have been sincere" (p. 296).

In Suzuki's *Clytemnestra* it is the bad mother who prevails and absorbs the child in her final fatal embrace, ironically a stabbing that catastrophically reverses the oedipal fantasy. The avenging mother is not to be exorcised or given a euphemistic name. She exacts a fatal even more than in most countries because few mothers work outside the home, and the father is so often absent. Suzuki's vision of a vengeful woman is reinforced both by traditional Japanese drama and modern Japanese movies.

Klein comments further, "The dramatist's capacity to transfer some of these universal symbols into the creation of his characters, and at the same time to make them into real people is one of the aspects of his greatness" (p. 299). Suzuki's tapping into the universal to mingle it with the particular both intensifies and creates a new dramatic flood that overwhelms the audience because the flow from without meets the flow from within. Suzuki shows no final reconciliation by Athena, "the good mother . . . who becomes the carrier of the life instinct," nor "a change in the furies towards forgiveness and peacefulness," expressing "the tendency towards reconciliation and integration" (p. 297).

In Suzuki's *Clytemnestra* it is the bad mother who prevails and absorbs the child in her final fatal embrace, ironically a stabbing that catastrophically reverses the Oedipal fantasy. The avenging mother is not to be exorcised or given a euphemistic name. She exacts a fatal toll as recompense. In Japan, the corporation is rather like the Olympian gods, a patriarchal substitute for matriarchy, embodying social and cultural ideals. But Clytemnestra is still at home, and retirement is an ever-present threat. The benign resolution is for the Japanese male after retirement to continue his life in companionship with male friends, drinking, playing Go, discussing politics, and so on, similar to the modern Greek male gossiping with his male friends at the *kafenion*. The women remain in the *oikos*, benevolent housekeeper mothers—Eumenides in their cave beneath the Parthenon.

Suzuki says that he was not interested in "reproducing" Greek tragedy, rather he was "recreating" it to offer commentary on problems he saw in contemporary Japan.[25] We have alluded to some of these problems. Kato Shuichi, the scholar who is well known for his frequent commentary on Japan, proposed his list: (1) the growth of a consumer society where everything is disposable, (2) the unchanging groupism and death of individuality, (3) the absence of a strong intellectual elite, (4) the continued low status of women, (5) the dangers of a gradual shift to the political right, and (6) the shortness of Japan's memory about the "unpleasant past" and the total absorption in the present.[26]

Suzuki symbolizes these problems using the vehicle of Greek tragedy. Orestes throws the knife he has used to kill his mother into a Marlboro wastebasket: modern disposable values clash with ancient stable ones. Orestes himself is another disposable, symbolic of Japanese youth in a society without traditional values. He is also the individual absorbed into a society that controls his fate and ultimately sacrifices him via the avenging mother who, in modern Japan, trains her child to be absorbed into the social mainstream. Orestes as puppet is a vivid symbol of the modern Japanese male. The modern Japanese woman concentrates on making her son succeed and in this way affirms her own value: by sacrificing her son's individuality for the social cause, her self-confirmation and vengeance are one.[27] Suzuki's play can be a ritual catharsis, as Emile Durkheim, Walter Burkert, and René Girard say Greek tragedy itself is, but it is more; it is an affirmation of qualitative human existence in a world where such existence is questioned.[28]

Suzuki presents a black view of the universe. His plays end in death; even the optimistic illusions of Greek tragedy have been eliminated. We do not see the defiance of an Aeschylean Prometheus or the anachronistic heroism of a Sophoclean Ajax; Suzuki is closer to Euripides in showing the sufferings of the victim rather than the struggles of the hero. But in Euripides we found hope (cf. Hecuba's telling Andromache that in life there is hope; *Tr.* 532–33) or the gesture of *philia*, one person helping another, futile though that act might be. At the end of *The Madness of Heracles*, Heracles says that person is mad who would prefer power or wealth to friends (lines 1425–26). Euripides seems to imply that in the face of an irrational universe, a human being's only hope is in another human being.

Suzuki, however, contrasts with Euripides in discounting the power of language. He seems to illustrate Roland Barthes' conception that truth is often obscured by language and also at times to illustrate Barthes' point about Japan itself, that it is an "Empire of Signs" (in fact, signs without significance). *Mu* or "emptiness" takes precedence over fullness. Only the sign is there.[29]

Whereas Suzuki's view of man and the universe is pessimistic, he still believes in the creative act. He has said, "To parody Sartre's words, I have finally been able to see at close range a few people who truly understand that life is a useless but passionate play, but who are driven by the fact that they too must continue on, to fight the battle of the defeated."[30] He has fought this battle and succeeded. He has created a drama with international appeal based on the ability of the actor to communicate nonverbally. Suzuki teaches his actors the grammar, but they create the sentence: "Technically speaking, my method consists of training to learn to speak powerfully and with clear articulation, and also to learn to make the whole body speak, even when one keeps silent . . . in short, this training is, so to speak, a grammar necessary to materialize the theater that is in my mind. However, it is desirable that this 'grammar' should be assimilated into the body as a second instinct, just as you cannot enjoy a lively conversation as long as you are always conscious of grammar in speaking."[31] The accident becomes the sign. Suzuki purposely sets up contrasts, such as between past and present or East and West, and considers the confrontation as creatively significant.

Thucydides and Euripides showed us the breakdown of cultural norms in the chaotic universe at the end of the fifth century in Greece. Suzuki has also noted the breakdown of traditional human values in contemporary Japan due to the stultifying victory of technology and the corporation; his art provides the organizing factor and the new mythology, so that we see his dramatic presentation as an existential act, existential in that by the dramatic act one affirms human existence. Men and women work together, realizing the possible futility of their gesture, but they make a communal passionate statement that is important for both the speakers and the listeners, the actors and the audience.[32] In the modern technological society, this drama as a creative act is a gesture of human defiance against the constriction that would make a person into simply a tool.[33] There is a certain irony in that this gesture of freedom is only in representation: primeval mimesis. But then, after all, as Rilke said, "Denn wir leben wahrhaft in Figuren," (We live truly in metaphors), a variation of Heidegger's, "Dicterisch wohnet der Mensch," (Man lives poetically)."[34] Self-consciousness also begins with representation in Lacan's "le stade du miroir."

The actor and his nonverbal language are Suzuki's priorities. Zen contributes its values. Language and logic are futile gestures in an incomprehensible and all-powerful universe. Emptiness and the accidental have as much value as content and the planned. There are no tenses in Japanese, as we know them, and no such thing as causality, in the Western sense.[35] All this may also contribute to the open-endedness of a Suzuki performance.

Besides his mixing of the ancient with the modern, Suzuki has been criticized for this open-endedness, as well as for his eclectic synthesis of the three Greek playwrights' visions. Jonathan Saville took this position in his review of *Clytemnestra*, which was titled "Hoarse Opera" (referring to the deep timbre of the actress Shiraishi's voice, derived, as he did point out, from Kabuki). He says this technique (with the voice "tense, constricted, hoarse") as compared with Western "naturalism" exhausts the listener; the mixture of ancient with modern in Suzuki's play is "confused and dramatically unsubstantiated" and "his literary tinkering with these ancient texts has resulted in nothing less than a mess," and the whole results in "dramatic chaos."[36]

This review is contrary to Saville's usual imaginative analyses of experimental theatrical productions. Many reviewers in the West rely overly on Eurocentric standards, some of which derive from Aristotle's *Poetics*, which call for clearcut beginnings, development, and endings. This "culturally imperialist" criticism is what Edward Said dealt with so brilliantly in his book *Orientalism*, what Miyoshi masterfully confronts in the case of misjudgments of Western interpretations of the Japanese novel in "Against the Native Grain."[37]

Miyoshi shows that in the artistic medium itself (the *shōsetsu*), the socially constricted Japanese finds freedom, and that this is opposite the case of the Western novel, which is restricted in form whereas the society seems at least to advocate, if not allow, freedom: " . . . The novel expresses the problematic of the individual in the contradiction between formal constraints and the ideological characterization of the individual as a free agent. The *shōsetsu* is the reverse: while the character is always defined in the close texture of society, thus imparting to him an approximation of a role, the plot is open-ended and spacious, as if man's true existence is irrelevant to the actual details of living, the acts and events of actuality. Politically and psychologically deprived of liberty and freedom, *shō-setsu* characters seem to inhabit a space unbothered by life's constraints."[38] This freedom is evident also in the way Suzuki breaks up the works of the Greek playwrights into fragments and reconstructs them in a fluid open-ended way mimetically to confront some of the political and sociological crises of modern Japan.

Suzuki's main actress Shiraishi, with her four-octave range, crosses language barriers and vividly communicates the dramatic message of each play. Timbre and movement convey as much as words. Shiraishi, as Clytemnestra, approaches Orestes and Electra in the final scene with a slight bent to her shoulder; her slow powerful progress (with costume and movements from Noh) makes her overwhelm the children even before she strikes. She herself is an all-encompassing symbol of primeval fears. The optimism of legalism and the day of cultural triumph is shattered by this modern representation of Mother Night's victory, a victory achieved in total silence. *Eros* has met *thanatos*. Agamemnon has been slain once again, this time as Orestes. The cycle continues.

III

Suzuki Tadashi's *Bacchae:*
No(h) *Bacchae*

S UZUKI TADASHI has taken Euripides' *Bacchae* and fragmented it, inserting it in a frame studded with generalized historical
shards to dazzle the audience. The result is a glittering mosaic of
particulars. It is a fantasy of the oppressed reenacted endlessly: one
beginning is taken from the final words of Euripides' play, and the
ending repeats Euripides' beginning. In addition to being a rewriting
and rereading of history, it is also a drama of miscommunication,
and opposition to the "other." Suzuki's manipulations of Euripides'
play are used to express ideas that differ from those of Euripides.
Both Euripides and Suzuki operate in their own historical and philosophical contexts, which they impose on an ancient myth, but these
contexts differ: Euripides' view of history is essentially linear,
but Suzuki's is cyclical. In Euripides, the gods will get their way,
perverse though it may seem, and humans suffer, but one has an
idea of finality. In Suzuki, Pentheus is a recurrent phenomenon.
Even after the apotheosis, men stupidly attempt to reimpose their
repressive regimes, and the leaders are interchangeable. The differences between Pentheus, Creon, and modern monstrous despots

are elided. The only thing one is sure of is that this phenomenon will recur.

Euripides' *Bacchae* shows us the god Dionysus coming to Thebes in the guise of a priest. He leads bacchants from Asia and drives the local women mad for their blasphemy (they have questioned his divine birth). Pentheus, the king of Thebes, refuses to allow rites in honor of Dionysus, even though his grandfather and mother are among the devotees. Pentheus is seduced by Dionysus (whom he has tried to imprison with disastrous consequences) into dressing as a woman and spying on the deranged women. They mistake him for a wild animal and, led by his maddened mother Agave, attack him and tear him to pieces. When she realizes what she has done she goes into exile with her father Cadmus, wishing "nothing to do with Dionysus" ever again.

Suzuki has many versions of this work, and at the time of this book's writing was working on a collaboration with Isozaki Arata and Roger Reynolds, possibly incorporating some elements of Samuel Beckett's drama. There are also versions without Dionysus' physical presence on the stage; his power is felt through his absence (much as Zeus in Aeschylus' *Prometheus Bound*). Suzuki has yet another version in which priests close in on Pentheus and murder him (instead of his being killed by his mother and her sisters, as in Euripides). Lines are rearranged and characters are not necessarily consistent: the chorus can play the role of a character and vice versa, and characters have interchangeable lines.

In this discussion of Suzuki's work I shall try to make it clear, when speaking of each protagonist in his various roles, which persona I am referring to (e.g., Dionysus as the god, as a character in Euripides' play, as a character in a version by Suzuki, or as an actor). I beg the reader's patience in trying to sort all this out.

Suzuki's version in which Dionysus' failure to appear produces the effect of an absent center might illustrate the thesis Roland Barthes made in *Empire of Signs*, that Tokyo is a city with a void in the middle (i.e., park, palace and emperor, all signs empty of content).[1] Isozaki tried to achieve the same effect in Tsukuba: "Instead of a towerlike projection, I have used this sunken plaza as metaphoric expression of the hollowness of the center."[2] In some senses the space is indicative of Japanese uniqueness, not simply absence of the West, but a creative void, a black hole whose absence is formed by profound presence. Karatani Kojin sees this black hole closed in on itself: "No matter what form the West's evaluation of Japan may take, Japan will remain for the West a place of exteriority rather than being what in fact it is: a discursive space filled with complacency and almost totally lacking in exteriority."[3] Suzuki in his various versions seems to be playing with the idea of East versus West (with Dionysus versus Pentheus), or an absence versus a presence, or perhaps an irrational "Eastern" deity versus a rational "Western" sovereign. In each case Pentheus abuses his power. Communication is replaced by force.

Suzuki has said of one of his earliest versions:

> This production is performed as a play-within-a-play, or to be more exact, a play-within-a-play-within-a-play. The basic story has been restructured into a fantasy embodying the hopes and aspirations of people oppressed by a totalitarian and despotic ruler. Thus Dionysus makes his appearance as the symbol of the dreams and desires of people deprived of their freedom by such a ruler (with nothing left to wait for but death). In order for them to express their desires for vengeance, they perform Euripides' *The Bacchae*, depicting the misfortunes which befall the house of Pentheus. But I have further added another frame to "distance" the story. At the very end, precisely when the oppressed people have begun to think that their revels are ended, Pentheus comes back to kill them. This is a nightmarish vision but a brutal fact repeated ever since the beginning of political history—a moment of festive liberation cruelly crushed down by the despot.[4]

This version begins with a people, crushed by a despot, deciding to perform Euripides in search of catharsis; they identify with Dionysus and the chorus, gleefully watching the murder of Pentheus, a stand-in for the despot. They revel in enacting portions of Euripides' play. After the climactic moment when Agave discovers that the head she is holding is not that of a lion but of her son Pentheus, there is a sudden break in mood. Agave and Cadmus revert to their preplay personae and drink tea together. While they are relaxing, Pentheus reappears and runs them through with a sword.

Each of Suzuki's reworkings of Greek tragedy ends in death, or some situation from which there seems to be no escape. He takes on political and sociological themes, such as the abuse of the defeated, particularly the abuse of the weak, such as women and children. The contextual circles close in—from country to city to family. But all contexts seem to end up as prisons. Both abuser and abused move in closed circles, with no promise that the abused will not become abuser (e.g., Suzuki's Dionysus, Pentheus, or Clytemnestra, and the general theme of vendetta in the *Oresteia*). There is no final curtain in Suzuki. He gives us no surcease for rest: catharsis is merely preparation for the next disaster.

Suzuki's *Bacchae* continues to depict the oppressor versus the oppressed, as we saw in his earlier *Trojan Women*. There is much debate about who oppresses whom in Euripides' *Bacchae*, whereas it is clear in *the Trojan Women* that the Greeks abuse their victims after defeating them in war. In *The Bacchae*, are we to blame Pentheus, who seeks to imprison the god as he tries to repress and conceal his own instinctual nature? Or do we fault the god Dionysus, who Agave claims went too far since "gods should not equal man in their passions" (*Ba.* 1348)?

Suzuki has eliminated some of the ambiguity and seems to be on the side of Dionysus. He portrays Pentheus as a tyrant; Pentheus will have none of this lawless god who has led the women of Thebes to the mountains, away from their civilized duties. Pentheus tries to repress the god, the people, and his own emotions. Yet they are bound to erupt: the god goes free, the man becomes psychotic, and the state is in revolt. The king becomes the scapegoat for the city and the people are spared; the king is not. Dionysus takes his sacrifice in the *sparagmos* of the victim, who is literally torn apart (as he was earlier mentally divided).

Suzuki's art in this case is not simply a commemoration of suffering as in the *Trojan Women*, where catharsis is reenacted in the vision of an old woman. Suzuki's *Bacchae* shows the temporary victory of the people, followed by the reinstatement of oppression.

Michael Cacoyannis, in the preface to his translation of the *Bacchae*, depicts Euripides as more optimistic than Suzuki does; to him Euripides' message—spelled out with prodigious versatility in *The Bacchae*—is that "all progress harnessed to the pursuit of absolute power engineers its own destruction."[5] But Suzuki shows us that ritualistic revolution results merely in the return of Pentheus, as strong as ever.

One can maintain that Euripides makes Dionysus the villain, so the ending with Dionysus' victory is a pessimistic one (derived somewhat from Euripides' experience of the Peloponnesian War). Dionysus, like Medea, has a case for what he does, but he goes too far. He represents passion carried to excess.[6] But obviously it is more complex than this: Euripides and Thucydides, as the philosophers of their time, were attempting to define the conditions under which evil or good might exist. Such philosophers as Jürgen Habermas and Jean François Lyotard have carried on this debate into the postmodern period. Dionysus and Pentheus continue to personify the forces at work here. As always, myth and tragedy embody and enact the absolutes of philosophical speculation.

One could claim, however, that Suzuki, like Cacoyannis, sees Pentheus as being even more evil than Dionysus. He is a repressive force, against the instincts, and in a sense represents excessive law or regulation personified. Thus, for the bleakest picture, Pentheus must triumph, and indeed he does. He is the paradigmatic tyrant.

Suzuki's *Clytemnestra* is similar, in that the mother in that play is depicted as even more evil than the Greeks represented her, since she murders not only Agamemnon and Cassandra, but her own two children as well. Suzuki shows us a Clytemnestra turned Medea.

I have been discussing the various versions that Suzuki has done of the *Bacchae*. Now I shall turn to the version that is the main concern of this chapter, namely the bilingual performance done in Milwaukee, Toga, and Tokyo in 1981. In this performance the part of Dionysus was played by Shiraishi Kayoko. She also played Agave. This fluidity of roles is a common device in Noh plays, and texts often alternate between the actors and the chorus with one speaking for the other. In ancient Greek tragedy, an actor simply changed his mask when he assumed a different role.

In this version the actor who delivers the prologue also plays the messenger who tells of Pentheus' death later in the play. So also the actor who plays Cadmus in the final scene is constantly onstage and not only recites lines that are his own, but also lines from Tiresias' part as well as miscellaneous lines from Euripides' chorus (his eyes are closed when reciting his early lines, perhaps to reinforce a notion of anonymity, but when he opens his eyes he is clearly Cadmus). The character Tiresias has been eliminated, but some of his lines are taken over by this actor whom I shall designate "Cadmus/man." No masks are used, but changes of costume, voice, and general physical bearing make the change in character if not always apparent, at least ambiguously suggestive.

A short summary of the version I shall be treating (which has been videotaped) is in order at this time. It begins with a narrator saying the word "shinyo," (meaning "faith"; *Baksu no Shinyo* is the Japanese title for the play so *shinyo* in this case may stand for the bacchants who worship Dionysus). The beginning narrator then repeats Euripides' concluding words (translated into Japanese): "There are many shapes of the divine, and the gods bring about much that is unhoped for; and what we thought to be done was not fulfilled, but the god found a way for the unexpected. That is what happened here."

Pentheus enters carrying a light and speaking of the turmoil that Dionysus has brought—how the women have left their homes and that a "magician from Lydia" is leading them in their orgies. Cadmus/man tells Pentheus he is wrong not to honor the "son of god born of the virgin," Dionysus, as wine, who brings peace to man. (Dionysus is seen sitting in the middle of the stage.) A chorus chants in English, "If I could only be in Cyprus . . . " while Cadmus/man tells more of Dionysus' blessings. Some of the chorus is recited in Japanese. Dionysus appears, saying he has come in the shape of a man to the house of Cadmus. He urges the bacchants on. Music follows and the actors interweave each other on stage: an actress draped with a red-and-white flag crosses the stage diagonally. There is a wordless confrontation between Dionysus and Pentheus (Dionysus' staff crosses Pentheus' body on the video screen). The nonverbal domination is clear.

Dionysus and Pentheus square off as Pentheus questions and taunts Dionysus. Pentheus advances on Dionysus with a sword, but at the last moment he puts it up; the nonverbal victory belongs to Dionysus. A messenger enters and tells of the miracles in the mountains. Dionysus looks content as the bacchants begin to cross the stage again to the same music. Pentheus is shown screaming silently.

Dionysus tempts Pentheus, asking him if he would like to spy on the bacchants. Pentheus refuses, but Dionysus throws a spell on him. Pentheus' head bobs under the spell. He goes inside (offstage), saying he will consider Dionysus' suggestion (part of which is that

Pentheus wear female clothes so as to escape recognition by the bacchants).

Suzuki gives us a choral interlude without words: the actors and actresses cross the stage quickly. Dionysus leads his followers like puppets; as he waves his stick and utters a grotesque cry, the followers respond to his movements. Pentheus reenters dressed in female clothes. Irony drips from the words and actions: Dionysus puts his hands on Pentheus' head; Pentheus says, "You set things right. I'm in your hands." Dionysus shows him how to hold the thyrsus and how to move. Pentheus becomes more and more madly ecstatic in his actions. He leaves the stage and Dionysus seems to enact Pentheus' destruction with his chorus of followers.

A messenger's speech in Japanese tells of the end of Pentheus. Agave, dressed in white, enters carrying Pentheus' head. She boasts about her actions to a bacchant and to her father. Her father forces her to look more closely. She recognizes her son and a silent scream precedes her words of recognition. She and Cadmus plan to leave.

The end shows Pentheus returning to recite his opening speech. Dionysus also recites his first words. This is a more abstract version, a *Bacchae* without a frame, but there is a clear suggestion that this is a cycle, one without escape. The cycle of confrontation and non-communication begins again. Nothing has been learned; nothing has changed.

The alternation of Japanese and English leads to the inevitable confrontation of East and West, as well as a commingling. Dionysus, who speaks Japanese, is dressed in Japanese robes, and carries a monk's staff; he confronts Pentheus, who speaks English, is dressed like an English king in red robes, and carries a sword. Pentheus is defined by violence and legalities, Dionysus by silent authority and oracular speech. Pentheus orders and threatens, even his followers, drawing his sword on everyone he confronts, from messenger to Dionysus. On the other hand, Dionysus' followers obey automatically. It is impossible to see this play and not remember Hiroshima, the ultimate speechless violence, the paradigmatic use of inhuman force against human beings. So also the bacchants follow Dionysus as the kamikaze pilots followed the emperor. Both leaders in this play suggest nationalistic and imperialistic overtones; both are tyrants suitable to their respective nations.

It is very difficult to speak of a nation without using terms and concepts that have been used before in a Eurocentric imperialistic (orientalizing) tradition, and the orientalizing vocabulary abounds.[7] Thus, speaking of the opposition between the rational and the irrational in the persons of Pentheus and Dionysus as representative of the West and the East respectively, one is led to the brink of racism, or trivializing. Karel van Wolferen, for example, claims that "the tolerance of contradiction is closely connected with a characteristic that, in the final analysis, is the most crucial factor determining Japan's sociopolitical reality, a factor bred into Japanese intellectual life over centuries of political suppression. It is the near absence of any idea that there can be truths, rules, principles or morals that always apply, no matter what the circumstances."[8] This, according to him, is in contrast to the West: "The occidental intellectual and moral traditions are so deeply rooted in assumptions of the universal validity of certain beliefs that the possibility of a culture without such assumptions is hardly ever contemplated." This recognizes the Platonic and Kantian tradition in the West, as opposed to Shintoism in the East, "a religion of nature and ancestor-worship that tolerated contradiction and ambiguity"(p.10). What of Heraclitus and Nietzsche in the West? And the overriding role of Japan, Inc., in the East?

Suzuki in his division of roles along racial and linguistic lines seems to utilize some of the stereotypes that have appeared in these East/West critiques. His choice of roles does not seem as random as that of Sellars in his *Ajax* (a black actress playing Athena), but rather something that emphasizes rather than reinforces East/West differences and misunderstandings. Thus the clash Suzuki presents is not only between Pentheus and Dionysus as state government and religion, rationality and irrationality, authoritarianism and freedom, reason and passion, chastity and profligacy, suppression and expression, anality and orality, and all the other usual oppositions that have been seen in Euripides' original drama.[9] In addition now, and perhaps ultimately, the conflict is between East and West, Oriental and Occidental mentalities, although one should not define these categories simplistically. One should also be aware that one can shift into the other, so that the cycle also involves a switching of identities. Pentheus is the clear bully at first. The moment of "festive liberation" described by Suzuki is from an occupying power, one that uses force: the Pentheus who carries "Fat Boy."

The respective clothes, language, and race emphasize these distinctions. The chorus who follow Dionysus appear wrapped in the *Hinomaru*, the Japanese naval flag with its reds and whites. Their puppetlike motions, particularly before and after Pentheus' *sparagmos*, seem derived not only from the Bunraku puppet tradition, but also from a political tradition that demands absolute obedience. In fact, the continued strength of the puppet tradition in Japan might lead to cultural speculations, if not a clearly developed sense of irony, in this representation by Suzuki. The Japanese nation is homogenized and puppetlike not only in its unquestioning military subservience during war, but it is also one of the most racist of all nations in its attitude toward the "other," whether toward the *Burakumin* (also called *Eta*, those who have outcast professions such as leather preparation) or the *Ainu* (an indigenous minority race of whites roughly comparable to the American Indians in that their land was seized and their race is socially ostracized, while romantically providing touristic opportunities). I am sure that Suzuki did not confine his irony simply toward Japan, but in showing the puppetlike movements of the chorus he was criticizing man in general for following a leader without question—from Nazis goosestepping to American know-nothings snapping to attention when the flag is unfurled: "My country right or wrong."

In the choral breaks Dionysus manipulates the bodies of the chorus with suggestions of deadly power. In the final sequence, one of the bacchants returns as Agave recounts her adventure on the mountain; with stiff puppetlike motions this Japanese actress enters carrying an arm (pure white, from a plastic mold?), which she drops as she awkwardly crosses the stage. One recalls the severed limbs of Agamemnon and Cassandra that were served to the citizens in *Clytemnestra* (in one version of that play, Orestes also entered with puppetlike movements).

The puppetlike motions of Suzuki's choral actors suggest not only limited freedom, but also a fragmentation of movement. Suzuki's choral actions substitute for the ancient words; the ancient themes are thus reworked to provide a new commentary on the present. Perhaps language has been exhausted for expressing basic human truths. Thucydides claimed that words had lost their usual meaning during the atrocities of the Peloponnesian War. But it seems even worse in modern times, when governments and the media have perfected the art of disinformation. Now we are the post-Holocaust and post-Hiroshima generation. We have violated the truth factor behind language so often, perhaps now the ineffable as expressed through the image is the only way left to approach truth.

Suzuki has cut and rearranged Euripides' plays, interspersing the acts with choral interludes without words to convey some of the major themes. The music is the same for each interlude, a theme beginning with an insistent drumbeat and gradually adding melody. The drums reinforce the notion of Bacchic ritual. Drums are also used extensively in Noh drama and punctuate the text in such a way that they provide additional commentary.

Dionysus is seen as a tyrannical god, in complete control of his human automata. The people have become machines and Dionysus as the Japanese state controls their movements.[10] And is Pentheus' *sparagmos* the West's, as it is bought up and dismembered by the Japanese? A fitting end to its bullying, which included Hiroshima? As Pentheus tries to subdue Dionysus with words and threatening actions, his menace is seen as child's play. He becomes another puppet of the god. In one grotesque scene, as Pentheus is dressed in Western women's clothes, Dionysus is shown to be in control of his every movement. When Pentheus laughs with joy, Dionysus laughs grimly, playing with the king who has become a puppet. Dionysus drives Pentheus mad; Pentheus, as he proceeds to the mountain, leaves the stage imitating Dionysus, rolling his eyes and uttering bestial cries. The king is dead and the beast rules, following the god's command.[11] He will be torn apart in a ritual performed by the god's devotees.

Faithful to the Greek tradition, as also to Noh, violence is rendered symbolically, in words and dance. Contrary to the Greek tradition, there is more action without words in this production. Horror is shown in silent screams; Pentheus' mouth gapes wide following the messenger's account of the miracles. So also, instead of a blood-chilling scream, Shiraishi/Agave, as she recognizes the head she holds as her son's, performs a silent scream with her entire body. This is in contrast to the Western tradition of clearly enunciated emotive screams (e.g., Irene Papas' in this role). Silence imitates the void at the center of this agony. Shiraishi/Agave, after she writhes in silent anguish, rises to spit out her first tortured words of discovery.

Shiraishi plays both Dionysus and Agave brilliantly. One might guess that the *Bacchae* had to be performed without Dionysus when she left the company. She is impossible to replace. She plays Dionysus rather as a samurai warlord, and the nonverbal confrontation of her eyes and body shows that she has won over Pentheus even before she enchants him (following *Ba.* 810, "ah," in Euripides' text). She uses the hoarse vocal mode of the Kabuki actor. When she becomes Agave her voice is at least an octave higher and she combines feminine charm as she boasts over her hunting feat. There is an obvious transformation from male to female. As one admires the range that Shiraishi presents in her portrayals, one must agree with the justice of the claim that Leonard Pronko makes: "The Western actor, inhibited by his realistic and psychological approach to acting, might learn a real sense of freedom from the Kabuki actor: freedom not to do anything at any time, but to use body and voice within a much broader range than Western theater practice permits."[12]

In the choral interludes one might also see Shiraishi as executing a *Mie* stance, rising to a height, and sneering to express her power. Her cries and laughter at times are bloodcurdling. When she exits preceding the messenger's account of Pentheus' *sparagmos*, she performs something like a *roppo* exit in Noh, conveying mingled violence and power in a nonverbal way. She contorts her face in accordance with the intensity of her demonic mastery.

Dionysus is dressed in black, white, and purple and this contrasts with Pentheus' red robe suggesting not only his royalty but the blood that will shortly flow. One of Dionysus' arms is free, in which he carries his staff, rather like a magic wand as it presides over choral movements and, finally, Pentheus. This is reminiscent in the Greek tradition of the Amazon who kept one arm free from her tunic for the bow and arrow, even removing a breast (a-mazon means "without a breast") so that it would not get in the way when the bowstring was fully drawn back.

Pentheus threatens first Cadmus/man, the actor that tells him to worship Dionysus, then the messenger, and finally Dionysus, advancing on each with his sword. Each attack ends in threats and empty blustering.

We have seen how the sequence of events in Euripides' play has been altered. The end provides the beginning and the beginning the end. So also Pentheus speaks of the scourge that has overwhelmed his country without Dionysus first giving us his account, as in the prologue to Euripides' play. Here truth is presented in a fluid way, much as we see in Kurosawa's film *Rashomon* (Japan, 1950). No version seems definitive. This further obscures communication, lending it a more paratactic structure, which resembles much of Japanese literature: there is no clear beginning or end; the organizational principles of Aristotle do not apply. Miyoshi refers to the structural fluidity in Japanese literature and a generalized "hostility to logic and rationalism"; he cites "Karatani Kojin and Asada Akira boasting to Derrida that there is no need for deconstruction as there has never been a construct in Japan."[13]

The Euripidean scene involving the destruction of the palace in an earthquake and the freeing of Dionysus is eliminated. The performance time of Suzuki's production is roughly the same as that of Euripides' original, but much of Euripides' text is eliminated and nonverbal sequences take the place of the words. Instead, the destruction of the palace, which prefigures the dismembering of Pentheus, and the dissolution of his ultimately fatal rigidity, is shown symbolically by the movements of the chorus. Pentheus' madness is a dissolution of another kind.

There are many interpretations of *The Bacchae*. Some see it as Euripides' recanting his criticism of the gods, and a document of his newfound belief. Others see it as the ultimate critique of the gods; as R. P. Winnington-Ingram, for example, put it: "Euripides recognized but hated Dionysus."[14] Suzuki has broadened the frame to contain sociopolitical problems, questioning the foundation of East-West communication.

The theme of communication was also broached by Euripides. What the bacchants call worship, Pentheus defines as licentious orgy (*Ba.* 210ff.). The god that Tiresias sees as a source of wine and peace for man (*Ba.* 279–81), Pentheus sees as disruptive of the smooth functioning of the city, a consuming fire, an outrage and blame for all of Greece (*Ba.* 778–79). The virgin birth of Semele is regarded as a lie and blasphemy by Pentheus (*Ba.* 242–47), but as a boon to the family by Cadmus (*Ba.* 330ff.). As in many Greek tragedies, perception is the crux, what Aristotle calls *anagnorisis* (recognition that is often only a cognition), or a knowledge bought at high personal price. Oedipus paid for his newfound sight with his eyes. Pentheus paid for spying on the bacchants by becoming their victim.

When Pentheus voices his adamant beliefs as if they were absolute knowledge, he is called ignorant by Tiresias (*Ba.* 269), Cadmus (332) and Dionysus (490). He is said to have true knowledge and sight only when his mind is subject to the god and he is to all outward appearances mad. According to the Greeks, knowledge and sight are interdependent, and we can see this linguistically in the fact that the commonest way to say "I know" in Greek is to use a form of a verb that means "I have seen." Euripides' text shows us the developing madness, and it is characterized as the proper way of seeing: *Pentheus:* "I seem to see two suns . . . " (918), *Dionysus:* "Now you see as you should" (924).

Suzuki also plays on the image of the blind seer who sees, by having the presenter who opens the play and later recounts the death of Pentheus in Japanese close his eyes as he speaks. The same is true of the actor playing Cadmus/man, who as a loyal worshiper of Dionysus keeps his eyes closed, but opens them when he confronts Agave, urging her to look at the sky and regain her vision. In this case sight is aligned with sanity. For the worshipers of Dionysus, when their eyes were closed they had insight, true knowledge of the god. So also when the first messenger appears to tell of the miracles in the mountains, Pentheus' back is turned, another symbolic representation of the "truth" he is unwilling to face.

There is another confrontation here, which is also in Euripides, namely that of male versus female, alongside that of barbarian versus civilized. Pentheus dismisses both barbarians and women as inferior beings who should know their place. When Dionysus mentions that "the whole East dances the god's mysteries," Pentheus counters by saying, "Oriental mentality is lower than ours." He also dismisses females, complaining, "This is too much to suffer from women." The barbarian, and in this case woman (Dionysus as played by Shiraishi), takes vengeance on Pentheus by forcing him to assume the trappings of those he dismisses: Dionysus dresses Pentheus as a woman and teaches him to hold his staff (thyrsus) and dance as the barbarians do, a final degradation by identification with the "other" before he is sacrificed.

The difficulties in communication and understanding are augmented by Dionysus' delivering lines in Japanese to Pentheus' English. East/West difficulties are obvious. As Dionysus understands Pentheus, but Pentheus does not even try to understand Dionysus, one is tempted to see a particular form of Western arrogance at work. The Japanese make an attempt to understand the "other," at least to the point of being economically effective in their interactions. Americans and Europeans have rarely made the reciprocating effort. The result is their economic dismemberment.

Suzuki may very well be investigating the whole problem of the "other," or the question of whether communication is possible. At times one feels no one is understanding anyone and we are watching meaningless words being mouthed. Only the cycle of life and death continues. Oppressed becomes oppressor and vice versa. The roles may alternate, but nothing is learned. Repetition replaces reason and the bully is a floating signifier.

Suzuki's criticism of excessive control and compliance in Japanese society should not be taken in a one-sided fashion. It is obvious that Americans are also liable to this control, if simply through the media. Noam Chomsky is not unique in showing the insidious ways our opinion is shaped.[15] Michel Foucault, Antonio Gramsci, and Eric Hobsbawm come immediately to mind among those who have traced the way Western tradition has been shaped, and essentially created. John Dower has shown the manufacturing of the "other," particularly the misrepresentation of Japan by America and vice versa.[16]

Suzuki also provides critical perspective on the traditional theater itself, undercutting the Japanese theatrical tradition by jarring modern and Western allusions. He also undercuts the Western theatrical tradition, particularly "naturalistic" renditions associated with method acting, by his introduction of highly stylized techniques clearly derived from the "performance" theater (e.g., Noh), which has ritualized its conventions in a way utterly foreign to the majority of modern Western theatrical genres. This is a postmodern pastiche that questions as well as incorporates conflicting traditions and ideologies. Pastiche though it is, his drama still has a ritualistic power and provides probing political questioning.

What Suzuki does by putting on the mask is to lift the mask from our social practices. In *The Trojan Women*, he asks us to look death and war in the face; in *Clytemnestra* he examines the fatal game in the playful/deadly war of the sexes in which the dice are loaded in favor of one side, but both lose; in *The Bacchae* he questions freedom and conformity. There are recurrent themes: children are slain by invaders in the first play and by a mother in the two that follow.

Is the past destroying our present, or is this the future? There are no answers. We may be shocked and confused, but above all we are involved. We cannot distance ourselves emotionally by solving the problems intellectually. We are the problems.

The play is now the thing in which to catch the conscience of the postmodern audience, for theater is one of the final places that encourages us to think. If conformity deprives one of freedom in Japan, in America this is equally true: in both countries the media deprive us of opportunities to think and reason, two necessary requisites for freedom. Comic books have replaced serious reading in Japan. Even more insidious is television, which seeks to enslave through meaningless images and mindless content.

If Suzuki's theater can only revive in us the ability to ask questions, it will have done us a service. Hell is no longer the "other," but the "other" functions rather as a Lacanian mirror, perhaps as our mother; we are reflected in her eyes but the image is reversed. The earth has become such that this mother of intercommunication is rewriting us all. This "otherness" can be regarded as deadly, or it can be accepted as an added richness. In his poem "Ithaka," C. P. Kavafy says, "May you ask that your voyage be long and full of adventure and knowledge." In seeing Suzuki, we go on such a voyage, and it is a *nostos*, a return to a place that we know. In perceiving the "other," we may also end up knowing ourselves.

IV

Peter Sellars' *Ajax:*
The Obsolescence of Honor

WHAT HAPPENS to Homeric heroes in Greek tragedy? In Aeschylus, Agamemnon is killed by a resentful wife and a family curse. He is a scapegoat caught in a divine mesh; his blood is a dew watering the fertile earth in spring (*Ag.* 1389–92). There is perhaps an optimistic message in the *Oresteia,* that man can learn from suffering, the "violent grace" (*Ag.* 182–83) afforded man by the gods. The hero is subject to and must learn from the gods. In Euripides, Agamemnon's weakness is exposed as he debates killing his daughter to obtain fair winds so that he can lead the Greek expedition to Troy. The traditional Homeric heroes are unmasked. If there are any heroes left, they are the women, slaves, and children.[1] Euripides' universe is bleak, since the gods are not benevolent, nor even neutral forces: they personify the irrationality of man and can be distinctly malevolent. *Philia* (benevolent love) replaces heroism: in an irrational, dark universe only man's consideration for man provides a flicker of light.[2]

In Sophocles' *Ajax* we have the story of a hero who is slighted by his own army. He is known to be the greatest warrior, second only to Achilles at Troy, but the arms of the slain Achilles are awarded to his rival Odysseus, who is known more for his cleverness than his bravery. Athena protects the Greek army from Ajax's revenge by driving him mad, letting him think that he is torturing and slaughtering his enemies rather than herds of sheep and cattle. Tecmessa, Ajax's concubine, finds him after he has regained sanity. He is resolved to die rather than live in a world where he is not appreciated. He commits suicide. The leaders refuse to bury his body, in spite of the protests of Ajax's half-brother Teucer. Odysseus finally convinces the leaders that it would be in their interest to bury Ajax. The play ends with this muted reconciliation.

Sophocles shows us traces of the Homeric hero, not one who wins victories as he did in epic, but one who in defeat shows the glory of a man who will not yield. Ajax says to Tecmessa that she is foolish if she tries to make Ajax not Ajax (*Ajax* 595–96). In the *Philoctetes*, Neoptolemos recognizes the disgust and difficulty one meets in all things when one is not true to one's nature (902–3).

Sophoclean tragedy is in part determined by character.[3] Aristotle said that Sophocles made men as they ought to be, but Euripides saw men as they were. It is the dichotomy of circumstance, the concatenation of gods, other men, and fate, as opposed to a type of ideal character—man as he ought to be—that creates much of the tragedy in Sophocles.

How do Peter Sellars as director and Robert Auletta as translator treat Ajax as an idea, as a character, as a play, and as a production? I shall be discussing the production done in 1986 at La Jolla Playhouse. Some of Sophocles' original remains, but this time the language is in modern English. There are many additions and changes, and refreshing new ideas help to bring this ancient tragedy into modern times. We shall look at the changes in and the similarities to Sophocles' play that determined this Ajax. In this version, we mourn Ajax's death, but can we afford his life?

In the Homeric epics that describe the Trojan War and its immediate aftermath, heroism provides a way of life. A hero is told that he is to act nobly—*aei aristeuein*, "always excel"(*Il.* 6.208)—so that he can acquire immortal fame. Achilles chooses a brief life filled with glory over a long one lived in obscurity. Unlike the epics that glorify the noble deeds of heroes, tragedy reflects on their consequences for others.

Ajax is a hero of the Homeric epics second only to Achilles; when the ideals of a warrior conflict with the ideals of the citizen, Ajax becomes a tragic figure. This play deals with the consequences of a soldier and hero having to reenter civilian life and learn to compromise.

Even the Homeric epics show the difficult transition from military to civilian life. The hero of the earlier epic, the *Iliad*, is Achilles (Ajax's model), a military hero who exemplifies bravery, despises deception, and dies in defense of his honor. The hero of the second epic is Odysseus, the survivor, who lives primarily by his wits, to the point that the goddess Athena says to him, "One man must be clever indeed to get the best of you, even a god, . . . when even in your own land you will not leave off deceiving and telling false tales which you love from the bottom of your heart" (*Od.* 13.291–95). Contrast this with Achilles, who says to Odysseus, "More hateful to me than the gates of Hades is the man who hides one thing in his heart and says another" (*Il.* 9.312–13). It is Achilles who dies and Odysseus who survives. In the modern world are compromise and negotiations necessary for survival? Plutarch quotes Lysander, a spiritual descendant of Odysseus, who also does not consider truth better than falsehood, but values each according to need: "Where the lion's skin doesn't reach, sew on the fox's" (*Lysander* 6.4).

After Achilles' death, his arms are awarded to Odysseus, the most inappropriate heir because his approach to life—negotiation and compromise—is more suited to the demands of civilization than to his own authentic being. This is first mentioned in the *Odyssey* (11.543–47), and later developed at length by the Cyclic poets (Arctinus in the *Aethiopis*, ca. 776 B.C., and Lesches' *Little Iliad*, ca. 700 B.C.). Ajax takes offense at this decision and kills himself on the dawn of the following day. It is in the *Little Iliad* that we first find the madness motif (see Proclus' abstract). Sophocles may have added the idea that Ajax offended Athena because he refused her help in battle, an example of *hybris* more suitable for Greek tragedy than epic.[4] Auletta gives Ajax an additional act of *hybris*—Ajax rapes Athena. This violation is more than just the violence of war; it is also sexist and racist (Athena is played by a black woman).

Ajax is a hero whose time has passed. As Rosenmeyer notes: "The hero does not count, he lives, and when life becomes a sordid

business of ticking off days, he sacrifices life. . . . The heroic nature
. . . seeks to perpetuate itself against mutation, and to stabilize the
world which it dominates. And to do this, it must oppose the agent
of change, time."[5] The hero is dead, but, as in Homer, heroism is
immortal: "Ajax stood with the gods, and fought against time. He
perished as a man, but his heroism survives, beyond good or evil,
beyond the reach of time, in the pure air of everlasting life which
even in tragedy is the reward and proof of an earthly existence
purposefully spent."[6]

Knox also describes the Sophoclean hero, pointing out that it is
no accident that there are numerous suicides in Sophocles' plays—
six in his seven plays, against four in Euripides' nineteen, and not
one in Aeschylus.[7] "The hero chooses death. This is after all the
logical end of his refusal to compromise. Life in human society is
one long compromise; we live, all of us, only by constantly subduing
our own will, our own desires, to the demands of others, expressed
as the law of the community or the opinion of our fellowmen."[8]
Not Ajax, who dies for himself in a defiant act of self-definition. As
Charles Segal notes, "Ajax thus fulfills the characteristically Sophoclean pattern: by apparently losing everything that defines 'himself,'
the hero becomes 'himself' in a profounder and truer way."[9] While
Ajax is a glorious hero in Homer, in Sophocles he becomes a tragic
hero who wins immortal glory.

In the Auletta/Sellars' reworking of the myth, however, we find
ourselves in a world where the rules have changed. War is no longer
fought by men, but instead by technology and computers: the hero
is faceless and nameless.[10] Homer and Sophocles commemorate the
glory of men who fight in war. Besides the Trojan War, Sophocles
remembers the recent victories against the Persians, where civilization (Greece) symbolically triumphs over barbarism (the Persians).
After the Peloponnesian War, Euripides wrote about the change in
the entire notion of heroism. No longer did one commemorate the
glory of the victors, but rather the suffering of the victims. Now in
the nuclear age, after a war there may be no victims left alive, nor
poets to lament.

The "heroics" of a nuclear war are generically different from the
heroics of a war before the invention of gunpowder. Now nations,
not individuals, square off. Auletta's text concludes with the chorus
saying: "It's not easy to be on this earth, with its warrior stars and

furious men; it's hard to pierce the night, and difficult to see the day; but if we aren't careful with every moment, every sight, the dark will come in with the tide and the future wipe us out."[11] In comparison, Sophocles' play ends: "There are many things that man can learn after he sees them, but before he sees, no one can foretell the future or fate." Against fate, heroic vitality still has meaning, but the context is different. The potential destruction of the human race is contrasted with the heroism of the individual; this is the main difference between the ancient and the modern play. Freedom is still a vital issue, but the rules, indeed the game itself, have changed.

Sophocles emphasizes the heroism of men who struggle against gods and fate; he shows the Homeric hero in conflict with fifth-century (modern for him) social demands. His heroes have faults, quirks, sometimes even hateful traits, but their nobility is unmistakable. They have our admiration and this is enough. His is a paean to the glory of man: the divine now is seen to be in man, who is superior to the gods *because* of his mortality. The price of heroism is death, but with it is purchased immortal glory in the memory of humankind. Memories can also be created, and Auletta's version deals with the construction of memory. He shows how a country creates its past, complete with constructed traditions, so that it can shape and control its future. It is the molestation of, and the authority exerted over, a text that then is used as a tool of power.[12]

Ajax embodies the greatness of man. Sophocles says, "There are many wonders in the universe, but none more wondrous than man" (*Antigone* 332). He uses the word *deinos*, which means both wondrous and terrible: the source of creation and destruction. And this is modern man's dilemma. Ajax says a noble man must either live with honor or die with honor (*Ajax* 479–80), and characters echo this in Sophocles' other plays (e.g., *Electra* 989). Now one man, or one nation, can make that decision for the entire human race.

Ajax is played by the deaf actor Howie Seago in Sellars' production. Here is Ajax the isolated scapegoat—the sacrifice that society demands for survival? Does he express the ambiguity of a hero/warrior needed by society and yet a danger to that society? Is he the lone hero, dead to the new requirements, whose day is over? Does the new day belong to Odysseus: the era of a Dulles, a Kissinger, and a Baker? Are heroics now dead so that humanity and the human race can live? Or is this modern compromise itself fatal? In what circumstances is suicide a viable alternative to life? For the individual? For the race?

These are some of the many questions raised by *Ajax*. Sellars places his drama in front of the Pentagon and shows the other characters with microphones in front of them, as if they were testifying before some senate committee or in a courtroom; but Ajax remains isolated. His words are relayed by members of the chorus, who perform the ancient function of the mask, a representation, yet clearly "other." The *Verfremdungseffekt* created by Sophocles' words is now augmented by this deaf actor whose lines are delivered by others.

The outline of Sophocles' play is preserved, but additions both in the text and the production do not simply translate the text to modern times; while many ambiguities from the original are reproduced, startling new ones are created. Athena, played by the black actress Aleta Mitchell, opens the play as she walks slowly toward Odysseus, performed by another black actor, here dressed in an officer's uniform. The choice of a black, white or oriental actress/actor seems accidental, aside from the choice of Tecmessa (whose race is more specifically suggestive in the play's context). She represents a woman from a "leftist" country just defeated by the Americans (an oriental woman in the role suggests Vietnam, Korea, the Philippines, Japan—wherever America has fought "for Democracy").[13]

Auletta's text describes the setting as "America" and says that it takes place in "the very near future." His Tecmessa is described as a Latin woman. He goes on to say: "America has just won a great victory in Latin America. The forces of the left have been decisively beaten. The war was a long and bloody one, marked, on the American side, by a great deal of bitterness, hostility, and rivalry between factions of the armed forces."

Auletta, by putting the ancient play in a modern political situation, has abstracted the conflict generated between those who manipulate truth and those who are their own standard. Truth used to be conveyed by the actions of the individualistic hero, but now "truth" is the propaganda of politicians. There are competing notions of truth, e.g., Ajax versus Odysseus, Plato versus Protagoras. In such situations, what do heroes do? What do politicians do? What is

Sophocles' truth vis-à-vis Sellars' and Auletta's? One establishes the ancient model and the other shows us modern practice.

The ancient play has been considered awkward in that the first part focuses on Ajax, his shame at losing Achilles' arms, and his mad slaughter of the sheep (instead of the Greek leaders), followed by his suicide. And the second part, it has been suggested, is merely a tacked-on denouement that depicts the wrangling of weak men over a hero's body:

> The second part of the play—the coda or whatever you like to call it, the dispute about the burial—is less concerned with purely theatrical considerations than the first. For it is certainly not just tacked on for merely external reasons, in order to make up the length of the play, as some have thought; nor is the relationship of this part to the whole satisfactorily explained by saying that the fate of the body was more important to an Athenian that it is to us.[14]

Some, however, have seen the second part as defining the first part, giving definition to Ajax, and revealing how his earlier faults are subsumed in his attempt to preserve a personal truth as a standard in a world now based on lies, rhetoric, and bad faith:

> the latter part of the play is not an arbitrary addition to the former, but a natural, indeed a necessary development of it.[15]
>
> The purpose of the finale is rather to contrast the genuine greatness of the tragic hero who was fated to die with the spuriousness and conceit of those who opposed him, triumphed over him, and lived on—their ingratitude, pusillanimity, envy, meanness and arrogance.[16]

Sellars presents an Ajax wallowing in blood, screaming his defiance to Athena. She reveals him to Odysseus, who is said to be so good at tracking that "no CIA man could be better fitted for the job." Athena calls Ajax "the force and heart of the American army," as she uses him to illustrate that men are "kittens, playing on a ledge above the sea; one gust of wind is all it takes." Ajax is encased in a transparent plastic box, which represents among other things his madness; it contains the blood of animals that he has destroyed. Indeed, when we first see him, Ajax is wading in the blood of the victims. The box disappears when he is restored to sanity.

The blood of the first part of the play becomes mingled blood and water in the second. Ajax's body lies close to the shore and water flows freely on the stage. The blood of the animals mixes with Ajax's own blood, but he is purified and cleansed in the water of his death.

Tecmessa "testifies" with a microphone, telling of Ajax's madness, and recapitulating her past when she was a child: "And my father and the leaders of my country were killed and trains were loaded with the dead; all because the Americans willed it." Ajax also recreates his past (via the chorus who speak for him): his father was a general, and his "father's father was a quiet man, a storekeeper," but "his grandfather was a Sioux chief, a warrior! And one Spring day wiped out an arrogant West Point lieutenant named Gratin and his entire troop outside of Fort McKenzie." Ajax feels that Sioux blood and is himself "The Great American War Chief." He is a fighting tool, and his skills, although derived from the original "enemy," have stood the army in good stead. We sense another political undercurrent. Not only does Ajax represent truth versus lies, he is the "true" American, in that he was descended from the original native people. The others came later, and introduced their own rules.

Agamemnon will later emphasize his ancestry and what constitutes proper birth. He says, "One doesn't become an American overnight, you know, just because one's father was an American general. My family has been here for well over two hundred years." The irony is obvious when one thinks how long Ajax's and Teucer's ancestors were in "America." Agamemnon's family came from Europe. Ajax, however, is a native American, but his people seem not to exist from the colonists' perspective. One is an American, it would seem, only if one can trace one's lineage to the European imperialists.

Agamemnon also threatens Tecmessa: "Recently some very incriminating evidence concerning your activities has surfaced." Once again, facts are manipulated. He argues: "Put your trust in us, your leaders. Try to forget your egos, your needs, your passions. . . . What we need now is loyalty and allegiance to those in charge. . . . Accept the democratic process." And the "democratic process" is defined by those who control the sources of information (the same ones who rigged the decision about Achilles' armor).

Both Sophocles' original play and this modern version indicate that the awarding of the armor to Odysseus was due to the corruption of the judges. Since it is Ajax and Teucer who make this claim, however, and since it is never admitted by Odysseus or the other leaders, one has to judge whether this is simply an ego-saving excuse on Ajax's part. In the broader scheme, the armor's being bestowed on Odysseus is symbolic of the new shift in power from the man skilled in war to the man skilled in politics.

Auletta also makes it clear that politics are what succeed now, and the manipulation of information. Menelaus and Agamemnon want to make the body of Ajax disappear. Menelaus explains, "Regions of the mind and the spirit must be cordoned off. America must be protected at all cost." Teucer asks, "And how do you explain his disappearance?" Menelaus answers, "We think of something, or we think of nothing and call it a mystery. As far as America is concerned, this night never happened. Every sign of Ajax's activities will be eliminated. Our agents are scouring every inch of the terrain right now. You all, by the way, are breaking the law. As of now, this is a total security area—off limits to everyone. A piece of radiation has fallen on American soil, and it is too contaminated, too dangerous to touch or to move. So we leave it right here, for as long as it takes, a thousand years, forever." Ajax's truth is the danger.

Odysseus finally wins Agamemnon over, by appealing to his political advancement, the only argument that can work: "I understand that you may be running for major office in the near future." Odysseus goes on to argue that Ajax has too many friends simply to disappear. On this basis Agamemnon gives in and the chorus congratulate Odysseus: "You know what you know, and you know it well. You play the game like one of the greats. We admire your skill and performance." The game is the information game. Now one wins through controlling the media.[17] As Auletta's Agamemnon says, "We all know that a dead man can be fiercer in combat than any living body." In the *Choephoroi* of Aeschylus the statement is made, "The dead are killing the living" (886). Memory was then, in ancient Greece, a goad to the living in the search for vengeance, and it still is. Sellars' play also shows us how to create memories.

Sellars's *Ajax* shows how the media shapes our thought through the value-loaded terms it uses. A legitimate protestor, one fighting to reclaim his land, is called a "terrorist," whereas, when those in authority do worse than any terrorist, they are lauded for carrying out "police actions," or "making the world safe." The orthodox media protects the delicate audience from deciphering the facts. Blame the victim and accuse the enemy before the enemy accuses you. Manipulate opinion through the media and conceal the power that shapes morality.

Ajax knows too much and the gods and leaders arrange that he will be silenced and that he will vanish. Others then testify, but are threatened that their testimony should be of the right kind. Tecmessa is told she may be deported and Teucer is tied up. Only Odysseus' political solution is acceptable: he bribes Agamemnon with the offer of power. Odysseus adopts the role of Clytemnestra, laying out the red carpet of political office . . . and Agamemnon begins to walk.

Odysseus also threatens Agamemnon with oblivion: "In ten or twenty years, we could be dead, and somebody may decide that we weren't the heroes that we were cracked up to be. And we need somebody in our corner. . . . Nothing is completely secure these days. Power and opinions are constantly shifting in this country." Odysseus is the gameplayer who plays to win. He knows that games are won though public opinion, and it is this opinion that must be created. Facts are still to be manipulated, and Odysseus is cleverer than Menelaus and Agamemnon at knowing which facts are to be manipulated.[18]

Auletta also varies the original by his emphasis on Athena's sexual connection to both Odysseus and Ajax; Sellars carries this even further by having Athena masturbate with a microphone as she watches Ajax and shows him to Odysseus. She also takes the sword from Ajax's body and gives it to Tecmessa; Ajax's death is in part Athena's rape of him, reversing Auletta's text, which claims that Ajax once raped her. Athena uses her sexuality in a kind of power play. She promises Odysseus, "I'll control him" (speaking of Ajax). She addresses Ajax directly: "General, is this the way you treat your date, stand her up like this? You should be ashamed." Ajax responds by saying, "How pretty you look tonight . . . " She asks, "Is your sword well greased with the blood of your enemies, General?" He answers, "It's still smoking and hot." He describes his supposed victory, finally asking, "Do you love me, Athena?" She avoids the question of love, answering, "I admire you deeply." He says, "But I want you to love me." She parries, "Love may come

Scene from Suzuki Tadashi's *Clytemnestra*
Clytemnestra killing Orestes
CLYTEMNESTRA: Shiraishi Kayoko
ORESTES: Tom Hewitt
ELECTRA: Takahashi Hiroko
Credit: Miyauchi Katsu

Scene from Suzuki Tadashi's *The Trojan Women*
CASSANDRA: Shiraishi Kayoko

Credit: Suzuki Tadashi

Scene from Suzuki Tadashi's *The Trojan Women*
THE GOD JIZO: Fueda Uichiro
TROJAN WOMAN: Ishida Michiko
WARRIOR: Kimura Yasushi
Credit: Furudate Katsuaki

Scene from Suzuki Tadashi's *The Trojan Women*
CASSANDRA: Shiraishi Kayoko

Credit: Andreas Pohlmann

Scene from Suzuki Tadashi's *The Trojan Women*
TROJAN WOMAN: Tada Keiko
WARRIOR: Kimura Yasushi

Credit: Andreas Pohlmann

Scene from Suzuki Tadashi's *Clytemnestra*
CLYTEMNESTRA: Shiraishi Kayoko
Credit: Furudate Katsuaki

Scene from Suzuki Tadashi's *Clytemnestra*
CLYTEMNESTRA: Shiraishi Kayoko
Credit: Andreas Pohlmann

Scene from Suzuki Tadashi's *Clytemnestra*
CLYTEMNESTRA: Shiraishi Kayoko
ORESTES: Tom Hewitt
ELECTRA: Takahashi Hiroko
Credit: Andreas Pohlmann

Scene from Suzuki Tadashi's *Clytemnestra*
(center) CLYTEMNESTRA: Shiraishi Kayoko

Credit: Furudate Katsuaki

Scene from Suzuki Tadashi's *Bacchae*
DIONYSUS: Shiraishi Kayoko
PENTHEUS: Nishikibe Takahisa
Credit: Furudate Katsuaki

Scene from Suzuki Tadashi's *Bacchae*
DIONYSUS: Shiraishi Kayoko
PENTHEUS: Tom Hewitt
Credit: Suzuki Tadashi

Suzuki's *Bacchae*
AGAVE: Shiraishi Kayoko
Credit: Furudate Katsuaki

Suzuki's *Bacchae*
AGAVE: Shiraishi Kayoko
Credit: Furudate Katsuaki

Peter Sellars' *Ajax*
AJAX: Howie Seago
Credit: Micha Langer

Peter Sellars' *Ajax*
AJAX: Howie Seago
ACERE: Justin Kidwell
Credit: Micha Langer

Peter Sellars' *Ajax*
TECMESSA: Lauren Tom
ATHENA: Aleta Mitchell

Credit: Micha Langer

Peter Sellars' *Ajax*
TEUCER: Khin Kyaw Maung
MENELAUS: Ralph Marrero

Credit: Micha Langer

Tony Harrison's *The Trackers*
GRENFELL: Jack Shepherd
HUNT: Barrie Rutter

Credit: Sandra Lou

Tony Harrison's *The Trackers*
Set at Delphi under Parnassos

Credit: Vicki Hallam

Tony Harrison's *The Trackers*
Peter Andrew, Christopher Beck, Stephen Bent, Jim Bywater, Lawrence
Evans, Billy Fellows, Dave Hill, Clive Rowe

Credit: Vicki Hallam

Tony Harrison's *The Trackers*
SILENUS: Barrie Rutter

Credit: Vicki Hallam

Theodoros Terzopoulos' *Medeamaterial*
MEDEA (in memory): Eyrikleia Sofroniadou
MEDEA (present): Sophia Michopoulou

Credit: Theodoros Terzopoulos

Theodoros Terzopoulos' *Medeamaterial*
Sophia Michopoulou, Dimitris Siakaras, George Simeonidis, Theodoros
Polizonis, Eyrikleia Sofroniadou, Akis Sakellariou
Credit: Theodoros Terzopoulos

Thomas Murphy's *The Sanctuary Lamp*
FRANCISCO: Garret Keogh
HARRY: Peadar Lamb
Credit: Fergus Bourke

Thomas Murphy's *The Sanctuary Lamp*
MAUDIE: Bairbre Ni Caoimh
FRANCISCO: Garret Keogh
HARRY: Peadar Lamb
Credit: Fergus Bourke

Thomas Murphy's *The Sanctuary Lamp*
MONSIGNOR: Peadar Lamb
MAUDIE: Bernedette Shortt
FRANCISCO: John Kavanagh

Credit: Fergus Bourke

Thomas Murphy's *The Sanctuary Lamp*
MAUDIE: Bernedette Shortt
Credit: Fergus Bourke

Suzuki Tadashi
Credit: Robyn Hunt

Tony Harrison
Jocelyn Herbert, Design and Lighting for *The Trackers*
Credit: Vicki Hallam

Piero Bordin, Director of Carnuntum Festival
Peter Sellars
Marianne McDonald

Credit: Piero Bordin

Thomas Murphy
Credit: Peter Reynolds

Olia Lazaridou
Theodoros Terzopoulos
Akis Sakellariou
Credit: Theodoros Terzopoulos

later." As Odysseus watches, she masturbates. Power over her victim has a strong sexual component. Auletta and Sellars have broadened the war between Ajax and the other leaders to include the war between the sexes.

A messenger tells of Ajax's treatment of Athena:

> And she comes to him when he's a young man, shy and gentle as a breeze, to be his sister, to be his friend. But he will not accept or understand her, nor let her befriend his heart, and he jeers at her sacred words, and then one day decides to use her as a woman, as a wanton, as a soldier would use his slut, caressing her breasts and her thighs. "Oh, Ajax," she cries, "Oh, dear Ajax, treat me like the sister of your soul, and not like the soldier's whore, twisted in foul sheets." "Then go off and consort with General Odysseus," he says. "I'll have none of you." But still she loves him, still, and comes this time to bargain with him. "Oh, listen to me, Ajax, and I will teach you the secrets of war and victory." And he tells her: "The secrets of war are mine and mine alone to find, and victory my gift alone to give to my men and my country. Go to General Odysseus, he needs all the help he can get." But still she loves him, and one day comes to him in a field, and rests her head upon his heart, and sweetly nuzzles his chest. But suddenly evil explodes within him like a bottle, and throwing her down upon the ground, he rips open her clothes with his dark shards, and then he rapes her.

This scene is a variant of Ajax's rejection of the gods as recounted by the messenger in Sophocles' play. There he refuses his father, who urges him always to ask the gods for help. Ajax boasts that he wants to win without their help. Then he specifically rejects Athena's help when she urges him on, telling her, "Go help the other Greeks. No one can break through where I stand" (*Ajax*, 774–75). Auletta translates this into the sexual arena, but Ajax is still Ajax. He will not be dependent on Tecmessa, nor even on Athena. He demands and takes love, as he would Achilles' armor. It is his due.

The two phases of woman are Athena and Tecmessa: mistress/goddess and wife/mortal. Ajax uses both for what he needs, sexual release and offspring. He will not owe Athena anything, nor will he protect Tecmessa if protection consists of his being a husband rather than a hero. He is deaf to their words.[19] When Athena hands the sword to Tecmessa it is a double victory for the two women, but also a double loss. Still, it is a loss of what they never had.

It would be easy to interpret *Ajax* as a Greek morality play, like *Jedermann* (*Everyman*, the most famous of the medieval morality plays), illustrating the vengeance of Athena; man goes too far, and the gods must have their due. "Know thyself," written on the temple at Delphi, means know your limitations as a man vis-à-vis the gods. But this is not Sophocles' meaning. Nor does Athena kill Ajax because he rejected her offer first of friendship, then of love on her terms. Ajax is master in his own terms. Ajax kills himself because he rejects a society where compromises and lies are the norm. He rejects a society where heroism is constructed by the media, by a rigged vote, and by falsified testimony. Ajax refuses to be a hero constructed by the gods, other men, and certainly not by a woman.

Ajax cannot hear, and Sellars' choice of a deaf actor is brilliant in conveying the character's majestic isolation. Another of Sophocles' sacred monsters. Ajax is debilitated spiritually and finally physically by his own restless internal power; he resembles Oedipus, Antigone, Philoctetes, and Heracles, likewise heroic monsters true to their own natures. It is Ajax's unique truth that blasts the compromising mediocrity of an Odysseus into insignificance.[20]

Ajax makes the familiar world strange. He shows it to us as a foreign land and creates a fresh perspective. The world of Odysseus and Heraclitus where up and down are one and the same (60 Diels-Kranz), or the world of Bias, where one treats the friend of today as if he were to be the enemy of tomorrow (Aristotle *Rhetoric* 2.13.4), is not a world for Ajax. He will never "yield to the gods or worship the sons of Atreus" (*Ajax* 666–67). He realizes the present impotence of the signified and will not accept the messages based on manipulated signifiers. Instead he chooses illuminating darkness: "O shadow, my light, most shining darkness" (*Ajax* 396–99).

Sellars adds an *angelos*, a messenger wearing wings (played by a large black actor, Ben Halley, Jr.), who recounts Ajax's blasphemous misdeeds, his rejection of the gods, and the rape of Athena. But Ajax is granted another chance: if he remains indoors for a day he will be saved. But could Ajax remain inside? It is outside, on the battlefield, that he is a hero. When the exterior comes to resemble the interior with its domestic compromises, life becomes unbearable for an Ajax. The angel (*angelos* means messenger in Greek) adds a familiar religious element; Ajax not only rejects the Greek gods, but the Judaeo-Christian ones as well. Yet Ajax is better than a god, because he can die.

Sellars has abstracted the content of the ancient play, raising questions about the possibility of honor and truth in contemporary political life. He has adapted the ancient themes to the modern world, where the manipulation of language has become more sophisticated because the capabilities of staging have been expanded by technology. Now the Pentagon looms behind the set, as Zeus loomed behind Aeschylus' Prometheus; words are conveyed by messengers, and their power is palpable.

The weapons of Ajax's enemies are words and time. Ajax lies (he has learned from the enemy) and dies (he will not be subject to time). Yet Ajax triumphs. His burial at the end of the play is a celebration, in a space consecrated by Ajax that will not include his enemies. Odysseus, the creature of the *polis*, the political master, the culmination of Aristotle's *politikon zoon* ("political animal"), is not invited.

V

Peter Sellars' Talk
at Carnuntum

I F I may just speak very briefly about the genesis of the production. I was the director of the American National Theater, in Washington, D.C., very close to the Pentagon, right across the river. It was the second term of Ronald Reagan and, as an artist with a public responsibility to permit the nation to think about itself, it becomes a question of what approach to take. In America, in the Reagan period, it is exactly the possibility of discussion that was not encouraged. Mr. Reagan was the first president to have fewer than four press conferences, and at these press conferences he would only answer questions from correspondents wearing red ties. Prearranged.

During this period, a very shocking event occurred. America bombed Libya, in an attempt, sort of an assassination attempt, I suppose. They tried to get Khaddafi, who for some reason was in another house that night. But there is a spectacle of this giant nation attempting to kill children, many miles away, because it was irri-

This talk was delivered at an international conference on Ancient Greek Drama, held in Carnuntum, Austria in September 1989. It followed the delivery of my paper (a version of the preceding chapter) on the *Ajax*.

tated. As a gesture, it was made without any consultation with Congress, without any of the normal kinds of discussion that precede, in our country, a large-scale military gesture. It was an event which made Reagan's imperial presidency complete, the idea that the President could operate independently of the rest of the government or the rest of the country.

When one is working in a theater that is called the American National Theater, one begins to think of Greek drama and the idea of a popular theater that is able to discuss issues that are very serious and, in fact, would be considered in our day undiscussable. This is our main crisis in America, where we live in a society that is almost the most censored society in the world. Very little information gets through that does not suit the purposes of the capitalist economic system. And the large-scale newspapers, and particularly television, operate under tremendous censorship. But again, it's a notion that is not an individual notion; it's no longer a question of individuals, but a question of a strange faceless collective that makes its decisions without asking anyone. So in America, it is a tall office building on the corner of 57th and the Avenue of the Americas (Sixth Avenue) in New York, where they make the decision in CBS News that it will not be this way.

This year in America, in every state in America, the budget for education has received its biggest cuts. Meanwhile, the largest single budget increase is for building prisons. So this becomes the shape of a developing society, where, frankly, most Americans are not educated enough to begin to enter a political discourse with any degree of sophistication. This is a crisis in the political life of the country because then George Bush and Michael Dukakis run against each other as the same candidate. And the election is decided on the basis of who looks best on television. George Bush has better makeup and he wears a tie. Meanwhile, we are sending troops to Nicaragua.

In this context, one asks if it is possible to make any statement that still has weight. Because, in America, there is a public that is now (and I feel this in Europe, increasingly) brought up through television to expect entertainment, and only entertainment. The task is to create an art that represents the public complexity, where one creates something that is, for example, as complex as the task of cleaning up a nuclear waste disposal site, which requires real thought, genuine expertise, and a series of very difficult decisions. It's not fun.

In this sense, one turns to Sophocles, because Sophocles is about the unresolvable questions in a human society, such as that notion that some things are permanently polluted, and may not be fixable. That after you have a toxic waste site, you have disposed of nuclear material in a certain place, it will never be clean; you have already ruined it for us. It is not that you can fix it; it is now ruined. And this idea, as it were, of two omnipotences meeting each other, if we can be Hegelian for a moment, this notion that you have two facts that come in complete contradiction, and in order to live your life, you have to choose which is true.

This is, of course, our crisis in a modern period, where we now know too much, where the myths we have are Marilyn Monroe and Donald Duck, where the notion of heroism that we have shows it no longer exists. We live in an age of the antihero, where Al Pacino and Robert de Niro are the big heroes, who for the public are larger than life. The movies make them exist on a mythological scale because their face is fifty feet wide. In every big Hollywood movie, these are not heroes, these are antiheroes. These are people who are against the society. These are people who are failures. These are people who are dangerous. These are people who are a menace. And this becomes the new hero.

We also have this strange notion where America has no sense of a past. For the Greeks, the generation of heroes were two generations, three generations before, where they were heroic once. In America, it's now science fiction. It's the future. You've already forgotten the generation past; you can't even remember them. Nobody was heroic before. It is the notion that in the science-fiction future there will be heroes. But the heroes are strangely selfish and think in a very primitive way.

So, in this period one turns to Sophocles for two things that were crucial to my survival in America. One is the ability to speak of the subject without flattery, because right now in the world, nothing is said without tremendous flattery. You have to entice the audience; you seduce the audience. You always say, "This will be fine; this will be OK; you'll like this." And Sophocles does not do that. Sophocles says, "Sorry, these are the facts; it's not attractive; too bad." Secondly, there is a sense that at the core of a society, and the core of a human being, is a moral question, and that the moral question cannot be moved. You can't shift it a few inches this way, or a few inches that way, to suit the convenience of the time. And if each of us asks ourselves seriously, How it is possible to live morally in this society?—you have to conclude that it is not possible, because the society itself is immoral.

For some people, this is not a personal crisis, but for others it is. It is a question of how can one allow one's own life, one's own very deep beliefs, to be gradually poisoned, gradually eroded, so that we have to pretend that we don't care. We pretend it doesn't matter, and it will be fine, and we will just look away. But here is the question of not hearing, and not seeing (and that is, of course, why I chose a deaf actor). There is the decision not to hear, the decision not to see, because each of us, when we get up in the morning, we see the newspaper. And you have to, just to get through the front page of the newspaper, decide, "I won't see this," and "I won't hear this," and then you drink your coffee. Because if you actually see it, and you actually hear it, it is not possible to accept this society. It is not possible to accept this disgusting debasement of what a human being truly is, what the genuine, heroic stature is of a human being.

A human being is the single greatest, most courageous, most beautiful moment of creation. And every day we foul it, we despoil it, we reduce it, we enslave it, and then we look away. But what happens if you insist on not looking away, and continue to look at a human being? This is, I must say, why I chose theater as a profession, because the work of art is man, is a person; and the question you ask is, How great can a single individual be?

In drama, in Sophocles, in Aeschylus, we have the shift of scale, which shows that the fate of one individual is the fate of a nation. And when we wake up and we tell ourselves every day that we ourselves can do nothing about this problem, that it is larger than we are, theater gives the light. Theater explains that one individual's decision, about how to live his life or not, is what makes the moral climate and temperature of a nation, and affects the political direction and the temper of a time. It's in the context of massive public passivity, and a feeling of helplessness in a world that we can no longer fix, that four years ago I turned to Sophocles for some help with the question of what is a single individual and is it possible to live? That is the background. For me the appeal of Greek drama is this insistence of those three playwrights to ask questions that our society rejects before you even ask. And yet they asked them anyway, and they asked them at length.

Marianne McDonald dealt with some of the structures that I used in order to present Greek drama today. I'll just mention a few of them briefly, because this is a conference on Greek drama. The masks are so important to present the scale of the human being in Greek drama. I felt a microphone was very important for the masks; I replaced masks with microphones, because the microphone is an amplifier, but also a cover. It enlarges the human figure, but it also creates distance and also is deceptive. It is the mask of our society, as it were.

One other reason to work with a deaf actor was, of course, he signs his role, and so there is a language of gesture. It was also very important that the Greek theater was dance, and that the emotional impact of the words was accompanied by the physical impact of a dance gesture. In having the central part of the drama expressed in very powerful, intense sign language, one got this sheer visceral rage and intensity that lies at the core of the drama. These Greek dramas are not intellectual problems, but instead they involve the whole human being. And again, every dimension of one's being is thrust into this intense conflict.

For the chorus, I used it as a commentary, as a translation. For me, I have to say, the most moving element of Greek drama is the last play of the *Oresteia*, where they invent voting. I do feel that Greek drama was instituted as a kind of biological survival mechanism about society, to teach people how to vote, to teach people what democracy is, and the gesture of voting for your favorite play was actually training for jury duty. As a citizen, if you have to sit on a jury, you have to decide, "Is this person lying or not," and pay attention to who is testifying. You have to decide if their case is just. Right now, most American juries are very sad, because Americans' only training is *Rambo* and *Hill Street Blues*. I think the Greeks invented this form of drama as a training for participation in society and for a way to understand jury duty. So the large construct that I place on the play was that it was an ongoing trial, where the chorus functions as a kind of jury and Ajax could present his case; but, of course, the bitter fact is that the judge is Athena. So Ajax, in court, enters his plea against Athena, and then looks and notices that, sadly, she is the judge, so he just lost. Because, of course, it's rigged in advance, but nonetheless you have your day in court.

I will just explain a little bit more the other images that Marianne mentioned, so you can have a sense of what they were. We spent almost a year designing the set, and it went through many different forms. There are four images that combine: first, I wanted, of course, the Pentagon—which was across the river. We chose, however, the back of the Pentagon, where they take out the garbage, the refuse—not the front. So on the back loading dock, near the garbage, we had the trial of Ajax. The stage floor was made of stainless steel, and slanted—very pitched—very steeply. Ajax was presented first in his tank of blood, where the actor sat there for a half hour before the show began, underneath a cover. When we started the show, we took the cover off, and he began "speaking." So it was terrifying both for him to soak in the blood, and the audience to see him. Then he stepped out of the box into the courtroom, and trailed his blood everywhere. Every time he'd make a hand gesture, blood would fly and spatter; he was just soaking in it, and the blood was just there on the stainless steel floor. And the image I really wanted, of course, was an abattoir, was a slaughterhouse, stainless steel counters, where, after the butchery of the animals, they'd wash it all away, and there would be more butchery tomorrow, and it's an ongoing abattoir. Then the release was when he went to the beach; the garage doors of the Pentagon flew up; you saw the sky through the windows of the Pentagon, and you saw the Pentagon facade as exactly that, a facade. Then, from the whole width of the stage, torrents of water would pour down while Ajax, after suiciding, lay there, and the whole bloody stage was just washed by this continuous stream of water, which occurred throughout the whole second half of the play for forty minutes. The whole rest of the play took place in the middle of this giant river.

Menelaus and Agamemnon were dressed as five-star Pentagon generals. And of course, in Washington, the fact that I could have five-star generals played by black people was incredible. [These were the days before Colin Powell.] But dressed in their very fancy military, shiny uniforms, perfect shoes, they had to walk in this bloody water to stand near Ajax. So, it was messy and it messed up their uniforms a bit. But the discussion took place over his body, and it's my feeling, my reading of Sophocles, that Ajax, during this entire discussion, is still alive. While these people haggle over his memory, and insult him, he's lying there alive, with his eyes open, as they decide to erase him from history. But they didn't notice. They are so happy to have the body that nobody bent down to actually look and see if he was still alive. They assume he's dead.

The only other thing I should mention is that what is so compelling in Greek drama, always, is what is not in the text. And one thing, which is not in the text, is the speech of Ajax's son, Acere's speech [Eurysaces, Ajax's son, in Sophocles' play]. I must say, in a way, many of the most powerful scenes in this drama, as in many Greek dramas, are scenes without words: where the son had no words to speak to his deaf father. The role of Tecmessa obviously is comparable to Virgilia in Shakespeare's *Coriolanus*, where the moral center of the play is mostly silent.

This play of Sophocles has been criticized for being strangely shaped, and I feel again that's because people are only looking at the text and not realizing that Sophocles was creating some of his most important dramatic functions through what is not being said. In the second half of the play, it is not these huge speeches of the generals that are significant, it is the silence of the wife and the child that is truly speaking. It is the silence of the dead body lying at their feet that is eloquent. I feel that the second half of this play is one of Sophocles' greatest inspirations, because the true argument is being made by the silent figures, while the speeches are, as usual, given to the generals.

VI

Harrison's *The Trackers:*
A People's Tract

Rainer Maria Rilke wrote of Orpheus words that could apply to Apollo, and to every poet:

> Die So-Geliebte, dass aus einer Leier
> mehr Klage kam als je aus Klagefrauen;
> dass eine Welt aus Klage ward, in der
> alles noch einmal da war . . .

> The one, so loved, that from a lyre,
> more keening came than from women keeners;
> that a world from keening appeared, in which
> everything once more was there . . . . [1]

Tony Harrison shows the power of the lyre to create and destroy, destroy and create, a song for the world celebrating creation over destruction, but also sending a warning through its blazing message.

A version of this chapter has been published in the *Proceedings of the Fourth International Meeting on Ancient Greek Drama* (Athens: European Cultural Centre of Delphi, 1989), pp. 170-87; another version was published in *Tony Harrison*, ed. Neil Astley, *Bloodaxe Critical Anthologies* (Newcastle upon Tyne: Bloodaxe Books, 1991), I:470-485.

In his *Trackers of Oxyrhynchus*, based on Sophocles' *Ichneutai*, he has taken the Sophoclean satyr play and broken the classical mold, allowing papyrological fragments to fuel a burst of tragicomic fireworks. As the ancient play is reconstructed in a modern frame, it becomes a commentary on elitist art and society. Cultural imperialism is lifted from its ancient setting, as modern punks put a torch to the salvaged manuscript and the trackers obliterate themselves along with their masters—a bitter warning to those who would like to reserve the benefits of art and society for themselves.

The satyr play was a comic play that regularly followed the tragedies at the dramatic festivals held yearly in ancient Athens. Tony Harrison held his premiere at Delphi on July 12, 1988, following the presentations of the tragedies at the Fourth International Meeting of Ancient Greek Drama. It is only that performance that I shall be dealing with. Harrison rewrites the play for each space in which it is performed, so far in the National Theatre, Salts Mill, near Bradford, England, and Carnuntum, Austria. An international tour was planned for 1991, when this book was in process. The "elite" and the "outsiders" vary from place to place, as does the text. For instance, the Burg Theater in Vienna has a statue of Apollo with his lyre on its pediment, so in the production performed near Vienna, Apollo says he can see his future as "Kultur Kommandant für die Burger von Wien." Each place has its own elite; each place, its own oppressed.

The only complete satyr play to survive is Euripides' *Cyclops*, but there are extensive fragments from Sophocles' *Ichneutai*, and a certain amount from Aeschylus' *Isthmiastai* (*Satyrs at the Isthmian Games*) and *Diktyoulkoi* (*Satyrs Hauling the Net*). We also have many titles and scattered fragments from others, often identifiable as satyr plays because they are indicated as such by words like *satyrikos* in their title. This suggests that Silenus and a chorus of satyrs, followers of Dionysus, feature as characters. The meter and vocabulary are often the same as in tragedy.[2] The plays are short (about 700 lines versus about 1400 in the usual tragedy).

Sophocles' *Ichneutai* tells the story of the theft of Apollo's cattle. Apollo enlists the help of Silenus and his satyrs to find them. The baby Hermes has stolen them, but a nymph, Kyllene, protects this precocious baby. The fragmented play breaks off, but we can tell from other sources that Apollo discovers the identity of the thief.

He strikes a bargain not to punish Hermes for the theft of the cattle. In return for the lyre that the baby Hermes has constructed out of a tortoise shell and gut from the purloined cattle, Hermes can keep the rest of the cattle.

Satyrs themselves are regarded as the offspring of Silenus and the nymphs. They are represented as bearded, but bald, with pointed ears, erect *phalloi,* and horses' tails. Sileni are often regarded simply as older satyrs. All are lustful, cowardly, and fond of wine, and are known for their vigorous dance called the *Sikinnis,* which Harrison in his adaptation renders through clog dancing, an old working-class dance of the North of England, executed by "hoofers" wearing wooden clogs.

The Greeks prized both dramatic festivals and sports competitions, and the stadium could be found close to the theater, as at Delphi. The ancient Greeks cultivated the arts of the body as well as those of the mind, and athletes were valued as much as the artists (too much, according to Xenophanes and Euripides). The goatish figure of the satyr himself symbolizes the meeting of a physical, or primitive, element with an intellectual or cultural component: he is half-animal and half-man.[3] The satyr play also provided psychological relief after the high anguish of tragedy.

Plato begins a discussion of the links between tragedy and comedy at the end of the *Symposium;* but in ancient Greece tragedy and comedy were separate genres with their own meters, structure, language, and purposes. The satyr play was a bridge between the two, parodying tragedy, yet using its meter and vocabulary.[4]

Euripides probably did the most to break down the distinctions, and one sees more comic elements in his plays than in any of the other tragedians' works. His was also the more "democratic" drama, and comedy can be considered a more "democratic" art form than tragedy. Tragedy itself may be seen as a "democratic" development after the aristocratic art form of the epic and lyric, if only because the audience in the fifth century almost certainly included women and possibly, on occasion, slaves.[5]

The satyr play contains both comic and tragic elements within its own specific form. Since it follows the tragedies, it often reworks tragic themes in a lighter vein, sometimes directly related to the tragedy immediately preceding (e.g., *The Sphinx* following Aeschylus' trilogy dealing with the story of Oedipus; and the *Ichneutai* was perhaps a reworking of the *Ajax*).[6] Jane Harrison saw the cycle of tragedy and satyr play as illustrating the alternation of the seasons, so the scene in the *Ichneutai* of Kyllene emerging in response to the satyrs' dance could represent "a form of the spring *dromenon*, the resurrection of life and nature from its winter death."[7]

The satyr play is often escapist: we delight in the folktale, especially in the stratagems of the trickster. Hermes is the trickster in this instance, and in Harrison's *Trackers* magic is provided throughout, with crates and cartons bursting open and satyrs appearing. Riddles abound. Kyllene only answers questions in riddling form — for example, speaking of the dead animal that has a voice but is silent when alive (the lyre, constructed on a tortoise shell with cow gut). There is also Harrison's magical wordplay and electrifying transformations: fellaheen (Egyptian workers) become satyrs, then punks; boxes range from Caligari cabinets to dance stages.

The satyr typically sees something new and is often amazed (e.g., at fire in *Prometheus Pyrkaieus*; in the *Ichneutai* at the lyre or in Harrison's version, at the ghetto-blasters). Satyrs are used to react to civilization's discoveries: one tests things out on the masses. They are required to serve, although they would rather participate. Harrison uses the statue of the satyr supporting the stage *skene* in the theater of Dionysus as a living symbol in this play. The satyr, however, would rather act than support; we have rumblings of this revolution as early as Aeschylus' *Isthmiastai*, in which the satyrs leave Dionysus' service to compete in the games themselves.

The plots of satyr plays are often derived from mythology. Sutton says, "The tragic hero is notoriously a linear descendant of Achilles, and the satyric hero is equally descended from Odysseus."[8] One might add Hercules, another "ambiguous" Greek hero, with his animalistic side and reputation for buffoonery, as well as Sisyphus (Odysseus' father according to the tradition followed by satyr plays). Harrison gives us Marsyas too, but he is more a tragic hero of the Euripidean rather than the Sophoclean type. We remember his suffering more than his heroic action.

Whereas most tragedies take place in or are centered about a city, the setting of the satyr play is rural, or *ek-polis*. The satyrs often take part in athletic contests (e.g., Euripides' *Athla* [or *Athloi*] and Sophocles' *Isthmiastai*). Harrison, in the premiere of his play performed in the stadium at Delphi, locates them under the cliffs of the

Phaedriades. Space is important for Harrison and his choices make the setting into something like a chorus with its own commentary. In the performance in England, one sees the homeless living under the National Theatre, and the papyrus is divided to provide bedding.

In ancient satyr plays, the satyrs are often prisoners and are freed at the end; so also in this play. In Sophocles' *Ichneutai* the satyrs seem to earn an unqualified freedom (although it is not clear from whom), but Harrison's Apollo sets down some limitations. The satyrs may be free only within the space determined by the god. In this way Harrison uses the Delphic space to express the tension between freedom and constraint. The "shining cliffs," the Phaedriades, are the "inrockation" of the god, and loom over the audience as Apollo looms over the satyrs.

The rural setting is particularly appropriate for a half-animal creature like the satyr. Shirley Strum, the anthropologist, has pointed out that man and the baboon are the only creatures on earth to thrive on the savannah, or in the open.[9] Man also survives in the *polis*, but one could hardly say he thrives there. Tragedy is more suitable for that setting. The country puts us in touch with the animals we share the world with, and the satyr reminds us of our animal side; comedy and the satyr play let us invent the memory of an atavistic utopia.

Harrison's Delphi location also allows for humorous play with audience participation, e.g. chanting, which echoes against the Phaedriades, to make the satyrs appear. The audience's chant is then taken up by the voices of eight thousand ghosts from the ancient Pythian games (as provided by a soundtrack accompanying the performance). Drama could not be more democratic in breaking down the barriers between stage and audience. In Delphi there was no stage. The ancient stadium, built under the Phaedriades, added supernatural/intranatural touches of light and sound and gave increased relevancy to such statements by Apollo as, "I'll be down in my temple. Give me a shout," or "I'm off to compose a new paean or ode / in my very own temple just down the road."

Delphi is sacred and the audience felt not only present at the discovery of the lyre, but at the birth of music, at melody added to rhythm, and ultimately at the scene of art given to man, a composite god and satyr, the rhythm of the primitive with the melody of the civilized, Apollo merging with Dionysus, form imprinted on matter.

We remember Nietzsche's claim that tragedy emerged from the spirit of music, and here we see satyr drama commemorating this birth of drama.

The actual production at the Phaedriades/stadium proved dangerous at one point. During the all-night rehearsal before the opening performance, a violent wind destroyed the set. Was Apollo preempting the punks? Dionysus protesting his omission? The premiere was charged with the knowledge that the performance depended on the gods.

Harrison personally supervised and directed the premiere performance, composing new verses until the end. No taping was allowed. The actors, exhausted and exhilarated, delivered a unique performance, drawing the audience into their magic. As noted, Harrison plans to revise the play for each venue where it is to be performed, so it will always be unique. But the premiere took place in Apollo's and Dionysus' space, and their presence was obvious to all. The space contained the satyrs, but the flames of the papyrus burned by the satyrs/hooligans at the end broke out of the space, as did the sound which rang throughout the valley. There was constant interpenetration of form and content; contained space became infinite space.

The stadium and the temple are both places of escape within the *polis,* and yet also the centers and foundations of the city; thus the escape they offer is based on a mode of theatricality. The satyr play, also, in contrast to tragedy, shares this ambiguity in its exploration of the wild outside the limits of the city. Harrison uses space and structure to contain and express the wild/irrational at the core of all civilization/rationality. Such dichotomies may be precisely what the synecdochic structure of theatricality puts into question (i.e., the mimesis and reflexivity involved in theater threaten a hermeneutic of binary oppositions; one structure encloses another, so that the enclosed becomes a new exterior). The NT production shows at the very end the satyrs outside the theater itself with the bright marquee reading "THE TRACKERS" in lights. We are thus inside and outside at the same time.

The structure of the stadium and of Harrison's text are transcended, his meter and rhymed words burst their limits, and again the vocabulary and appearance of Kyllene (a living caryatid) define by contrast the wildness of the satyr. Harrison quotes Stravinsky's *Poetics of Music* with approval:

> My freedom thus consists in my moving about within the narrow frame that I have assigned myself for each one of my undertakings. I shall go even further: my freedom will be so much the greater and more meaningful the more narrowly I limit my field of action and the more I surround myself with obstacles. Whatever diminishes constraint diminishes strength. The more constraints one imposes the more one frees one's self of the chains that shackle the spirit.[10]

These words can apply to textuality itself. How does the word trap or destroy reality? A word is a trace and we are dealing with trackers who follow the track/trace (*ichneutai, ichnos*). As Plotinus says, "The trace is the form of the formless" ("to gar ichnos tou amorphou morphē," in *Enneades* 6.7.33.30). Harrison's "tracks" are an incantation to avert the ultimate disappearance of humankind. But if a trace is the form of the formless, these tracks/words may have a more ominous side; they may be the incantation naming, summoning, and fetishizing the disaster.[11] Somehow the final erasure must be averted, the erasure described by Cassandra as a wet sponge removing the writing ("bolais ugrōssōn spoggos ōlesen graphēn," *Ag.* 1329).

There are no human beings in Sophocles' *Ichneutai*. It would seem that we are the signified behind the signs of the gods and god/animals in this play. As Socrates wondered if he were a monster more wild and complicated than a Typhon, or instead one more civilized and simpler, sharing in some sort of divine and tranquil lot (*Phaedrus* 230 E), so are we also caught between Apollo and the satyrs. Harrison makes the trinity visible: god (Apollo), man (fellaheen and scholar), and in-between (satyr). Here, Bernard Grenfell and Arthur Hunt (the two who found and edited the papyrus that contained Sophocles' *Ichneutai*) and the fellaheen are humans who are metamorphosed by Apollo into nonhuman projections.

What else does Harrison do with these Sophoclean fragments? He has rescued Sophocles, for one thing. Aeschylus is already known as a master of the satyr play, and many have seen the ironic genius of Euripides in his *Cyclops*, a masterpiece of comical *Machtpolitik* ("politics for power"), but not many have seen Sophocles' genius in his satyr plays.[12] As Ussher claims, "It cannot be said of *Ichneutai*, as it was of *Iliad XXIII* by Schiller, that no one who has lived to read it can complain about his lot in life."[13] The new *Trackers* by Harrison has rescued the old one.[14] These new trackers must be taken seriously in this play as a work of art and as social commentary.

Here is Harrison's version: Grenfell and Hunt with a team of fellaheen search for papyri at Oxyrhynchus. The fellaheen chant syllables from the *Ichneutai* (including titles of Sophocles' lost plays) and their chant sounds rather like an invocation. A rhythmic percussive background punctuates. Time is also fragmented and as photographs are taken the action is frozen (image and time as fragmented papyri . . . pure rhythm without melody or flow). Rhythm also seems to be the satyr's prerogative, whereas melody will be Apollo's; the fellaheen toss the papyri, showing their talent at sport, while Grenfell and Hunt show theirs for scholarship (one throws, the other reads).

Grenfell becomes possessed, as Apollo gradually invades his mind. Hunt expresses concern for Grenfell's health. After a tedious cataloguing of petitions and the more mundane and prosaic papyri, suddenly there's a discovery: Pindar's *Paean for the People of Delphi* (*Paean* VI), which the fellaheen chant with passion. Apollo begins a frantic interior monologue/dialogue with Grenfell and urges him to find the god's own play. In desperation, Grenfell tries to shoot Apollo, and a relay race ensues in which the chants of ancient spectators are heard.

And this was but the prologue. Now Apollo/Grenfell emerges from the rubbish heap and the *Ichneutai* proper begins with Apollo looking for his stolen cattle. He cries "Hunt," and Hunt answers from the tent, "Just a minute, just getting dressed," but then emerges from the tent *as* Silenus, who promises, for a reward, to retrieve the stolen cattle with the help of his satyrs. The satyrs (former fellaheen) are summoned with help from the audience and emerge from boxes that have been brought into the acting area; they begin a vigorous clog dance on the flattened sides of the boxes, marked with the tracks of Apollo's stolen cattle. The sound of the lyre is heard, to the consternation of all. Silenus urges his satyrs on, then leaves, saying he's too old for this but he'll be back for the reward.

A stage is formed on the back of the satyrs, imitating the sculpture at the theater of Dionysus in Athens, and Kyllene appears dressed as a caryatid from the Erechtheum in Athens. She tells of her predicament in caring for Zeus' child Hermes, and finally reveals the secret of the lyre. She is tipped off her stage and the satyrs become suspicious about the cattle being used to make the lyre. She falls, and as she retrieves her elaborate headgear she finds herself suggestively astride a satyr, whereupon the group takes up an erotically rhythmic chant (not unlike Stravinsky's *Rite of Spring*). Kyllene exits, pursued by the satyrs, protesting she is not in the right play.

At this point the papyrological fragments peter out. Harrison illustrates this by having the Greek fragments dwindle down to darkness, and it is Apollo who appropriately brings back the light.

Apollo enters and confronts the baby Hermes (a full-grown man although "not yet six days," as Sophocles' fragments say). The baby finally admits the theft of the herd, but Apollo is so charmed by the sounds of the lyre that he is willing to accept it in exchange. But he refuses to share his art with the satyrs and gives them, via Kyllene, ghetto-blasters instead, which they look at "like Cheetah in the Tarzan films getting hold of a camera" (as Harrison has said about them).

The satyrs exeunt clearly dissatisfied and Silenus appears. He kicks in all the ghetto-blasters. A powerful speech follows protesting against satyrs being used for the purposes of the elite: as simple servants to test things, and after they have tested them to hand them over and never dare to use them. Silenus uses Marsyas as the paradigm, (the satyr who dared to play a divine instrument—the flute—as well as a god could). The satyrs come to represent those who protest against the abuse of power, and who are tortured for their trouble (Marsyas was flayed for his daring to think he could equal a god). Silenus warns us against modern satyrs, those who, because they are deprived of power, will react violently. Indeed, the former satyrs suddenly turn into punks and destroy the set, painting the papyrus screens with the name Marsyas, which they then set on fire. The skinheads ignore Silenus as he makes a last plea for some compromise: What is so bad about a satyr's life if wine is provided and the body satisfied? But these modern raging satyrs act more like Dionysus in the *Bacchae* than even the Bacchic chorus in that play, who like Silenus praise moderate happiness ("I admire the happiness of the man who enjoys life from day to day," *Ba.* 910–11). Like

Dionysus, the satyrs here choose to destroy if they are ignored. The last of the papyri are used as a football. Apollo's words are heard ending in omega, the final "O," a type of moan, which is taken up by the eight thousand ghosts. Harrison writes of this, "There is the sound like a dying firework of *Ichneutes* off the Phaedriades." Once again the place is important: the "shining cliffs" at the spiritual and cultural center of Delphi are the sound board for the title of the fragments which, like a verbal firework, fades away into the landscape of culture. We have the word, and then just the memory.

In the epilogue, the satyrs/hooligans take a curtain call and reprise the paean while holding up the tops of the crates to spell the name Sophocles. They misspell it, but Grenfell and Hunt appear to make the correction.

The performance at the National Theatre transforms the final "Oh" to "Woe," uttered by Silenus, followed by, "Not bad for a Satyr for his first go." Then he starts to tap his clogs, more and more in nervous fear, as he looks up into the darkening space where Apollo has gone. Our last vision is of a vanishing Apollo, the god in power who can still dictate, but who no longer needs even to be visible.

While Sophocles' *Ichneutai* provides the basis for Harrison's play, there are allusions to many other classical texts: Pindar's *Paean*, for instance, while the *Ichneutai* plot is filled out by suggestions from the *Homeric Hymn to Hermes* (although in the hymn the lyre was invented before the cattle were stolen). The satyrs as searching hounds resemble Aeschylean Erinyes sniffing out Orestes. Harrison translated the *Oresteia* in vigorous verse, enlivening the ancient text for moderns. He uses the same meter for "sniff, sniff," as he did for "seek, seek, scour the ground" from the *Oresteia*. The Erinyes were the trackers of the soul:

> Furies the trackers fulfilling the blood grudge
> trip the transgressor tread him into the ground.[15]

A complicated operation takes place when ancient texts are used for modern ends. The ancient text in its ancient setting is perceived by the modern from his modern perspective; it is an interpreted sign. It is drained of its ancient significance and becomes a sign in a new modern context. Both past and present inform each other and provide ways to interpret each other; these lenses distort but also enhance.[16]

Tony Harrison uses the past as a vehicle for modern social criticism and conveys in his poetry dismay over an elitist system of culture. He was born in Leeds, and subjected to purified English (cf. "Them & [uz]," I and II).[17] This was well depicted in his play called *The Big H* in which a boy is forced to add H's to his local dialect — the boy is a hero in contrast to Herod, heroin, and the H-Bomb, all threats to the "civilized" world, and its quality of life, if not to existence itself. "Classics Society," from his *Selected Poems*, speaks of the English that schools required for classical translations (so well satirized by A. E. Housman):

> We boys can take old Hansards and translate
> the British Empire into SPQR
> but nothing demotic or too up-to-date,
> and *not* the English that I speak at home . . . (p. 120)

As Harrison's father said of his son:

> Ah sometimes think you read too many books.
> Ah nivver 'ad much time for a good read. (p. 141)

And many good reads the son has had indeed. We have the translation of the *Oresteia* mentioned above, and also of Palladas and Martial.[18] And now we have a satyr play by Sophocles — demotic triumphs. Whereas Apollo, Kyllene, Grenfell, and Hunt come from London, the satyrs definitely come from Leeds. As Harrison wrote *V.* (verses versus a constricting British society), so the satyrs and fellaheen oppose the cultural and social elitism of Apollo and Grenfell/Hunt.[19] Harrison calls Silenus an Uncle Tom. He likes his drink and his position as big fish in a small pond, and for this he is willing to sell his own services and those of his offspring.

As Grenfell and Hunt offer gold to the fellaheen, Apollo offers gold and freedom to Silenus and the satyrs, in return for their finding his stolen cattle. We have seen that Apollo keeps the lyre for himself. As in the past when Marsyas dared to pick up the flute that Athena had discarded and was flayed for trying to rival the gods, so the gods and upper classes have kept sophisticated art for themselves while allowing the lower classes limited access; their art was allowed as long as it was inferior. Scholars hardly open Oxford to the fellaheen, and for a long time the inner sancta were barred to those from Leeds.

What can't be shared is eventually destroyed, which is one way of eliminating rivalry, and perhaps an ironic variation of creativity. The satyrs were content to make love not war; they provided the antidote to civilization's ills:

> When the world seems hurtling in the wrong direction
> remember the satyr with his wineskin and erection,

another version of:

> Bad weather and the public mess
> drive us to private tenderness,
> though I wonder if together we,
> alone two hours, can ever be
> love's anti-bodies in the sick,
> sick body politic.[20]

The satyrs' values and demands are not to be ignored, for if we deny this animal part, we can well end up like Hippolytus or Pentheus, and if society is deaf, it will end up in revolution. Apollo must compromise or Marsyas will flay Apollo, or at the very least, burn up the satyr play which is his vehicle for expression.

With an ending that resembles that of the *Trojan Women* more than a satyr play, we have clearly left the world of Sophocles' *Ichneutai*. Harrison often uses his art as a political vehicle, a conscience for man. His *Phaedra Britannica* shows the English abuses in India. In the words of the princess Lilamani:

> I, last of Ranjit's noble household, forced
> to watch my brothers face the holocaust.
> My father bayonetted! The redcoat guns
> killed my six brothers. All my father's sons . . .
> Smoking smithereens! India's red mud
> churned even redder with her children's blood.[21]

Harrison has taken up feminist causes, stressing the patriarchy in his *Oresteia* and in *Medea: A Sex War Opera*, in which he gives various versions of the Medea myth and adds a character, Hecules, to show that the males are certainly as much at fault as females when it comes to killing children (a theme he also takes up in *The Big H*).[22]

Political abuse of the "other" is a frequent theme in Harrison's writings, but he is most eloquent in his opposition to global destruction. Abuse is one thing, but one needs people for abuse: annihilation is the ultimate evil. He has a trilogy, with the overall title *The Common Chorus*, comprising his versions of *Lysistrata*, *Trojan Women* and finally *Maxims*, his own play about the invention of the machine gun. Euripides suggested in the *Suppliants* (lines 481–85) that if we could see our own death when it comes to a vote for war, we would never vote for it. Harrison shows us, as Euripides and Aristophanes did, the reality of war not through the heroics of the heroes, but through the suffering of the victims. We "see" our own death, and hope that we can persuade the rest of the world not to vote for war. Through his use of the classics, Harrison has found an ally to fight his battles.[23]

But there is more. Harrison fully realizes the dialectic between celebration and mourning. He begins his Introduction to *The Trackers* by recalling the bonfire that celebrated the end of the war with victory over Japan. There was left "a black circle of scorched cobbles with thick scars of tar." There is also the memory and living testament of Hiroshima. It is the mutual secret of fire—"One element for celebration and terror. One space for the celebrant and the sufferer." And fire is also found in the sun, which lit the ancient performances in the orchestra of Dionysus. We still can see the disasters in the ancient dramas, yet we celebrate the performances. This was the same dialectic noted by Shelley in his *Charles I* (quoted by Harrison), describing the anti-masque of the world's abuses:

> 'Tis but
> The anti-masque, and serves as discords do
> In sweeter music. Who would love May flowers
> If they succeeded not to Winter's flaw;
> Or day unchanged by night; or joy itself
> Without the touch of sorrow?

The satyr play, like comedy, shows a world in chaos, or at least a world of extrasocial fantasy that is reconciled by the end of the play to the social norms. This is the reverse of tragedy, which begins in what seems to be the social track, but is derailed at the end.[24] The trackers in tragedy blaze their own trail to chaos through their defiance of the norm; obvious examples are Oedipus and Ajax. Harrison shows us a derailed world that blows up at the end. Ominous? Yes. But a warning, and a revelation, as is all drama.

Harrison shows us the tragedy of "otherness" via comedy, or "satyr-edy." Class distinctions, language, sexuality, sport versus art, tragedy versus comedy or satyr play, all the imposed arbitrary barriers collaborate to bring about the final conflagration. There is a tragedy in "otherness," but there is also definition: the light of the final fire illuminates as it destroys.

In the meantime the vehicle is delightful, as Harrison says in "A Kumquat for John Keats":

> Then it's the kumquat fruit expresses best
> how days have darkness round them like a rind,
> life has a skin of death that keeps its zest.[25]

And what a zest in the rest of this play! Harrison's language is playful and daring (e.g., rhyming "think us" with "Oxyrhynchus"; "track" with *sebakh*, Arabic for "fertilizer"; "byre" with "*Oresteia*"; and "satyr" with "patter"). In an early version, Harrison even invented a new word for hunting, called "grenfelling."

The fragments themselves yield delightful wordplays, and the beginning postulated by Ernst Siegmann provides the delightful lacunae g..l..o (*grenfello*) and the play ends on the "o" (alpha to omega and a long drawn sigh, "ohh". . . .).[26] This "ohh" is taken up by the "crowd at the Pythian Games" (who are sitting in the stadium and it develops into something like a football cheer). The private "o" of Apollo develops into the public "ohh" of the stadium.

Harrison uses the beginning for the end: the beginning implying and necessitating the end, the alpha becoming omega (and the "I"— omega signifies "I" in Greek as the ending for the first person singular of verbs—which remains elite and leads to the destruction conveyed by the final omega). Apollo's—*o* [I] is not willing to become -*omen* [we] with Marsyas. Should we say the ending of the play is an "omen" for us all? Is it an ecstatic "ohh"? Is it a victory for the group over the individual—the "I" obliterated in the final "ohh"?

We mentioned that the epilogue shows the name of Sophocles misspelled by the satyrs/hooligans, and then corrected by Grenfell and Hunt, who reappear showing that there is still a place for scholars next to the poets. But from sound and sight the final message is the poet's, or as Hölderlin has said, "Was bleibet aber stiften die Dichter" (What remains, however, the poets establish). So now also Heiner Müller says, varying Shakespeare's *Hamlet*, "Der Rest ist Lyrik." Harrison's published text ends, "This is the curtain call of Sophocles." But it was Harrison who used Apollo's lyre to recreate this lost world, and it is Harrison, in fact, who took the final curtain call that evening.

There are elements in Harrison's reworking that are more Aristophanic than Sophoclean. We find actual people, Grenfell and Hunt, as modern Cleons who usurp political power. Grenfell, in fact, finally did end his days in an asylum, as the text foretells:

> Grenfell was torrential. So dazzlingly fast
> I sometimes think his sanity might not last.

So also in his text we have made-up words that are more appropriate to comedy (e.g., Harrison gives us the masterpiece "Satyroboucelloniphone" to describe the lyre, with reference to what it owes to satyrs, cows, and tortoise [*bous* and *chelōnē*]). Apollo and Silenus want to include themselves and so come up with, respectively, "Apollosatyroboucelloniphone" and "Apollosilenosatyroboucellon-and-all-the-bloody-rest-i-phone."

The language here is more Aristophanic than is usual for satyr plays, and Sophocles' *Ichneutai* is even more faithful to tragedy's decorum than Euripides's *Cyclops*. Harrison's text has scatological and sexual explicitness. Once again this is a Harrison tradition; *v.* ends with an epitaph:

> Beneath your feet's a poet, then a pit.
> Poetry supporter, if you're here to find
> how poems can grow from (beat you to it!) SHIT
> find the beef, the beer, the bread, then look behind.

In true oracular tradition, like Orpheus, Harrison still intends communication from the grave. And certainly in his own living poetry Harrison spins fertilizer into the gold of words.

Harrison also plays on the theme of the baby Hermes' hermeneutics and the traces or tracks found by the scholars and satyrs. The tracks of the past scrawled on papyri, the excrement of antiquity, are paralleled by the droppings of the cattle of Apollo, and the baby Hermes continues Freud's *Fort/Da* game with his own excrement and lyre.

Harrison in *v.* says the language in Leeds' cemetery ranges from:

> how people 'fell asleep in the Good Lord'. . .
> to CUNT, PISS, SHIT and (mostly) FUCK!

His language can also reach lyrical heights, as for instance in "A Kumquat for John Keats":

> The dawn's molasses make the citrus gleam
> still in the orchards of the groves of dream.
> The limes, like Galway after weeks of rain,
> glow with a greenness that is close to pain,
> the dew-cooled surfaces of fruit that spent
> all last night flaming in the firmament.[27]

So also in *The Trackers of Oxyrhynchus* the language ranges from the caryatid-like Kyllene:

> Are you not they
> wherewith of old you made your master glad
> clad in the fawnskin and with thyrsus high
> was wont to chant of yore the holy hymns
> with, for escort, nymphs and youthful throngs.

to the satyr's translation of these same lines ("She means Dionysus pissed sang us old songs!") or even Leeds dialect ("summat's been flayed") to

> Ay, bugger the whatsit, and the miraculous boy,
> wanking about with the dead creature toy
> . . . and what we need's not some plaything to pluck.
> Satyrs need to get drunk, and then fuck.

Language establishes the class distinction: the language of Oxford versus the language of Leeds. The language of the folk has richness and living vigor, but perhaps a poverty of variation and sophistication; yet in Harrison's poetry the language of Leeds keeps its vigor while also achieving lyrical and conceptual sophistication.

Language can of course be used as a weapon. The purpose is no longer sex but annihilation; "fucking" as verb becomes "fucking" as adjective (in one Harrison version the phallus of the satyr is transformed into the "double-bulbed klaxons" of bikers who destroy the papyri and the entire set at the end of the play).

What we have is vigorous fun that turns sinister, and glorious poetry followed by a serious social message. Harold Pinter well characterized Harrison's poetry as "brilliant, passionate, outrageous, abrasive." Harrison is aptly and often also acclaimed as England's greatest modern theatrical poet. He has the blood and vigor that many new Brechtians and modern aesthetes lack. His works pulse with the rhythm of life, and his verses work to preserve the life he celebrates. His words are music with meaning.

The tragic ending allows us to experience joy: "the skin of death which keeps its zest." In the modern world, perhaps hope and joy can only be experienced in the context of death. The ancient satyr play is defined and more forcefully experienced within the modern tragic frame. Humor is simply transformed and in the modern context is itself tragic, like Lukács' irony which allows us access to a lost god.[28]

The ending in which the transformed satyrs destroy the fragments recalls some of the destruction we find in Old Comedy (the *catastrophe*), such as the burning down of the *phrontisterion* at the end of *The Clouds*. This type of ending fits T. W. Adorno's idea of art: the monad of the work of art is destroyed by the workers.[29] One sees the image of Odysseus having access to the sirens while his sailors row; but in Harrison's text the satyrs refuse to act in the elitist drama and destroy it. They resent what Stendhal speaks of as "la promesse de bonheur." The time is over for promises.

VII

Tony Harrison's Medea: *A Sex War Opera:* Internal, External, Eternal Medea

TONY HARRISON has written a powerful indictment of traditional male representations of the female in his *Medea: A Sex War Opera*.[1] He uses the myth of Medea as a focus of male fears, and we see her punished as a scapegoat for all threatening mothers, wives, and women in general.

Medea is every wandering husband's nightmare. Euripides cast this powerful princess in the mold of a Sophoclean hero and shocked Athens with the words and actions of a wife who criticizes and destroys her husband, fully aware of what she is doing.[2] In Euripides, she tells the women of Corinth that a wife's lot is not to be envied: "It is better to face the enemy in battle three times than to give birth once" (*Med.* 250–51). As the chorus sees her bravery and loyalty in contrast to Jason's treachery, they say that now a new song will be sung about women, one that will praise them as it exposes male perfidy (*Med.* 410–30). Tony Harrison quotes this

A version of this chapter has been published in Tony Harrison, ed. Neil Astley, *Bloodaxe Critical Anthologies* (Newcastle upon Tyne: Bloodaxe Books, 1991), I:470-485.

chorus several times in his *Medea*. Harrison shows that men kill their children too and adds Heracles, as a FATHER who slew his children.

The universal themes of ancient drama must be particularized for each age: they need new language and new performances. Poetry must constantly be rewritten by modern seers, and performed in ways that touch hearts. Harrison has done just this for Euripides' Medea—two poets, one ancient and one modern, have shared their dark vision.

Euripides' Medea is a princess who has left her home in Colchis to help Jason steal the Golden Fleece, in the course of events murdering her brother and scattering the remains to delay her father's pursuit. She follows Jason in love, and bears him two children. After years in Corinth, he decides to marry the Corinthian princess. Medea sends a deadly gift to the princess, a diadem and robe, which consume her with an acidlike poison. Her father dies also, glued to his daughter's body in a gruesome embrace. Medea then kills the two sons she has had by Jason and escapes to safety in Athens by means of a chariot drawn by dragons.

Who or what is Medea? Is she a living being? A goddess? A character performed by an actress? A symbol? A text? The ancient text? A modern recreation? Many texts? Words heard on the stage or words read in a book? How do we translate her for ourselves? Do we give her life by personally rewriting her text? Has she only transcendental significance? Or is she only significant because she resonates internally for each of us, "une Madeleine Médée"? Or is she, indeed, as her desires define her, all of these: an externally oriented hero (Knox), a godlike witch (Page), and an internally focused woman and mother (Kawashima)?[3]

The internal, external, eternal Medea is all of these and none; each proposition is refuted by the dichotomy of character and person. One eternal Medea is a perishable text, or many texts, potentially surviving as long as humankind (possibly thus an eternal indictment of the audience which never understood her). Let us look at some aspects of Medea and try to recognize the complexities of her role as a represented woman.

As a psychological symbol Medea is the monster mother who has taken various forms in mythology from Medusa to Scylla.[4] She represents the female who instead of mothering the male child, challenges him and becomes infanticidal rather than nurturing. D. Winnicott and others speak of the mother accurately reflecting the child, in the period that the child is dependent on the parent for a construction of his own image, but Lacan's mirror is always a distortion, an inversion of the subject's desire to be recognized; Euripides shows us Medea as a mother who refuses the mirroring role (indeed, this mother steps out of the mirror with a knife in her hand). Robert Wilson has carried on this image without words: in *Deafman Glance*, both in his film and play, his Medea gives her children milk and then stabs them. What makes Medea so particularly horrible for a male-dominated society is that she represents a woman, wife, and mother who consciously chooses to put her own needs and passions above those of the men in her life; she carries out her destructive plans rationally and efficiently, then escapes without punishment.

Bruno Snell, in tracing the development and progress of Greek thought and self-consciousness shows how Medea and Phaedra (*Hippolytus* 375–83) figure prominently because they know that what they choose to do is wrong according to objective ethical standards, but they still choose to do it. They thus refute Socrates' maxim, "If one knows the good one will do it."[5] Medea says clearly, "I know what evil I intend to do, but now my passion dominates my reason [controls my plans], which is the cause of the greatest evil for men" (*Med.* 1078–80)[6]

James Diggle further develops this theme in his insightful lecture, "Euripides the Psychologist" (Delphi, 1989). He shows the progression in Greek thought from destruction by *Ate* or an externally induced blindness (e.g., Agamemnon in *Il.* 19.86–89) to an internally chosen commission of evil with concomitant external (other) and internal (self) destruction—which in Medea's case was partly self-affirmation. Phaedra is characterized by passivity, but Medea chooses to do what she does through *thumos*, an active passion. Perhaps they are both confronting male standards, and affirming themselves by refuting those standards.

If one were to generalize crudely about conflicting "rights" in Greek tragedy, one might say that in Aeschylus god confronts god (e.g., in *Prometheus Bound* and the *Oresteia*), in Sophocles man confronts god (e.g., in *Antigone* and *Oedipus*), but in Euripides man confronts man and most often man confronts himself. Euripides gives Medea an interior monologue that reveals her conflict about killing her children. As Conacher says, only Medea can stop Medea.[7] And it is the public Medea of the *polis* that defeats the private Medea of the *oikos:* Jason's actions lead her to a vengeance that will reinstate her public image, although at the cost of destroying the house, her children, and contradicting her feelings as a mother. The external world does not validate her internal one, so she sacrifices her internal feelings for her children to her desire for external recognition, thus definition. Jason claims that *he* brought her fame, but Medea chooses to be the authoress of her own fame.

Our externally oriented Medea is Euripides' heroine who is modeled upon the Homeric and Sophoclean hero/heroine. This Medea is concerned with appearance, what other people think of her. She seeks immortal fame; at least, her enemies will not laugh at her.[8] She is angry with Jason not so much for his sexual adventure, but rather for his leaving her and taking away her prestige as wife, thus making her a laughingstock. One does not abandon the princess Medea for another princess, at least not with impunity. Medea taunts Jason: "Why didn't you discuss this with me in advance if you had my best interests at heart?" (*Med.* 585–87). Jason makes the mistake of thinking that Medea's anger is due to her abandoned bed (*Med.* 555, 569–70, and 1367). That may be a factor, but what matters most now is being deprived of her honor—becoming an object of scorn, and losing house and country after she has sacrificed everything for honor.[9] Euripides was also questioning that Greek institution of marriage which had created such dependency and vulnerability; Harrison further develops this theme, showing that Medea was blackened by male mythmakers interested in maintaining the status quo. In his *Medea* he has his chorus say:

> Men's hatred had to undermine
> MEDEA's status as divine
> and to reduce her
> to a half-crazed children-slayer
> making a monster of MEDEA
> like the Medusa.[10]

In his notebooks Harrison quotes Erich Neumann: "The ancient mana figure that most clearly represents this principle of transformation is Medea. But in her the declining matriarchate is already devaluated by the patriarchal principle, and the mythical reality she represents is personalized, that is, reduced to a mere personal level and so negativized. Like Circe, she was originally a goddess, but has become a 'witch' in the patriarchally colored myth."[11] Euripides is seen as contributing to Medea's devaluation.

A wife's primary function in ancient Greece was not as an erotic partner. As Apollodorus said, "One has a mistress for pleasure, a concubine to take care of one's bodily needs, and a wife to bear children and run the house" (Demosthenes, *Against Neaera* 59, 122). Plutarch quotes Solon's law: "A man should have intercourse with his wife at least three times a month, obviously not for pleasure, but in the same way that cities periodically renew their treaties" (*Amatorius* 769a). Jason's main mistake was not his leaving Medea's bed for Glauce's, but exchanging Colchis for Corinth. As Euripides' heroine says to Aegeus, Jason's "love" was for an alliance with kings (*Med.* 700).

Euripides' Medea not only laments the lot of women, but she understands how she was wronged and exacts her vengeance as "only women can," thus verifying male slanders said about women (cf. "There is no bloodier intelligence/heart [*phren*]," *Med.* 266; also, "most wise fashioner of all evil," line 409).[12] Worst of all, Medea escapes without punishment to begin a life in a new city where she may threaten other children. Her myth continues with her being exiled after attempting to kill Theseus, son of Aegeus, her husband and king of Athens. She escapes with Medus, her son by Aegeus, to found the country of the Medes.

How does Tony Harrison shape Medea? He concentrates on the sex war, and shows that the blame should be shared with the men. He contrasts Medea with Hercules, who in mythology was also a monster, a father who slew his own children; nevertheless, his general reputation was one of a hero. Bachofen, however, sees Hercules as "the irreconcilable foe of matriarchy, the indefatigable battler of Amazons, the misogynist, in whose sacrifice no woman takes part, by whose name no woman swears, and who finally meets his death from a woman's poisoned garment."[13]

In Sophocles the statement is made that Hercules conquered all, but was finally defeated by love (*Tr.* 488–89). His wife slew him ("inadvertently," in trying to win his love back) when he attempted to import a princess to share their marriage bed, thus making an interesting contrast with Medea. He was a man who slew monsters, thus contributing to civilization, but, as Harrison claims, these monsters were all forms of woman, maiden, crone, and goddess, and in slaying them he resembled the final monster:

> All the monsters that I ever slew
> were only the great EARTH MOTHER, you!
> The one in the end I couldn't subdue.
> If I lopped off its head, it grew another.
> I killed all the monsters, but can't kill the MOTHER.[14]

The shocking directness and simplicity of these lyrics—they are sung to musical accompaniment, of course, and not declaimed—adds to the mythical dimension. Hercules could not "kill" his wife either, who delivered him a fatal cloak (the mirror image to Medea's cloak, which eliminates HER rival). The cloak in Hercules' case was the ultimate embrace of the mother. He asked to be burned in a pyre, a burning externalization of his own passion, which Lichas says was his only master, the only monster he could not slay. But this pyre also frees him from the embrace of the mother. He will NOT be buried in earth, HER ultimate imprisonment. He says, "At last in death I shall be free / of enfolding Femininity."[15]

The mythmakers are also to blame for making women into monsters:

> As the sex-war's still being fought
> which sex does a myth support
> you should be asking.
> What male propaganda lurks
> behind most operatic works
> that music's masking?[16]

Harrison unmasks the attempted validation of power behind the words, as Euripides did earlier, by showing how men make myths to justify their abuse of women. Jason, as author, is cited by Hippolytus in his wish that men could find sources for children other than women, "such an evil they are for man" (*Med.* 573–75). Medea does not pray for the destruction of men, but rather that a sure sign might be given to women to discern which men are evil and which are not, as one can recognize a counterfeit coin (*Med.* 516–19). Pseudovaluations through communicated texts need constant vigilance, as well stated by Edward Said in *Orientalism*: "Systems of thought like Orientalism, discourses of power, ideological fictions—mind-forg'd manacles—are all too easily made, applied and guarded."[17]

Harrison prefaces his opera with a quotation from Lévi-Strauss: "We define the myth as consisting of all its versions," and goes on to include original text from Euripides, Buchanan, Corneille, a Prague translation, Seneca, Mayr, Cherubini, Calderón, Studley's Seneca (a version from 1856 called *Medea: Or the Best of Mothers*), and even a version by Hosidius Geta. There are many other versions, from Grillparzer to Heiner Müller, and Medea festivals abound.[18]

Harrison feathers his magpie nest of Medeas with mixed languages and mixed versions, having the children vary in age from two to fourteen. Medea is executed in his opera, and Hercules is killed by Deianira in a way that parallels Creusa's death: the passion that obsessed them in life eats them alive as they don Nessus' cloak and Medea's coronet and robes (the cap used for Medea's electrocution is the bowl she had mixed her poisons in). So no one goes free in this "final" version, which defines but does not resolve the sex war. Blaring headlines conclude the opera, first with news of mothers who have slain their children, then of fathers (one of Wilson's expanded versions of *Deafman Glance* shows the father also killing his child, following or inspiring Medea). Can we now in modern times revise our ancient texts, and truly sing a new song about women, one that includes men?

Not only is Harrison's *Medea* a compendium of former Medeas, it also adds characters, such as Hercules and Butes, the beekeeper, Argonauts from the original voyage. Here they represent, along with Jason, three approaches to women. Butes loves one woman and has had a happy marriage and longs to rejoin his wife in death. Harrison makes use of the symbol of the bee and its relation to women, quoting Bachofen in his notebooks: "This makes the beehive a perfect prototype of the first human society, based on the gynocracy of motherhood, as we find it among the peoples named. . . . The bee was rightly looked upon as a symbol of the feminine potency of nature. It was associated above all with Demeter, Artemis, and Persephone. Here it symbolized the earth, its motherliness, its never-resting, artfully formative busy-ness, and reflected the Demetrian earth soul in its supreme purity."[19]

Harrison's Hercules for the most part loathes women and will die at their hands. Jason loves women, but mixes one too many into his marital scheme. All three perish, either actually or spiritually, at the hands of women. Since Medea is electrocuted at the hands of men, at least there is some equality here, sparing one the resentment felt when Medea goes free with impunity in Euripides' play.

The theme of male versus female parallels the theme of life and death in Harrison's version. As Terzopoulos also showed in his production of Müller's *Medeamaterial*, there are obvious similarities between death and marriage, and many articles have been written about these similarities from an anthropological standpoint. We see this link in Medea's statements describing marriage and childbirth (e.g. her opening speech to the women of Corinth, *Med.* 213–66). Hipponax offers a male opinion that relates his happiness to marriage AND death: "Man enjoys two happy days with a woman, the day he marries her and the day he buries her" (frag. 68). For a woman the day of marriage is a type of death because she is exiled from a friendly world to that of a stranger: "And after one single joyful night of love, we are compelled to praise this arrangement and consider ourselves lucky" (Sophocles, *Tereus*, fr. 583).[20]

Harrison appropriately has his opera begin with two processions, one of marriage and one of execution. Death as a means of defining life is not new to Harrison. His Butes echoes the sentiments of the earlier "A Kumquat for John Keats":

> When a man gets to the age I am
> Death seasons every day
> as honey might taste of marjoram
> or my dead wife's soup of bay.[21]

This is a variation of

> Then it's the kumquat fruit expresses best
> how days have darkness round them like a rind,
> life has a skin of death that keeps its zest.[22]

Snakes represent both life and death in Harrison's opera, paralleling the writhing fire and the dragoness with her sibilants. Harrison directs at one point: "The text for the DRAGONESS uses the Greek, Latin and French texts . . . but given a more 'snake-like' setting. Another ancient aspect of the 'female' like the GODDESS, and should have some musical connection with those linked 3 voices. The 20 voices are one continuous voice, writhing, squirming, fierce, fiery, threatening, ever-wakeful, coiling, and unwinding, making sudden darts with its head . . . The separate words should be considered its 'vertebrae', the total sound its continuous glide."[23]

Earlier Harrison had noted the snake/mother parallel in *The Fire Gap*:

> The sainted heroes of the Church
> beheaded serpents who stood for
> the Mother whose name they had to smirch
> to get their own foot in the door.
> We had to fight you to survive:
> Darkness versus Light![24]

But for the poet:

> Darkness and Light to you are one.
> You link together death and birth.

The snake in this case becomes the "other":

> All earth embracing snakes that slink
> whether poisonous or not;
> the fairy, pacifist, the Red,
> maybe someone who loves the Muse
> are all forms of the serpent's head
> their GOD tells them to bruise.

Medea and the sex war is a universal theme, a war to conquer the "other"; but finally, insidiously, this "other" defines, creates, and destroys—mask absorbing character, and character absorbing the person. Mother is the source of life and death, as is the father, as is the human race. Death is the rind that gives life its fresh succulence, the ultimate external that finally wins.

Freud, in his essay "The Three Caskets," says that they represent the three ways the man knows the woman: as mother, bride, and "the earth that receives him." Harrison tries to correct "vulgar Freudianism" by adding Hercules to Medea. There is, of course, something more primitive about the male's fear of a woman for the very reason that it is more radical. A man's fear of death at the hands of a woman takes him back to his early childhood and cancels his being at its source. By killing his sons, Medea kills Jason "root and branch," his future heirs and his own primitive self. The very fact of his infidelity to her—with a younger, less threatening woman—shows his failure to face the figure who represents to him both love and death, and that strange in-between, sexual person.

Harrison has written an opera libretto that delineates polarities or oppositions set up in conjunction with the logic of parallels: life and death, male and female, all juxtaposed against the universal, the character, the person, and the particular. Euripides wrote an acutely accurate psychological portrait of a woman who understands the inner workings of men. When her external world is threatened she takes vengeance in a devastatingly internal way (with all her psychological acuity) and she destroys her enemy's external power as he had destroyed hers. But her inner world is destroyed also by her external weapon, as she says words to the effect, "Forget your children for this short day, but mourn them for eternity" (*Med.* 1248–49). Jason's princess and realm was "other" and external, but the children are self and internal.

Jason may well understand the *polis,* but Medea understands the family (cf. Clytemnestra telling Agamemnon in the *Iphigenia at Aulis,* "You may arrange all outside, but the house is mine"; line 740). Even Homer spoke of a man's virtues being exercised on the battlefield and in public discourse, as a "doer of deeds and a speaker of words" (*Il.* 443), whereas a woman's virtues were clearly exercised in the house (e.g., Penelope). Medea, whose house was violated, engages Jason in public conflict, and destroys his public life with a woman's weapons, insinuating her way into the new domestic interior that was to secure Jason's future public success. The price of her external victory as hero/wife is her destruction as internal woman/mother, an ironic affirmation of self by validation of the mask.

Harrison, as Euripides, universalizes Medea's story by showing her conflict with Jason as the eternal conflict between men and women, which in antiquity, and in particular fifth century Athens, entailed a conflict between a public and a private life. Boundaries are blurred and women now fight in public as men fight in private. The implications suggested by Euripides are fully developed.

The power and beauty of Harrison's poetry is inescapable; the resolution is a song that has dissonance creating harmony. Medea, as trope or representation as guaranteed through her fictionality, is eternal, becoming *das Ewig-Weibliche,* now a warning, now a reassuring song, as Harrison ends *The Fire-Gap:* "The only real eternity is a tale (like your tail) in the mouth," and now also, again, on the stage as an indictment of the world offstage.

VIII

Tony Harrison's Interview

WE BEGAN discussing performances, and how the ideal was simply to have one performance, as was the case of *The Trackers* as performed in Delphi.

HARRISON: One should never repeat. But I have to know that I am doing *Trackers* again.

MCDONALD: Will you just do one performance per place? Or will you do several?

HARRISON: Heaven forbid! They would never allow me to do just one!

MCDONALD: No, that's true. How will you burn down the set each night . . .

HARRISON: That was devised for the Delphi Stadium. When the papyri disappeared, the flames created a sporting image of two football goal posts. And there I wanted to create an eruption of what seems to be opposed to "culture," in a place which was designed ostensibly for sport, but at a period when there were no divisions between, say, poetry and track-running. This was a time when people didn't feel that there was a huge division between sport and culture like poetry and music. So that was designed for that stadium.

Now, in the National Theatre, in the Olivier Theatre, I use other images. I don't have the full-length stadium. I don't have to burn down the papyri to create an image of a football field, but I have found another image of modern, cultural rejection. Now, fortunately, or unfortunately, socially and politically, that image is ready at hand at the National Theatre in the South Bank complex, because beneath the place where people flock to listen to Mozart, or modern music, or go to the National Theater, is Cardboard City, where most of the homeless live, and in cardboard boxes. And, it seems to me, the way *The Trackers* is rooted in the National Theater, the satyrs become those people. Many of those people who are homeless are also alcoholics and winos and so on. That's the kind of negative version of the Dionysiac inspiration. And we, the satyrs, are—seem to be—celebrating the positive part of it. Of course, the satyrs have been excluded from culture. I see a lineage from excluded satyr to the satyrs in raincoats who live in the cardboard boxes beneath our theater, a little like that image I have in *Trackers* of the satyrs supporting the *skēnē*. It will be different in other places. I work things out in each new space.

MCDONALD: I see: it's an ironic exclusion from culture; people are seeing a play on top, whereas below, people are worried about their food.

HARRISON: I wanted to write a piece for the Festival Hall, where you just imagined the Festival Hall turned upside down and you heard the orchestra underneath and you saw the life of the homeless on stage.

MCDONALD: Fellini has a similar juxtaposition in one of his films, *And The Ship Sails On* [Italy, 1983]. There's a striking image of people putting coals in furnaces while the opera singers entertain them from an upper balcony.

HARRISON: *Trackers* as performed at Delphi was actually written for a very specific space. That's why that performance can never happen again. For the Olivier stage we draw on this very obvious, social, cultural exclusion: that people walk by the homeless, living in their boxes, which reflect the crates of the satyrs. They walk by those people on their way to the theater. So I end by creating the outside of the theater inside. If the American tour takes place, and if we do it in a sporting stadium, we could go back to a sporting theme, and divide sport and culture, mind and body, so that there are alternative endings.

MCDONALD: Yes, that makes sense. That combination of mind and body relates to Plato's image in the *Phaidros*, namely, a chariot where the rational element drives and the irrational horses pull the chariot forward. Ancient Greek philosophy saw no isolation here. And many Greek festivals had this model: sports were included besides dramatic performances.

HARRISON: Well, also what inspires me about a place like Delphi, and many places in Greece, is that you get a sense of a festival where the person who would now be the football supporter and the person who would now be the concertgoer is the same person.

MCDONALD: Absolutely! You have large crowds, but there wasn't the same sociological division between the people.

HARRISON: And it's a destructive division.

MCDONALD: You see it clearly in the beer-drinking groups that go to the stadiums now and the wine-drinking groups that go to the opera.

HARRISON: Right, and what *The Trackers of Oxyrhynchus* play was trying to suggest was that you can find this same division in the way scholarship has talked about Greek drama. Many of these scholars feel that there is a high spiritual form of tragedy, which is followed by a satyr play, which, certainly to the Victorians, did not seem to belong to the same high spiritual category. And these decisions were being taken probably as early as the second century A.D., because those people who made up the syllabus did not feel that the satyr play was worthy of inclusion.

MCDONALD: Which is ridiculous. Because there are even comical moments in the tragedies. For instance, in Aeschylus' *Choephoroi*, the nurse speaks of Orestes wetting his pants. And then, in Euripides' *The Trojan Women*, Hecuba tells Menelaus, "You can't take Helen back on the same ship with you," and he asks, "Has she gained so much weight?" And then again in Aeschylus' *Persians*, the ghost Darius speaks charmingly about his returning to Hades, "Come, make your speeches short because I can't be late getting back." There are lots of little things like that which undercut the solemnity for dramatic reasons. Should these parts be eliminated because they are not worthy of Greek tragedy? Somehow, it seems easier to tolerate these comic diversions in Shakespeare's tragedies.

HARRISON: It is not uniformly solemn. People read the Greek dramas through a kind of High Anglican Church mist, it seems to me, so that everything is portentously serious, but in fact, I don't feel that was true. One of the most amazing facts about Greek drama is that someone like Aeschylus, who flourished in this hugely high-minded art form, was also regarded as the best writer of satyr plays. So what is it? We are used to contrasting the Shakespearean imagination, which is supposed to be uniquely English, something rather like Dickens' ability to marry the sublime and the sordid, whereas the Greeks found a different way of doing that. But we cannot understand tragedy without always positing that it ended with the satyr play.

MCDONALD: Yes, and satyr plays used the same metrics as tragedy, so there was an intimate relationship with what went before, if not a thematic relationship. Some people thought *The Trackers* followed *Ajax*, and both had the tracking idea in hunting down cattle.

HARRISON: Well, that's what intrigues me, you see, to take the same form in which people, who might well have appeared in a tragedy, have certainly wandered into the wrong context, but the poetic form would probably be the same. Now, my own preoccupation with it: my poem *v.* is very formal, the form of a poem which probably everybody knows, Gray's *Elegy [Written] in a Country Church Yard,* and into that strict classical form I put some of the filthiest language, so that the language of the most extreme hurt and aggression goes into a classical form.

Now it seems to me that our struggle with life has to be opened to both . . . both what is called sacred and what is called profane, or what is called scurrilous, or obscene. And the Greeks found a form, but the secrets of that form are largely lost to us because somebody decided that the satyr play wasn't fit to be preserved, and that's what sent me in my preoccupations as a poet, looking to fragments like Sophocles' *Ichneutai.* How does Sophocles have such a spiritual reputation? What is there left? Just a few fragments. But what do they tell us? I use the Oxford papyrologists, who are committed to a higher ideal of Greek culture, in a way, being overthrown by their own discovery. If they followed the logical conclusion of their discovery it should give them a certain sense of insecurity. But having isolated myself in a satyr play, I felt, curiously enough, it couldn't exist only comically. What happens in that play is it ends with a very dark ending because the form is indivisibly linked to the tragedy.

MCDONALD: The language of your satyr play is more Aristophanic than Sophoclean, or typical even of the satyr plays we know. Your language suits comedy more than the typical satyr play, particularly in the use of obscenities.

HARRISON: Well, just the sense of it; I mean I did it the wrong way round. I have a satyr play which darkens.

MCDONALD: We know so little about the satyr play. At least, we know that it derives its meter from tragedy. And then doesn't the prejudice against this type of play involve complicated attitudes toward the class structure, and physicality versus the intellect? In a way, these are dualities that you have been dealing with throughout. So you have the so-called obscenities . . .

HARRISON: It's the idea of a word like "refinement" . . . someone being "refined," this means that you purge away the things that really are too difficult to absorb, it seems to me. So that you have an art which is "refined." And what happened to history's view of Greek theater was that it became refined. And our view of culture became one about refinement. Now, it seems to me, that by making culture a matter of refinement it stops doing the job of culture, which is to allow us to unite, even for the brief duration of a play, or a novel, or a poem, those elements of ourselves that we are always encouraged to separate by religion, or refined culture, or by social convention.

MCDONALD: But in a certain sense you are partially making a new art form, one that bridges both tragedy and comedy as the ancients had, whereas you still are using the mold, but making it even richer, in some sense, aren't you?

HARRISON: It's really also dramatizing the preoccupations you find yourself locked into when you have done versions of Greek plays for contemporary theater. I did the *Oresteia*. Most people's expectations of a chorus of Greek drama were, again, so terribly refined, best spoken by very well-bred ladies in white nighties, all speaking together. That kind of refined expectation which I felt was performing a Christian operation on Greek drama. And the expectations of the kind of voice in English corresponded to what the level of refinement was supposed to be in the culture. I got different voices. I wanted different voices so that the reactions to that were very mixed and very strange. The people reacted as though the wrong guests had been invited to the party.

Now, it seems to me, that what I am dramatizing in *The Trackers of Oxyrhynchus* is that the tradition of Victorian scholarship was suddenly, in a sense, threatened by the satyr play . . . and that is what I am saying. The satyr play really is related to the idea of culture being refined, therefore being the special, privileged possession of an elite, of a certain class, of a certain group of people who are also refined, and who also keep at bay the sort of things that have been refined away from culture. A class of people who don't have that religion are deprived of all those things.

MCDONALD: So you've restored a certain vigor and actually, in Greece, the idea of democracy. There was a limited democracy— although women and children were excluded—but there was democracy. And in *The Persians*, Atossa asks about the Greeks, "Who's their shepherd and who commands their army?" And the chorus answers, "They are called slaves or servants of no man." Well, they did have leaders, people were selected because of merit rather than birth. And the idea that men should all share in power and art is what you are going back to in your play. We have the dignified language of tragedy, but you also have the erect *phalloi* of the satyrs, and in a way don't you translate those *phalloi* into the text through your use of obscenity?

HARRISON: Oh, yes, because I also am not sure, you see, what refined language is. I am not sure if anybody has really done the proper work on this in Greek culture. It is something that really has to be done. It is very convenient that Greek is a dead language because we can't estimate what degree of relationship there is between the language of tragedy and the languages that were spoken. We don't have enough evidence to know that.

MCDONALD: We don't know the demotic, but we do have comedy.

HARRISON: We have comedy, but comedy itself is also a selection, because it is formal and metrical. There has to be a selection made in order for the meters to work.

MCDONALD: It is probably a little closer to the people. Because we get dialects.

HARRISON: It still pushes toward this notion that culture is a refinement although we don't know what it is refining. Now, my feeling about culture, about drama, about poetry, is that I find form, the classical forms, very inspiring in many ways. But I don't find them inspiring because of refinement. I find the language that they can contain is actually as unrefined as you like, once you understand the form.

MCDONALD: It's a beautiful postmodernist gesture to revive a culture that no one knows existed, in a sort of substratum of language that we also don't know, but which you have revived. You've signified the trace.

HARRISON: Yes, right. And my interest as a poet is to use the most "refined" forms and fill them with a language that has not normally been granted permission to inhabit those forms.

MCDONALD: So you put blood back in the veins . . . along with the rhythm, the heartbeat.

HARRISON: Well, it's also not just for the benefit of reviving the form which has gone through long, historical survival, but in order to grant the same dignity of focus to the language of the so-called underfolk.

MCDONALD: Yes.

HARRISON: You know, my parents were very uneducated, and because they were uneducated and inarticulate, I was passionate about all the forms of articulation, whether they were other languages or poetry, which I see as the most supreme form of articulation. But when I came to a more sensitive . . . and when I had assimilated some of the education and some of my yearning to become a poet, my sense of their language, the language my parents spoke, was every bit as rich, in fact, richer, than the language I was being taught, which was a kind of neutral language.

MCDONALD: I would think that you would feel closer to Euripides than Sophocles—Euripides, who depicted men as they were, rather than Sophocles who depicted men as they ought to be, the abstract idea of man.

HARRISON: Well, yes and no. I think behind any perception of men as they are, and as loving as it can be, and I find that things as they are, are best depicted with love, and love takes away that judgmental part, nevertheless, any description of men as they are, in some ways is also searching for a vision, where men as they are, can be men as they are together, in the best possible way.

MCDONALD: Artistic structure, and artistic framework.

HARRISON: Artistic social framework.

MCDONALD: Yes. The function of the artist would seem to be that, rather than a photographer . . . it goes back to the whole theory of realism versus artifice. I guess this has been a dialogue that has always gone on, even the most natural reproduction, obviously, even in taking a picture, there is an imposing structure.

HARRISON: Yes, I understand this more and more as I work in film and television even though I only work in those as a poet. What I've found, having first thought that film and television—and this was partly a myth promulgated by people that work there—that it was actually inimical to the word. In actual fact, film and television were much like poetry because there is a rhythm of editing, for in editing you choose what you show, so it is only an illusion of being complete.

MCDONALD: The audience has much less freedom in a film than in a play in some senses for in the latter they can choose whom they are going to look at, but the other imposes its editing.

HARRISON: That's why it is always unsatisfying to film theatrical forms.

MCDONALD: Yes, it would be, because you do not have that holy space.

HARRISON: That's one of the reasons I resisted filming the *Oresteia*, and I did not want *The Trackers* to be filmed in Delphi. Because what would have happened when they had that irresistible urge to go into close-ups? We would have had close-ups of the actors and in fact, what we really wanted, or needed, was the grouping of the actors in that enormously long space, backed by those Phaedriades, under that sky.

MCDONALD: And the wind.

HARRISON: And the wind, all that. And the choosing eye is often an inferior one in that sense, because it is narrowed down to a choice of successive close-ups, and an occasional wide shot to show and remind you where you are. What's weird about being a spectator at a performance, is that you do both of those things. The ear goes into close-ups sometimes, but the eye stays in a panoramic wide shot if you like.

MCDONALD: Theoretically, one could zoom in with the eye, but you are advocating keeping the totality.

HARRISON: Well, certainly for a place as special as the stage of Delphi. It was for that place I devised the piece.

MCDONALD: I love the special light of Delphi and the way it changes too. I think also of the *Oresteia*, which begins at dawn, and a watchman keeping his post throughout the night. Both the play's intrinsic time and space and the spectator's coincide: you begin in darkness and suddenly the day emerges. In your *Trackers* we began with some light and then went deeper and deeper into night; that, too, added to the entire presentation.

HARRISON: It was important also to me, from the beginning, that it was a theatrical event in a sporting stadium. It does not matter that that sporting stadium is no longer used for sporting occasions but has been "refined" into a theater. I know that there were ancient performances of poetry in that stadium, and no doubt they did put up a platform, but I always found that putting up a platform at one end, and, as it were, pretending that it was an ancient theater, was the wrong way of looking at the Delphi space. In any case, the curves are much sharper in the stadium so you don't have that embracing arc (which I think is essential to tragedy) that you get in the great Greek theaters: Epidauros, the theater of Dionysus.

My piece was a response to that space and I wanted to remind people that you are actually taking over a sporting stadium from a period when sport and culture were not considered divided. I wanted to remind the people that races were being run there, and that this was a sporting stadium. What I wanted was that when a sporting image ends the piece, that was what was expected from the very beginning, because that's what that place was created for. And that's why it can't be done anywhere else, that particular version of it. I can do a version that ends in the kind of Britain I've written about in other poems, where you have an actual theater around which you have several hundred homeless people sleeping in cardboard boxes.

MCDONALD: What about the race at the beginning of the play?

HARRISON: I wanted a gun to go off and a race start. What I planned was that there would be three teams of four. The original plan, if you look at the design, was to have it marked out with white lines like a race course, and when the gun went off, the fellaheen began a race, a relay race, with a baton, which eventually became the papyrus.

MCDONALD: So now you're planning the *Alcestis* taking place in a *kafenion* and a *Prometheus* in a slag pit, so here also space and setting obviously seem to be an important factor.

HARRISON: In the *Oresteia*, I've done the very formal mask—

language of the chorus. The *Trojan Women* I've done and the *Lysistrata* were deliberately set at Greenham Common so that I would have a real group of women who would never lose their modern reality when they played the legendary women of Troy. In the *Alcestis* I was interested in a situation which was a choral situation, which would have natural language that I could make formal.

If you go to any Greek town or village, the people in the *kafenion* are not looking toward each other, or inside, but all look outward watching life go by. They may be reading the newspaper, or drinking coffee, or playing with their worry beads or whatever. I wanted that sense of a modern male chorus at tables, so that I could also use very naturalistic language, which is nearer, maybe, to what Euripides is about. If I went for the most formal and invented a language for Aeschylus, then I want to go to find a language for Euripides also. Although it's still formal, I want to try and find a colloquial way of doing it. It would be almost like a modern *kafenion*, but, just as in a *kafenion* you have the people who might read something from the newspaper, they just read it out, and he picks it up over here, somebody knocks their spoon against his cup. . . . I would make the music out of those kinds of natural noises also. They often have a television in the corner of the *kafenion* and I thought that the equivalent of the television in the corner of this *kafenion* would be a very classical formal play being played onstage. I would have the *kafenion* down here and the formal part up there, which is the story of *Alcestis*. Now what draws me to the *Alcestis* is again, its uncategorizability, if that word exists.

MCDONALD: Well, it was in the place of a satyr play, wasn't it? In the fourth place, following three tragedies, and Euripides gave it a happy ending along with comic features.

HARRISON: What happens is that a character from the satyr play, Hercules, strays into the tragedy, and I love it. It's like they've concertina-ed tragedy and the satyr play and made a new form so that most people look at it without remembering that it was given, served up, by Euripides as a satyr play, so that it really is uncategorizable, therefore very interesting. It doesn't conform to the holy "here" and the unholy "there."

MCDONALD: *Helen* is a little bit like that.

HARRISON: *Helen* is like that, sure.

MCDONALD: The comic element. It seemed toward the end of his life Euripides turned more to fantasy and comedy; a sweet antidote to the bitter war. But the *Alcestis* was an early play.

HARRISON: Yes, but it's got a darker subject somehow, the *Alcestis*, it's like juxtaposing death and life.

MCDONALD: Also, the Homeric heroes come off so badly, and this woman comes off so much better than the Homeric heroes. This is usual for Euripides, who takes the social inferiors and casts them as heroes, while taking the usual heroes and casting them as villains. Admetus and Pheres take off each other's masks and wrangle over trivia in the same way that Agamemnon and Menelaus do in *Iphigenia at Aulis:* one ends up respecting neither. We respect Alcestis and Iphigenia, however: both are victims yet still heroines.

HARRISON: It's so funny that blackness you see in Admetus and Pheres, his father. But it's all so very funny and it has to be very funny.

MCDONALD: That's true. Each one sees so clearly the other's faults, and they are both right.

HARRISON: It's the absurdity of the situation, you know. I mean Admetus saying, "You're old anyway, you can die for me."

MCDONALD: Yes, and Pheres retorts, "Are there new laws that say that a father has to die for his son?" And the other one to have even suggested it in the first place.

HARRISON: Imagine that, you know, in white robes, in a solemn dialogue; it's just nonsense.

MCDONALD: Both Admetus and Pheres are so much in love with their own lives that there's no question they'll accept anyone's life in place of their having to sacrifice themselves, and certainly a woman's, if she's silly enough to want to give it for them. This use of woman as substitute seems a constant motif in tragedy, as Nicole Loraux notes in her *Tragic Ways of Killing a Woman:* so many gratuitous deaths. It's a wonder that the women come off as nobly as they do, and mostly by contrast with the standard heroes.

HARRISON: The *Alcestis* has always drawn me as a play.

MCDONALD: Why?

HARRISON: Because it didn't fit the categories I'd been told to slot Greek plays into; therefore, it was a clue to tell me that the keys I'd been offered were wrong. So just as I'm drawn to the satyr play, I'm drawn to *Alcestis* as a way of saying, "Well, those critics, those categorizers are actually wrong."

MCDONALD: Well, Aristotle was wrong in . . .

HARRISON: Well, Aristotle was wrong from the beginning. I think he's up the pole.

MCDONALD: And it's appalling what people made it into, they even went one step worse.

HARRISON: Well, I don't see why we should think that Aristotle had the better idea.

MCDONALD: No, and then the sixteenth century French saying that you have to have all the unities, it just seemed to get worse and worse and worse. Aristotle's favorite play seems to be the *Oedipus Rex*, which then became the procrustean bed for all the others. I find him too restrictive.

HARRISON: His approach to a section of Greek drama doesn't give to me a drama that I would find very interesting . . .

MCDONALD: No, in fact, even the Aristotelian notion of tragedy having a beginning and an end is constricting. I find that your plays and your reworkings don't end the same way, and this would suggest that you do not consider the ending as such a definitive thing. I think we now realize that completion and endings are illusions; cycles are the closest thing we have to wholes. The modern age seems to be more Heraclitean than Aristotelian: a category or frame is clearly an imposition. Your plays seem to flow out of the frame. You had several endings for *The Trackers*, didn't you?

HARRISON: Yes, I will have to have more than one ending if we're going to perform it in London and other places. Even the version that was played in Delphi ended three times.

MCDONALD: It was fun. I loved it, but that's the way to do it, that destroys your ending. If you see that one ending is immediately followed by another ending, obviously, the last ending is not the last. . . .

HARRISON: The last thing is you hear the fragment "O . . . " again . . .

MCDONALD: The omega . . .

HARRISON: The omega, which is supposed to be final but to the English ear is also "O," is also a beginning, "O," an address. It's a vocative. It's like an invocation. And then, as a curtain call, but the curtain call was itself part of the play they discovered, and they put together the letters of Sophocles' name and gave him back the authorship.

MCDONALD: I liked your going up and taking a bow then, too, because it would have been empty without you filling the frame.

HARRISON: I didn't want to. I didn't like that.

MCDONALD: So *Prometheus* then is in a slag pit. That's probably one of the most morbid, the blackest of all the plays; it has an idea of light and freedom but . . .

HARRISON: But a light and freedom which haven't been realized.

MCDONALD: Well, he's cast into the pit with only the prophecies, the blind hope. He's an illustration of the same blind hope he brought to man, and a concrete illustration of horror, suffering, torture, as is Io who is victimized by a tyrant.

HARRISON: By a tyrant, yes, and Io is an amazing part. It could be someone returning from prison in Latin America; it could be anyone returning from any prison; the role of Io has always drawn me for that reason. It's like someone who escaped from tyranny to tell their story, who's had electric shock treatment or whatever, and although that's always been in my mind, it wasn't primarily the reason I wanted to do it.

It came out of the preoccupation I had with changing the expectation of what were cultural voices, such as, for example, my reinstating the Northern classics, *The Mysteries*, in the voices of the people who created it. There's nothing to say that ancient Greek should be done by a lot of middle-class ladies. To disturb that expectation, I then thought, well, why can't I then take a Greek play back to Yorkshire? And wouldn't this be the obvious thing, as there are so many mines and coal fields in Yorkshire, that are also now being closed, which was one of the great issues of the miner's strike, as you know from my poem, *v*. This was one of the most devastating symbols of national division in Britain. So why not take the play, which talks about the gift of fire and minerals, to a place where fire and minerals are created? And think of the refuse of that creation of coal, mining coal, these vast pit hills, which could be a Caucasus, if you like. And I envisaged a golden Prometheus—like the Prometheus outside the Rockefeller Center in New York—all gold, high up in these pit hills. And I would use some of that machinery of the mines close by finally to dispose of Prometheus.

What you're also raising is, what have been the social results?

What are the commensurate social layers to the separation of tragedy from satyr plays? What have been the results of the Promethean gift? Why not do the play, one of the earliest plays of European civilization, in the place of the earliest industrial revolution? Where the gift is there in the technical arts, minerals, fire, coal. So let's look at it in its real environment and we have a Caucasus which is both a physical Caucasus in theatrical terms but also is the detritus of the Promethean gift, and that gift is not just something that you bestow on everybody. Its bestowal meant that certain people have controlled the rights and other people have to work to bring these minerals and these Promethean gifts out of the earth. This seemed like a perfect setting for all my preoccupations.

MCDONALD: Why do you use tragedy and myth to illustrate these modern things?

HARRISON: Because they're received in our country as so-called unchanging measures of our experience.

MCDONALD: Poetry is more philosophical than history because it deals with universals rather than particulars, as Aristotle claimed.

HARRISON: Right, but you have to feed the universal particulars, it doesn't stay universal unless it gets a diet of particulars.

MCDONALD: So you want the interplay, which is lovely, because in a way, that goes along with your rational/irrational, intellectual/physical dichotomies. But why Greece? There are myths of so many places.

HARRISON: Well, that goes back to my earliest education. As I said, I came from a house without books, an uneducated family, and I was doing ancient Greek at the age of eleven, so that the idea of reconciling, or measuring ancient Greek against the particularity of working-class life, for example, is my earliest struggle to accommodate one with the other. I've always presented the one to the other since I was a child.

MCDONALD: You also have branched out; *Bow Down*, obviously, is a conglomeration of myths.

HARRISON: That takes one story which was, and follows, the idea is . . .

MCDONALD: Permutation . . .

HARRISON: Every permutation . . .

MCDONALD: Is included . . .

HARRISON: . . . is part of the story . . .

MCDONALD: . . . because a myth consists of all its versions.

HARRISON: Right. A myth consists of all its versions, which I used as an epigraph to the *Medea*, and for *Bow Down* I collected hundreds of versions and also wrote my own.

MCDONALD: Why do you have all these languages? For *Bow Down*, Danish and English, and for *Medea*, Greek, Latin, and French.

HARRISON: Well, to show that there's no one version of the story. The version is the present teller's. Or, the present teller's dialogue with past tellers. It's a chorus of past and present tellers. But in *Bow Down*, even the name of the girl becomes different in every line, even her name changes and that's only emblematic of our accounts of reality. If I tell you a story of something that happened to me it might be a different version if I tell it to somebody else, who has maybe a different kind of interest, a different kind of background. Not only will I slightly adjust the story, the reception will be different.

MCDONALD: It's the elephant as interpreted by blind men, or *Rashomon*, or *M. Butterfly*: different perceptions and versions of reality which create that reality. So also with Medea; I think she resembles a Homeric hero in that her external role shapes her internal desires. The mask can become the "reality," which in certain cases can be dangerous. There's an interesting interplay between external presentation and internal perception; one informs the other. Your presentation is in part molded by your audience.

HARRISON: Well, there's no one version, just as in the end there is no once-and-for-all truth about the world.

MCDONALD: No, you can't put your foot in the same river twice.

HARRISON: Well, I prefer Heraclitus' idea to the one that claims someone came along and received the word of God and that was life, solved, once and for all. I remember when I was living in northern Nigeria for four years, in an Islamic country. I put on the *Lysistrata* and I quoted from the Koran at the beginning the sura about the Greeks, and it says, "'The Greeks.' They care for the outward show of this life, but of the life to come they are heedless." It's as though that's a terrible thing. According to the Koran, the Unbeliever says, "I love this fleeting life." Well, I love this fleeting life. I think that some of the health of the Greek culture and the Greek mind was that it was heedless of the life to come, that it didn't posit an afterlife, that it didn't throw its energies into creating an afterlife that was better than this one; in fact, the image of an afterlife is totally shadowy.

MCDONALD: Aristotle said of happiness, "What every man aims for in a life, is the activity of the soul in accordance with human excellence."

HARRISON: And not divine.

MCDONALD: Even Aristotle's notion of the good, and ethics in general, improved on Plato's absolute by being considered a mean which depended on the human being, his character and its disposition (*hexis*) and choice (*proairesis*). People are still writing about what that mean could possibly be. You don't have it defined as one truth that people contemplate. But of course philosophy has gone between these poles for almost all time. There's Kant and then again there's Heidegger, showing the age-old conflict between the eternal and the ephemeral, the unchanging and the changing.

HARRISON: I love that poem of Wallace Stevens, "Sunday Morning," it's one of my favorite poems—which is a rejection of the other world; you know it's such a sensuous apprehension of this world, which, I feel, is very important.

MCDONALD: I like Cavafy's "Journey to Ithaca." It's the journey that counts, not the arrival; Cavafy bids you to wish for a long journey, full of adventure, full of knowledge. Life, not the afterlife.

HARRISON: Teresa called me yesterday and said she made a slip of the tongue, but it was a very creative one; she said, "All roads lead to Ithaca."

MCDONALD: Instead of Rome; so the Greek instead of the Italian route.

HARRISON: Yes, that's right.

MCDONALD: Absolutely, and it's not where they lead, it's how long and what's on the way.

HARRISON: Right, it's what's on the way that matters.

MCDONALD: Was the *Oresteia* your first reworking of Greek tragedy?

HARRISON: No, the first one was the one I did in Nigeria in 1966; it's called *Aikin Mata*—a reworking of the *Lysistrata* by Aristophanes. Have you ever seen that?

MCDONALD: No, I haven't.

HARRISON: Well, I remember when I first went to Delphi, there was a man who gave a paper which mentioned that it was the first Greek play that had ever been done in West Africa. I did it in collaboration with an Irish poet, James Simmons, who was there, living in Nigeria, and we really wanted to do a European play using Nigerian music, dance, theatrical modes, and so forth. We did the version very quickly and we used a setting which tragically came true not long after the play, in that intertribal conflict broke out between North and South, just shortly before the Nigerian Civil War.

MCDONALD: So your play was prophetic.

HARRISON: Well, not so much prophetic, in that you are always aware of the tensions between the tribes. But that was the first Greek play I did. It was published by Oxford University Press and I used African music, and dancing, and film.

MCDONALD: In the *Oresteia*, were you taking a social stand? You did it in masks, and it seemed more abstract than some of your other reworkings, but you did use some of the wonderful Northern dialects.

HARRISON: I think if you're looking for social ground, I think it's in the struggles between men and women and looking at *Oresteia* in the light of feminism, feminist history, or feminist historiography. You realized that if you began to go deep into the sexual antagonism of the play—and this came out in the workshops we did when it was open to the actors of both sexes—that when women played the parts, the usual empathetic root of an actor identifying with the character seemed to break down in some places, especially, for example, in the chorus in the *Choephoroi* on how dreadful women are. Gradually the idea came to me that it should be, as it were, vacuum-sealed in maleness because the play seemed to have been written in order to overthrow the dynamic female images that seemed to dominate the imagination in the Athenian culture at that time, and to present some kind of male image liberated from this defeat of the female principle. Somewhere there is that meaning; it's quite clear in the trial, and it's quite clear in the fact that Orestes kills his mother; and then that leads to the choice in the trial between the ties of blood and the ties of the marriage bed and to the virtual sort of pensioning off of the furies.

I think I got into it through Strindberg, who is the dramatist who most had his finger on the pulse of the sex war; he really wrote about how terrible the sexes could be to each other, and he was really obsessed by the *Oresteia*. He'd read in a French anthropological magazine an article written by Paul Lafargue, who was Marx's son-in-law and who had written on kinship systems in the *Oresteia* and the idea of matriarchy. No, it doesn't necessarily matter if there were historical societies which were matriarchal; the fact is that there were very powerful female images. Strindberg, who was horrified, began writing *The Father* and *The Pelican*, as kind of counter-plays to those, because, if you remember, in *The Father*, the idea is that he goes crazy because he's not sure that he's the father of his own child.

MCDONALD: Even Telemachus in the *Odyssey* said his mother told him who his father was, but he's not sure, because no man can know himself who his parent was; this seems a strangely apt remark for the son of wandering Odysseus.

HARRISON: That's how monogamy probably grew, so that man could be certain about his paternity. I mean, Engels links all those things together, speculating that monogamy grew with the growth of private property in order to transmit it to a male heir. If it was not a matrilineal succession but a patrilineal one, how would you be certain? A woman always knows that she's the mother of a child. And all those things are obviously in the *Oresteia*. I also wanted theatrically to find out what kind of language would be spoken in masks, because that's something that most scholars never even give a thought to; they don't investigate what it means that these plays were masked.

MCDONALD: Didn't masks function somewhat as an amplifier?

HARRISON: No, that's a falsehood. They didn't. I mean they had their existential use, I think. I've brooded about their use for a long time but it's very difficult to brood about use without working to find out what kind of language works through the mask. It's no good imagining that people spoke as they spoke in ordinary conversation, you know, in a vast theater with masks, which always forced you to turn outwards, toward the audience. I was interested in exploring the world of masks and the language that was spoken in order to get a better idea of what the poetic nature of the language was.

MCDONALD: Do you think the language has to be more graphic because the features are frozen?

HARRISON: I think it throws so much focus on the language. In actual fact, the mask, even though it's static, changes according to what it says. There's no doubt about it.

MCDONALD: The mask fulfills the observation by Kulashov that the same expression can mean different things depending on its context, or montage; it differs if it appears next to a knife, or a smiling child.

HARRISON: Well, yes, the same mask changes depending on who wears it and what is said. In this case, also, I wanted men to play the parts, as they did, not out of archaeological interest but precisely because it reflected the fact that the play was a play written for the male-dominated society, about male preoccupations. And it was not even ready to admit women to play their own parts.

MCDONALD: What about your *Medea?* It carries on the sex war.

HARRISON: Right, all I learned about the sex war in Greek drama went into writing the *Medea,* but in a different way.

MCDONALD: The sex war then, do you see it ending in a draw? It seems in your *Medea* you at least have fathers killing their children also.

HARRISON: Well, that's a negative draw, isn't it?

MCDONALD: But the *Oresteia* seems to be a clear male victory.

HARRISON: Well, I think what I was doing with the *Oresteia* was, as I said, vacuum-sealing it in maleness. It seems to me that that dramatizes the beginning of what is now known as patriarchy, and that patriarchy has been socially and ecologically disastrous. I think there's no doubt about that. I'm certainly not a supporter of male domination.

MCDONALD: Do you support a form of matriarchy?

HARRISON: No, no, no, on the contrary, but what I think I am, is something that has always been with me since I was a child, since I was writing poetry in an area which didn't really have much regard for those kinds of sensitivities, a person that knows we do need, both individually and socially, the male to honor the female within himself and the female, the male, whatever those categories mean.

MCDONALD: In Jungian terms?

HARRISON: Yes. The play I was engaged on—which was going to be produced but I didn't find the composer—was called *The Indivisibles* and that was about the *anima* of Oppenheimer, who developed the atomic bomb. It was about relationships and how the unchecked animus could run riot. Although Oppenheimer had originally wanted to be a poet, and was in touch with, in Jungian terms, the *anima,* through his reading of Sanskrit, the *Bhagavad Gita* from which he quoted when the first bomb was dropped, it was the *animus* in him that led to his contribution to creating the bomb in the Manhattan Project. I think it's simple-minded to think that matriarchy would be an alternative to patriarchy, and of course, these are symbolic terms.

MCDONALD: Oh yes, so there will always be a tension . . .

HARRISON: We, in Britain, know that to have a woman in a key position in politics doesn't always lead to a gentler culture or a more caring culture; on the contrary.

MCDONALD: It seems to me there were a couple of Greek comedies on the theme of women in politics, from *Lysistrata* to the *Ekklesiazousai*, frequently subtitled, *Women in Power*.

HARRISON: Right, very hard to do either of them. How's the tape?

MCDONALD: Oh, it goes on forever, you can't turn it off; You see, it's open-ended.

IX

Theodoros Terzopoulos' Production of Heiner Müller's *Medeamaterial:* Myth as Matter

HERE HAVE been many analyses of Heiner Müller's use of myth in his plays. Manfred Kraus, for instance, gives a summary of some of the conflicting theories in relation to Müller's *Philoktet.*[1] Some claim that Müller is faithful to the original myth; others say that he distorts it for his own ends. I think both claims are true.

Müller has often turned to myth for his subject matter: the *Philoktet* in 1965; then *Herakles 5* dealing with the cleaning of the Augean stables; *Ödipus, Tyrann* in 1966, a reworking of Hölderlin's version of Sophocles' *Oedipus Tyrannos.* Then we have a *Prometheus* based on Aeschylus in 1968. We have two works based on the Medea theme, *Medeaspiel* in 1974 (a pantomime), and finally, the subject of this chapter, *Verkommenes Ufer Medeamaterial Landschaft mit Argonauten* (1982), "Despoiled Shore Medeamaterial Landscape with Argonauts." From 1968 we also have a piece called *Der Horatier,* which was based on the mythologically oriented history of early Rome.

If we scan the bibliography of Müller's plays, we find an impressive list of reworkings of classics, from Shakespeare (*Hamletmas-*

chine) to Laclos (*Quartett*). Why? When Müller himself is asked, he parries with jokes or counterquestions. He says that realism simply does not suit the GDR: "Here actors cannot even say *Guten Tag* without it sounding like a lie."[2] He claims that actors in the West are much better at naturalism, and good in films, whereas, "Here they are better in productions of the classics, i.e., in anything that entails a stylized removal from immediate reality" (p. 137).

So also American drama rarely concerns itself with the past, but European drama does, perhaps simply because of the richness of the European past. Müller claims that since the dead outnumber the living and literature is a democratic tool, it should be respectful of the majority.[3]

In general Müller fends off critics. He says that he enjoys drama because, "Writing drama you always have masks you can talk through. . . . I can say one thing and say the contrary." And further, "My texts are frequently written so that every—or every second—sentence shows only the tip of the iceberg—and what's underneath is nobody's business." He complains about the theater people who put on "their wetsuits and dive down, looking for the iceberg or building their own" (p. 19). So we are told we are going to be presented with contradictions, and we are advised not to try to discover what is underneath the surface, nor to invent our own alternative.

I enjoy diving and have an Irish imagination, so please join me now on what may be a cold swim, but I promise that if we don't see the beauty of crystalline shapes, we shall at least appreciate the shock and horror of the overall mass. Hope still follows fear and horror. Müller himself said, "The first shape of hope is fear, the first appearance of the new, horror" (p. 30).

Contradictions are part of the new reality. In our critical journey from Saussure, through Adorno and the Frankfurt School, to structuralism with Lévi-Strauss and Barthes, to Derrida and deconstruction and the postmodernists, we have come through elaborate explanatory schemes to realize finally the futility of some explanations. Müller is right, when asked about his relation to postmodernism, to answer, "The only postmodernist I know of was August Stramm, a modernist who worked in a post office" (p. 137).

Euripides used the theme of Medea to show, as he often does, how a woman is the true representative of the virtue (*arete*) that used to be found in the Homeric hero. Now men, the city dwellers, show their corruption in the elaborate language learned from the sophists, language used to deceive rather than as a sacred repository of truth. Medea invokes the gods and the sanctity of language as oath. She is not as jealous of Jason's new bride (contrary to Müller's emphasis) as angry at having been deprived of her status. She who created Jason's present can also destroy it. She appears at the end as a goddess in a dragon-drawn chariot, out of Jason's reach, holding the bodies of their children. In Euripides man has become god—in fact woman has become god. In Müller man becomes landscape.

Many have used the Medea theme as a dramatic tool since Euripides, from Ovid and Seneca to Corneille, Anouilh and Grillparzer, and to the present. Almost all have eliminated the gods. Lukács said the novel is the new epic, but without gods.[4] Modern drama also lacks gods and often man is at the center. Müller will expand this focus to include man's tools, his *Produktionsmittel;* this includes the earth, which finally absorbs man.

Pier Paolo Pasolini's *Medea* (Italy, 1970) shows the confrontation of male and female, barbarism and civilization, and the blurring between the two. Dassin in his film *Dream of Passion* makes the story into a melodrama, individuals into generalizations. Tony Harrison has written *Medea: A Sex-War Opera*. Robert Wilson has made a silent film of Medea as mother, silently giving life and taking it away in his *Deafman Glance*. Müller also has a silent play done first in 1974, called *Medeaspiel*. This shows a woman tied to a bed, wedded: the sexual act is followed by birth. There are three projected titles: The Sexual Act, The Act of Birth and The Act of Killing. The final act is described in these terms: "The woman takes off her face, rips up the child, and hurls the parts in the direction of the man. Debris, limbs, intestines fall from the flies on the man."[5] A truly nightmarish conclusion to what Müller sees as man's primordial victimization of woman.

Other modern reworkings have echoed this fear: Suzuki has Clytemnestra return from the dead to kill Orestes: Agave kills Pentheus. There was a fear of woman in antiquity, and the catastrophic fantasy of a wife killing her husband, and a mother her son, was a concrete reflection of the fear of a rebellious woman. A woman of fifth century Athens was kept prisoner in her house, but she might exact revenge. Women's history is, of course, a long variation on this theme, so the nightmares of males have a long history. In fact, it was Euripides himself, often called the first psychologist, who first made Medea consciously murder her children in response to Jason's abuse. There are many other "wicked women" Euripides made into heroines (e.g., Melanippe, Auge, Phaedra, Stheneboia, Canace, Aerope and Pasiphae).

As our past shapes our present, our present reshapes our past. History organizes that past, and mythology colors it. The resonances derived therefrom will also inform our future. I see Heiner Müller using these tools as dramatic devices and also as warnings. About his *Philoktet,* he said, "Damen und Herren aus der heutigen Zeit, / Führt unser Spiel in die Vergangenheit" (Ladies and Gentlemen of modern times, our play will lead back to our past).[6] His art may not change the future (Euripides' *Trojan Women* did not stop the Athenians from continuing their disastrous war), but it is a sign that can inform us. It is a warning. And this is the beginning of hope: the fear that may alter our present destructive rollercoaster ride—a ride if not to nuclear destruction, then to the destruction that results from the misuse of our means of production (both the people and the material). Perhaps we shall end in a trash heap, "not with a bang, but a whimper."

Müller's earlier work was more easily accessible, at least superficially. After he was expelled from the Writers' Association, following his presentation of *Die Umsiedlerin,* a comedy (1956), we find less humor in his plays (but more in his interviews) and also more use of the abstract and stream-of-consciousness delivery. Personal and public events (1956 was also the year Brecht died) seem to have contributed to Müller's black vision, which I see culminating in *Verkommenes Ufer Medeamaterial Landschaft mit Argonauten.* Müller says this work "presumes the catastrophes which mankind is working toward. The theater's contribution to their prevention can only be their representation."[7]

Now for my view of the iceberg: Medea is the mythological sign, a woman violated by Jason, used by him as a tool to further himself, then discarded. Taking her vengeance, she destroys him through his future (his children), and also destroys the princess who could give him more children, as well as the princess' father who has bestowed upon him the kingdom. Müller's Medea takes away even Jason's identity, by refusing to recognize him: Jason: "Medea." Medea: "Amme kennst du diesen Mann?" (Nurse, do you know this man?)[8]

Medea refuses to be his reflective other, and Jason ceases to exist. This section makes up *Medeamaterial.*

The frames—*Verkommenes Ufer* and *Landschaft mit Argonauten*—complete the picture and bring us into modern times. Man has violated the earth, as Jason did Medea: we see the *Verkommenes Ufer* ("Despoiled Shore"). In *Landschaft mit Argonauten,* we see the earth taking vengeance on Jason for its violation, as Medea did for hers. The matter (material cause, to borrow the Aristotelean phrase), the *Produktionsmittel* (means and materials for production) will now destroy the worker who used it. The result is "meines Todes" (my death). Will this death come from from man or stone? "Wer hat bessre Zähne / *Das Blut oder der Stein?*" (Who has better teeth, blood or stone?)[9]

What are Müller's devices and what sets his treatment of the Medea legend apart from other versions? In an interview with *Der Spiegel,* he said that text material in the first two sections was old, but the last section, *Landschaft mit Argonauten,* was new, and semiautobiographical. He added, "As in every landscape, the 'I' in this segment of the text is collective."[10] He also sees the myth in a colonial perspective, saying, "The end signifies the threshold where myth turns into history: Jason is slain by his boat. . . . European history began with colonization. . . . That the vehicle of colonization strikes the colonizer dead anticipates the end of it. That's the threat of the end we're facing, the 'end of growth.' "[11] The vengeance of and absorption by the *Produktionsmittel* signifies the ultimate revolt of the colonial. The source of life becomes the source of death: Medea is the boat, the earth, the wife mother, and the executioner who ignores the executed. Death is impersonal, mechanical, automatic, and identity is effaced along with life.

The class war is also evident. Jason the capitalist exploits Medea the worker; the worker is historically victorious. But the final scene concentrates on Jason and total loss, so Marxian optimism is absent. Optimism, if there is any, is to be found outside the play; we have the potential as collective inhabitants of the world, to recognize this reckless rush toward destruction and to stop it. The worker and the workplace—the *Produktionsmittel*—must be valued, treasured, respected, and preserved. The disastrous effects of noncommunication must be avoided, because now they can be fatal to the world.

Müller has said of his *Philoktet,* "Dass die Vorgänge, die das

Stück beschreibt, nur in Klassengesellschaften mit antagonistischen Widerspruchen möglich sind," (The events which this play describes, are only possible in a class-based society with antagonistic oppositions).[12] So we have these social confrontations in this version of the *Medea* also. Odysseus is like Jason, as an emblem of *der Politik der Macher* with the *Maske der Manipulation* visible.[13] The past is interpreted in terms of the present and in turn is used to give perspective on and, indeed, even to shape the present. The tragedy of Medea is a useful vehicle. Jason wishes to possess Medea as a slave, just as man wishes to possess the Earth; both are to be abused and discarded when they are no longer needed. Only their continued use can ensure mutual survival. The *Arbeit* must continue, not just the *Besitz*—work, not just ownership—activity in addition to the static.

Müller also suggests that the three sections of *Verkommenes Ufer Medeamaterial Landschaft mit Argonauten* be performed simultaneously. It is as if war were being symbolized by its very representation: text obliterates text (depending on how this is performed). This would be a loss because of the concentrated beauty of the text. It shows great subtlety, with historical references both to the history of Germany (e.g., reference to the deserters who were hanged at the end of World War II) and also to earlier works. There are also references to specific German products and pollutants: popular brands of condoms and cigarettes (Fromm's Act and Casino, for instance). Then again the Medea myth is interwoven with all, past with present: the fatal Argo waits in a hangar. In a simultaneous performance the valuable text would be obliterated like Medea, like the earth.

Verkommenes Ufer shows us a landscape filled with the dead who are identified with the earth and walked upon by the living, as they are sailed over in *Landschaft mit Argonauten*. The dead of the past are mentioned: women in their blood, and corpses dangling from lampposts (those who were thought to be cowards during World War II). The dead of the future are mentioned: the collective Argonauts and Jason as representatives for all mankind. The living appear as an interim between the two groups of the dead. Pregnant women squeeze out children "gegen den Anmarsch der Würmer" (as a defense "against the advancing worms"), a futile gesture against death.[14] Human effluences and other liquids water the earth, feed and smear the living; there are images of a lake, menstrual flows, ejaculated semen, vomit, urine, blood, sweat, tears, feces, and poisons. Human effluences are mentioned: babies, vomit, sweat, tears, semen, blood, feces. We are also told what a human can absorb: food, liquids, penises, bullets, poisons and so on. All human activity is seen in terms of ingestion in or expulsion—*Produktionsmittel* used properly and improperly. Man consumes food and sex as a machine uses gas and electricity, and he automatically produces, until at last production is cut off and the abused resources turn murderous (i.e., poisonous).

The final image of *Verkommenes Ufer* is of Medea cradling the brother she has killed to help Jason—Medea the expert in poisons. She had served Jason as the *Produktionsmittel* for his power and his posterity. When she is discarded she turns the poisons against him, as will the earth against man. We are visually and audibly overwhelmed by the sheer waste and abuse of human and material resources.

Medeamaterial begins with a dialogue between Medea and the nurse, then between Medea and Jason, then a monologue by Medea triumphant: she acquires an identity and a famous name, whereas Jason is obliterated. Medea begins with reference to Jason as her first and last love: and now he is already with Creon's daughter, because Creon has the power. Medea asks her nurse if she is crying or laughing. The nurse who functions rather as Medea's mirror, an aged Medea, says that she is "beyond crying or laughter." Medea then asks for a mirror and says, "Das ist nicht Medea," "That is not Medea" (p.36). Medea is immortal although she will die.

To Jason, Medea complains about his absence and asks if he will drink her blood. The blood motif continues (it began and will end the play). Jason tells her what he has given her: power and position, the recognition of others. She says she sacrificed a brother; he gave her something lifeless. She gave him life and power, but not enough. Like the true capitalist, he must continue to amass beyond his needs for survival. *Besitz* over *Arbeit*. This can only end in death for all, if everyone overaccumulates and wastes the resources that should be shared (one thinks of the changes in Eastern Europe in 1989, where there was a drive for shared accumulation). How will Medea exact repayment? Will there be anything left to repay when the resources are seen as finite?

Jason counters he has given Medea two children for her brother; Medea says she will give them back. She was his slave, his tool (*Werkzeug*). She killed for him, gave birth for him, but she is merely a rung on his ladder. She has given him the blood of her kin and the blood of her body, for which he returns only ashes and sand and death. He has on him the stench of the other woman, the other bed. Medea suggests he stuff his bride's womb with her children, whom she now also sees as using her; she gave them milk and is now their footstool. Suddenly, she changes her tone, and, dwelling on Jason's lovemaking with his new bride, persuades him to take her gifts. But Medea's gifts for Jason's bride are imbued with the fire emblematic of the passion which in this case will only bring death. The bride's skin will melt away, liquified by the acid which permeates the robe and the fire that descends from the divine coronet. The result will be ashes and death, as Jason had given Medea ashes. She will engrave her history on the young bride's body, as Kafka's protagonist had his sin and sentence carved into his skin in "The Penal Colony."

Medea wants to hear Jason's laughter at his bride's screams (an ironic variation of Euripides' Medea, who said she did what she did so that her enemies would not laugh at her, the bane of the Homeric hero). Not just blood, but screams come out: the screams from the past and the present. Laughter for Medea; screams and tears for the new bride. Now Medea asks the children for her blood back. She was cut off from home, and seeks a way to do the same to Jason. She was the barbarian, exploited by the colonizer. Now she will kill, drain the blood, and silence the screams. And she no longer knows or recognizes Jason. He is no man; his past is destroyed. Here we see the core of Euripides' play reproduced in a freely associative text, with Medea at the center, jealous and raging at being used and abused, paying back blood with blood: the *Produktionsmittel* demanding recompense in death.

A spurned woman is not new with Müller (it has been a favorite theme since at least Euripides). But Müller's Madame de Merteuil poisons Valmont. And in *Hamletmaschine*, his Ophelia, the final figure on stage, says, "Down with the happiness of submission. . . . When she walks through your bedrooms carrying butcher knives you'll know the truth."[15] This is a feminist vision bound to strike terror in any male heart. Ophelia calls herself Electra, and Müller wrote (in *Projection 1975* during an American visit): "In the century of Orestes and Electra that's rising, Oedipus will be a comedy" (p. 29). He said that one used to be able to fit death into verse (and we recall Adorno saying poetry is no longer possible after Auschwitz). Müller also comments that only now have "killers ceased to scan their victims" (p. 29). Impersonal death is the ultimate horror. We are not even confirmed as having existed when we die: modern death is incidental or accidental.

Now we turn to the final section of the play we are investigating, in which Jason takes on the persona of the author, an identity we (the audience) also come to assume. As Medea denied Jason his identity, so does Müller ask who he is: "Auswurf eines Mannes" (the outcast of a man), "Ein Flattern zwischen Nichts und Niemand Wind vorausgesetzt" (a floating between nothing and no one, a supposed wind).[16] He claims his father was an idiot in Boeotia (and we think of Hesiod who, while tending sheep on Mount Helicon in Boeotia, was called by the Muses to sing of the gods). Now Müller has been called to sing of man. Is the poet considered the idiot? Did the Writers' Association pass judgment on him?

This Jason/Müller has an anchor as his umbilical cord; tied to the horizon of memory, he sails over the dead as earlier man walked over them. Suddenly, we find ourselves in modern times surrounded by the garbage of civilization and war: trash, rubble and beer cans. Children play the ghosts of the dead to come. Hope is sought between the thighs of a woman. Müller himself produces "Wortschlamm aus meinem Verlassenen Niemandsleib" (verbal slime from my abandoned noman's body) (p. 37). He is the successor to Odysseus, renowned for his wily words, who taunted the Cyclops, Polyphemus, and called himself Noman. How can "ein fetzen Shakespeare" (A ragtag Shakespeare) be found "im Paradies der Bakterien?" (in bacteria paradise?) (p.37). Like Nero, he creates art while observing destruction. One-eyed Polyphemus is seen directing traffic; he is a traffic light, a sign without words. Jason/Müller makes allusions to television, theater, and film, what he calls the theater of death: "unser Hafen war ein totes Kino . . . das Theater meines Todes," (Our harbor was a dead film theatre, the theater of my death)(p. 37)—and memory is destroyed, "DO YOU REMEMBER DO YOU NO I DON'T"(p.38). Cf. the end of *Medeamaterial*: Jason: "Medea." Medea: "Amme kennst du diesen Mann?"

Jason/Müller sees dead comrades around him: an airplane comes (what his grandmother called God), and blood flows from his veins as his body turns into the landscape. The rest, in this case, is poetry (contrary to the silence that ends Shakespeare's *Hamlet*). There are no flights of angels, there is no god—only a plane, a tool of man, consigning the poet to the landscape. Poetry is now a sign of death; teeth now blood and stone.

This is powerful imagery. The words both alienate and seduce, and are more like stream of consciousness than dialogue. Müller's *Medea* may now have three characters (Medea, her nurse, and Jason), but given the nurse's function as "Medeamirror," we can see Müller has reduced Euripides' play to two main characters. In this case, a dialectic is created—Medea and Jason: male, female; capitalist, worker; master, slave; colonist, subject; worker, tool; poet, subject matter—and the message is not optimistic.

Also one must, of course, mention Brecht, since Müller is his obvious heir. Müller has said, "Brecht gebrauchen ohne ihn zu kritisieren, ist Verrat" (To use Brecht without criticizing him is to betray him).[17] And Müller has truly not betrayed Brecht; he has more violence and poetry, but less humor than his predecessor (at least in *Medeamaterial*). Brecht established space between himself and his audience, a kind of aesthetic distance, so as to transform the stage into an "other" that could be recognized and have its clear message understood. He also used antiquity for a model—for example, his *Antigone*, of which he tried "aus dem ideologischen Nebel die höchst realistische Volkslegende auftauchen zu lassen," (To have the most realistic people's legends emerge from the ideological fog).[18] Müller has made the message more complex, to reflect a reality that has become more complex, and contradictory. He taps the resources of the unconscious to both entice and estrange his audience; language and images are used as weapons that assault and disturb the mind. Characters are not sympathetic figures who easily lend themselves to audience identification. The language and focus that are taboo for a bourgeois audience may repel, but drive away at the same time they excite, which involves the audience in a form of ritual. Müller sees the theater as "Prozess," and, Kraus notes, "Die auffassung von Theater als Prozess bedeutet für Müller die Miteinbeziehung des Publikims in die dramatische Produktion," (Müller's concept of the theater as process means drawing the public into the dramatic production).[19] The audience is a crucial element in every performance.

Müller says he is neither a dope nor a hope dealer, but I don't believe him. I think he drugs his audience with poetry and shows them hope in the possibility of change. Perhaps it is not too late for us to understand the message. Müller's final message is powerful theater. As he says, the rest is poetry. *Medeamaterial* may show us the specter of death, but there is hope, not only between the thighs of a woman but between the lips of a poet.

There have been many productions of Heiner Müller's plays, which are suggestive enough to allow for many different interpretations. One of the most interesting has been done by Theodoros Terzopoulos, the Greek producer who has spent much time in Germany studying their dramatic techniques. He has combined these with his Greek background and training to merge theatrical traditions in a way that resembles Suzuki. Terzopoulos has also reworked ancient Greek tragedies, such as *The Bacchae.*

Like Suzuki, Terzopoulos believes in rigorous training for his actors, and he creates a holy space in his hypnotic presentations through repeated and ritualistic actions. From his own experiences after World War II in Greece, and also in the country's civil war, he saw the way that people dealt with their overwhelming sorrow. Through bodily movements, they would exorcise their suffering in a kind of atavistic dance. His experience of the fire-walking ceremony (in his native Thrace) helped him learn the limits of human endurance, and also about the bodily transfigurations of which a human being is capable.

Theodoros Terzopoulos has made Heiner Müller's *Medeamaterial* into a ritual of death. He is brilliantly faithful to the principles that were established in his performance of Euripides' *Bacchae,* but he goes even further. Myth is again made visible through the use of the human body. He goes inside man and conveys the internal truths that indeed are eternal truths, and we come to see that the tragedy of mankind is indeed a collective tragedy. Distinctions are blurred; Medea's lines are given to Jason and vice versa. The personae flow back and forth. There is no longer a distinction between male and female (something that could be interpreted as liberating) but horror sets in. There are no distinctions made between the sane and the insane, between the living or the dead.

Through the repeated gestures or motions of the characters—often seemingly without meaning or relevance to any text except some inner indecipherable one—man is seen to be a victim of his compulsions. We witness his repeated meaningless motions in a world that is itself devoid of meaning. This is the paradigmatic deconstructed landscape: signifier represents signifier in endless regression and man represents the dead and vice versa.

We are shown a near barren stage strewn with the debris of civilization: a television running with no picture, bottles, cans, papers, and discarded tools. The characters are dressed in rags, and what is seen of their exposed skin is filthy: they resemble more disposible objects, trash that walks. We hear the Blue Danube waltz, an idyllic promise that mocks the reality. Heavy-metal rock music invades at one point. We hear the sound of an airplane flying overhead and rolls of film drop from the sky (modern bird and droppings?).

Jason sucks at a balloon/breast which bursts over him as he basks for a moment in symbiotic ecstasy. Medea compulsively strikes her breast as if trying to remove it while she endlessly fondles it. She wears the poisoned bridal dress as if it were a straightjacket and this poisoned dress will be her legacy for the next bride. Repetition. Repetition. Shoes are endlessly polished.

A young bride is contrasted with the old Medea; images of sexuality and fertility, and decay are conveyed by a young girl who beats a sheaf of wheat between her legs while the old Medea can barely raise her head from the mud. Youth and age, both at the end of their compulsive acts, become the dead—and what is worse, the living dead.

Just as soon as identities are established, lines from the play are exchanged and Medea speaks for Jason, Jason for Medea, and "nurse" and "argonaut" for both Jason and Medea (there are three actors and two actresses in Terzopoulos' production). Through this exchange, all identity is lost. Identity becomes another disposable item.

Terzopoulos has made the modern nightmare flesh, and to our horror we realize that this collective nightmare landscape is our own. Man is reduced to landfill, and the earth to debris.

X

Theodoros Terzopoulos' Talk

I WANT to talk about the origin of my work, and my need to be involved with the theater, and to practice the kind of theater which incorporates the energy of the body, human memory, and life experience and images which have been stored within the human body. All this predisposition which I have felt since the time I was very young, and which now is being manifested—years ago it was a tendency—and now it is being manifested as a point of view on art, comes forth clearly from a deep need of mine to remember again things, images and life experiences which have been dormant within me, buried in a type of amnesia, in an era which is our era, where memory does not exist, where only amnesia exists and everything has been forgotten. The more man becomes civilized, the more he forgets what he has experienced in life. Very often he forgets bad times and remembers only what he learns from outside information. He learns from the outside world, in a society which keeps developing, which progresses, which is dominated by technology, in a technocratic era which automatically is self-destroyed. It is the subject of *Medeamaterial*.

I come from a family which, after World War II and after the civil war in Greece, was on the side of those who lost the struggle—not the victors, but the defeated. I come, that is, from a social unit which has been defeated socially and psychologically and culturally, from within the official established notion of social psychology of the official civilization, from within the official order of things. From the moment I had been on the side of the defeated, and those who had been on the side, on the margin of things, I had the potential of seeing my surroundings with a critical eye. I had been automatically in a natural position to observe very critically—since the time I was very young—all things. What does this mean? That I was creating images since the time I was very young, that I was a spectator. Since the time I was very young I'd been a spectator of social theater. This helped me, because from this position of mine, where I am the spectator and opposite me is the society where I observe the victor, I observe the woman, I observe the man, I observe the daily things, I observe the mores and customs which must be preserved, I observe all these things. I began little by little to create my own stories, my own inner *scenaria*, my own themes. And all these themes gathered, gathered, gathered, and all these stories at a certain moment had to be expressed. Which realm [medium] would be able to express this accumulated matter which was an accumulated, gathered material of memory, which had many images, many themes, many stories? I found, therefore, the path which is theater itself. Theater is the realm par excellence where one can express his natural need to unfold all these life experiences, images and a notion of despair and society. The story with the theater began, from that source, the inner source; I thought immediately to get involved with the theater, finding the parameters, finding the correlations in theater.

Well, which was the closest thing to me, my closest realm of research? The Berliner Ensemble. It was the theater of criticism; epic theater; the theater which at that period, the decade of the sixties, was perhaps the most significant member of the worldwide theater. I had the opportunity of joining the Berliner Ensemble, and little by little, all that anguish, all that inner, deep psychological chaos I had, all that information that I had gathered from Kafka, Milosz, or Rilke, or Joyce, or Rimbaud, I was able to put into practice. With them [in my mind] I went to a school where the

Marxist concept of art is taught, and since that time I know Ernst
Schumacher. Well, however, little by little I had to organize that
material I had within me, which was anarchic, and I needed some
system. All this methodology of Brecht was very useful for me in
order to classify the material and organize it, so that I could bring it
out and use it later in my work, in creation, in staging.

Surely, this tired me very much, because when you are anarchic,
and you want to make this German strictness fit into your inner
world, it is very difficult. It was painful for me. But during these
four years I managed to give a more specific form to what I am, to
what my need is, and what materials I have at my disposal. At great
cost and pain I learned from what point I had to proceed in order to
develop.

I started with Brecht and I brought his ideas to Greece and then I
produced two plays, one of which was *Aufstieg und Fall der Stadt
Mahagonny* [*The Rise and Fall of the City of Mahagonny*]. I had
two great successes in Thessaloniki [Salonika]. I staged the shorter
version, not the opera, but the blueprint for the opera, and little by
little I began to evolve. There comes a point of satiation, that is, to
have my fill. I grew tired from this austere Germanic concept and
Brecht's absolutes about things, and I could not find any way to
escape. I suddenly felt within me the time had come to stop; I was
exhausted so I began finally to research other plays, other texts. I
passed on to Lorca, his *Yerma*.

Little by little, I began to see again all my internal material and
to try and organize it with all the Brechtian methodology and the
experience I had gathered from those two performances. I kept
trying to advance and to develop, and I felt always unsatisfied. The
only artistic gratification I felt was with *Yerma*, where indeed I got
to the point of working internally with the body and little by little
to get rid of all those constrictions which came from the information
I had from Brecht. Well, what did I do? I'd climb the ladder; I'd
stand at the verge of insight, and then I'd throw away the ladder
inside me with all its information—because the ladder is the information which props us up in our climb—and then I would fall inside
myself and begin to grope deeply.

Little by little all these problems began to be solved, and I tried
little by little not to use a ladder, but to find myself by myself. This
indeed requires continuous awareness and continuous sensitivity to

the material itself. I started, therefore, another period, and I turned inevitably to ancient tragedy. And I found myself at Delphi where I had the possibility in the first year to see certain performances, and to be excited by them, and to decide what direction I would take.

And from there begins another story, my relation with ancient tragedy. Well, for me it was something which frightened me and which I also loved. I knew that this relationship was simultaneously both erotic and self-destructive, because ancient theater draws you inside, and does not leave you any leeway to escape. And if you escape, and betray it for a while, you find that escape was simply an illusion: you will return again to ancient drama. It has all this dynamic material, and it is unique in this respect. And of course I knew all these dynamics. I had delved theoretically into the dynamics of the drama. I could see all the magnitude of tragedy. I could penetrate sufficiently its essence.

In earlier years, I had made great efforts also to see the parameters of contemporary life, and this experience helped me to understand the role of tragedy in today's world, which is destroying itself and dying—where all values have been abolished and where in the place of the great magnitudes we have conventional magnitudes, not the essential ones. And I could see that the correlations with today's world are very interesting but very distant. Namely, the concept of depth has an entirely different dimension in ancient tragedy, from the concept of depth today. Depth today extends to a certain point of the outer shell, sometimes to the marrow and sometimes a little bit deeper. But the concept of depth in ancient tragedy is different because it encompasses the entire structure. So when you interpret a phrase, an image, a situation, a magnitude, at the same time you also interpret structure. The interpretation of an isolated word leads to the splendor of a whole process; one word, or a dynamic phrase is inseparably bound to structure. On this I have been influenced, I may say, by the Bauhaus, and from all the philosophy of the midwar years, and from structuralism, and from all those efforts which were made in central Europe in order to see things structurally. It was important to see the *structura*, and eliminate all the additional elements, which in my opinion are all superficial functions which are not the essence, but simply sentimentalism.

The key is the word, but usually we apprehend only a reflection of the word, because each word is also a trauma in the tragic speech, it is a wound, it is a blood clot. It is a lexicon of a language, of the tragic language; it is ready to die and yet lives on. It always lives on, but you have the feeling that it is ready to die.

I have this idea, that exterior sources account for only a little of our knowledge and give commands only to the instrument of expression which is the mouth. But the real source of our energy and knowledge comes from the interior of the body, from memories which have been printed inside us from long ago. There exists an inner energy which carries images and repressed memories of other lives and of other eras. Namely, there exists all the knowledge of the world inside our very bodies, and there is no need for us to refer to a hundred books in order to extract this.

Intellectual analysis of drama is not sufficient. Action creates its own unity and its particularity nourishes me. The performance opens something within me and I say, "Yes, that's it!" Even a word of yours or a phrase can give birth in me to such an eternal situation and a creation of something new. Sometimes we agree, sometimes we go different ways, but we develop together. That in my opinion is what is interesting in theory. That's why we can differentiate between philologists: some give you insight into the life of the words, and let them flow; others desiccate the life of the words.

So I found in the *Bacchae* the origin of my own memory, even the origin of things, of images, and these became the foundation for me to make correlations, and decisions. I accepted the Bauhaus, but not Stanislavsky. I accepted Meyerhold, but not Barrault. I accepted Grotowski, and all Artaud's perspectives, even the philosophy of Julian Beck, and the various concepts of cruelty, which operate in everyday life. I saw human pain in its real form, not simply its appearance; and I found my own text, not the text of somebody else. I began to see the things which would help me develop.

What does this mean? I see correlations in myself. I begin to see my own parameters, without which no artistic function can be conceived. I escape theoretical thought which is an artificial escape from the deeper anxiety. I only know a small part, but I search myself for the lost utopia. And I try from within art to connect myself with a vision which the ancients had and practiced in their lives. Like the ancient Greeks, we too try to live a moment of utopia. This gives some meaning to our lives and makes it beautiful. And searching I found indeed inside the body hidden potentialities which were indeed the impetus for the second period of my work, which begins with the *Bacchae*, goes to *Medeamaterial* and continues in *Quartett* and will go into the *Alcestis*.

I began to delve and search for the small intervals which exist between two points, as in music; in two tempos there exists a hidden tempo, in between. Behind the black line what does there exist? That is what I want to research. What exists behind that interval, behind that void? Which is a period, which is a diaeresis, which is a stop? There are possibilities hidden behind the word, behind the syllable, behind the letter. We, in the theatrical group Attis, are searching for *ecstasis*, and we try to find the energy components of the body and from within them our origin, our memories, and our visions. Because no vision exists without this knowledge, which must be found in each person's veins, in his blood, and in his own energy, which has many forms and is infinite.

This was what I was looking for in the *Bacchae*. We searched in all this boundless field, and boundless stretch of land of self-knowledge which is the most painful. That is, many times theater is a cause, a pretext, for proceeding to the internal knowledge, the knowledge of the cell, of our blood, and it is painful.

I began to search into the mysteries, the Greek theatrical events, to explore the popular festivals, to search for all information about Dionysus. I found some vital information in a book which was found in Leipzig, an edition of the seventeeth century. I read there that in Attica, where there is the hospital of Asclepius, the patients had to follow a certain ritual. When the sun was setting, they had to walk naked in a circle on wet sand, on wet earth, one around the other. In the second hour, they had to quicken their steps, in the third more. In the fourth, they had to bend their knees just as in Kabuki. In the fifth, they had to bend the elbows, and little by little advancing and quickening this motion, with the extremities bent, the physical pains started to go away, and the clots to break up. One had pain in the heart, another in the stomach, and suddenly it was gone. Little by little these people, for eight hours, did this same thing and they began to have so much energy. This is like what happens in Kabuki. The Kabuki actor can walk with bent knees for ten hours, and plays with the same secret. And from this, gradually, the pains began to break up and go away.

Those who the next morning were to be operated on were in a

state of *ecstasis* and happy, under the influence of Dionysus, just as in the *Bacchae*, but not with wine, nor with words, but with the wine of their body, with their blood. Blood is wine, the blood which circulates in all veins correctly is happiness. Through this circulation of the blood, they went to the operating room and the operations were performed with a small blade of grass for anesthesia. And this secret was very significant for me.

I started with my group in a circle at Delphi; then we went to Mount Kithairón, and we performed this circular ritual, and we found astounding secrets in the body. It was a very deep search and painful.

From this movement of energy and *ecstasis* I tried to resurrect the word. Elevation of the word means exaltation of speech, not speech as a proper expression—academic speech, explanatory speech —but speech of pain, speech which comes from the soul. We had success with this during our recent tour of the Soviet Union. Now with *Quartett* we have developed it even more. Therefore, it is a path which helps me research the source of sound.

This is the story in the *Bacchae*. One finds energy points, and places from which to breathe. This part can participate in breathing, or this finger may want to move. A tiny little finger, when the hand is independent, will dance its own dance, or perhaps the palm, just as the Sufi dance, just as they dance the *Zeibekiko*. Some part is cut off and dances, as in the Noh play, which formulates codes, and so also the Sufis who perform these things.

The palm remembers its own memories, just as my father used to dance a hundred years ago, my grandfather, and my great-grandfather. They were people who dance, who were not ashamed; and it was not only the body which had to move in this way. All these things found dynamic expression in the *Bacchae*, where my theme was exaltation, whereas in the *Medeamaterial* my theme was the burning of energy. There energy was born and was sent out around the body and it seemed to reach three or seven meters. Burned energy filled *Medeamaterial*, and even more the world was burned, was destroyed. It might be Strassburg, it might be Palestine, it might be Athens, it might be New York, a point of the world after the Third World War which must not occur. After a war where a group of people with burned energy try to live, to remember, and they remember the most shuddering story of passion, this is the story of Medea. Medea is the greatest energy—the big energy is Medea, the big pathos, the big engine, the universe. It is the world and Müller grasps this world, the shuddering world of Medea, and of passion. Little by little, through this story, they remember the world which was burned and they denounce the destructions, all the fires. Here energy tries to come out of the body but it is again entangled within. An effort is made to liberate the energy, but again it is constrained within the body. Here, man has been turned into ashes. Euripides' *Medea* has been dismembered, and all this speech which has fever within, and is broken up into pieces, which is a madness, is a shell through which the brains of those who perform might burst out. It is a gesture of self-destruction. This was an opportunity for me to research another boundary, not of the positive energy which is emanated by tragedy, but of the energy which is burned.

In *Quartett*, energy is even more burned, and thus when I will go to *Alcestis* or to Euripides' *Medea* I'll know much better how to proceed. Medea is another aspect of Dionysus; she is a dialectical continuation. Müller eliminates all the explanatory elements, all the repetitions and descriptions, and is deeply influenced by Hölderlin, who points out the value of the essence of Greek myth and goes deeply into the mythical realms of *Existenz*. There archetypes emerge, unique images emerge which are primeval, and whereas Müller appears to be cerebral and intellectual, he is, however, going very deep into the human structure and psyche. Müller is very deep. I disagree when they call him simply intellectual and cerebral. He is deep and he searches for deeper memories. He makes use of events for this voyage which he makes in the realm of deeper memory. This is an astounding path where one may go and sit with Alcestis or with Medea, on the raft that goes to the other world.

This is also my work, and this is not the theater of death. It is the theater of the antechamber of death. It is before death. It is also a passage through. Sometimes this passage is very narrow, and that's how I myself feel it internally. Sometimes it is a raft in a dead sea, boiling from within. Sometimes it remains motionless on the Acheronian lake. Another time it is beyond the time of passion and the time of the death of Medea and of Alcestis.

This concept of death has preoccupied me from my childhood years, which I also sought to elucidate in Sartre and in Lorca and I also seek in tragedy, in Müller. So also I search in Genet, Beckett,

Euripides, and Sophocles. There are very few playwrights that I will stage. There are very few of those whom I thirst for and whom I have some relation with. That's why no one can say that I am a researcher, that I proceed, taking into consideration world theater, or the contemporary needs of theater studies. I am simply motivated by internal needs. I have a personal theater. In my effort to go deeper, to research deeper the structures of my own existence, this makes me particularly bold, and encourages me.

And now punctuation marks. For me there are no punctuation marks in art. There is no full stop. There is no comma, there is no exclamation mark; there are no brackets. All these things which the bourgeois theater uses abundantly, and uses as the dynamic elements of its language, do not exist. There always exists a sliding scale beneath speech, an internal temperature with very many gradations. These create a tree or a bird that flies. They create a flash of lightning; they create all the destructions of nature. At this point I should refer to my great teacher, to Katina Paxinou, who showed me this internal human raving, which abolishes the academic way which uses punctuation marks, and advances into a language which is only limited by the tempo of nature, and shares its rhythms, the tempo of spring, but of catastrophe as well.

Now I shall speak of my own need for my work. I go deeper at precisely that point when something is about to be born. That's why I go to Attis. That's why Attis is the death-bearing Dionysus. It is the Dionysus of winter. It is the seed, it is that point precisely which says that something will be born, that is, it is the effort for birth, it is the birth after nine months. That's why all my performances, their rehearsals, last about nine months. It is a birth, and from within that inner state I try to see other times, achronic with conventional time, or natural time.

Last year I had studied together with my group the seven catastrophes of nature. I wanted to discover the law of the wave and how the wave breaks, how lightning is born, what energy is spilled over, and how an earthquake takes place. All these physical phenomena, all these elements of thermodynamics, all this information of cybernetics, all these elements are indispensable for my work, and for the work of everyone. Sometimes this experience passes through my staging, at other times this experience is simply retained as research knowledge.

And what I want to research is precisely the small interval, not the moment when the explosion has occurred, when the explosion has taken place, and we see the spectacular result as if it were a fanfare, as if it were very beautiful fireworks. The bourgeois theater relies greatly on these fireworks, but I instead search out the point exactly where all the forces, those outside and those within, are about to explode, and where one wrestles against the other, leading to the explosion. I want to research this process of fermentation and conflict. That is why in my performances there is no solution, there is no catharsis. There exists a despair, there is a gaze looking out onto the spectators, a staring somewhere at a point of nature. Even in my latest work, *Quartett*, there is this. This is the moment where Merteuil licks Valmont. He has shed tears and she licks his tears with her tongue, and that's how the performance ends. There the model is generalized. And I mean to say that inside this realm, precisely before the explosion, there exist tiny, unseen, invisible, tiny intervals. One can see them also in the minimalist music of Philip Glass. We find them also in painting and in general in contemporary art.

For me all this story of passion, of the magnitude of passion, of the external magnitude which we exaggerate so greatly is only in order to cover up our own void. We enlarge the picture of the tragic in order to protect ourselves. It is an umbrella under which we can invest our own needs and pursuits, but I believe art must explore those tiny intervals, shortly before the explosions. One must use delicate nuances, to search out the things which elude. But from this minimum, little by little, a much bigger picture of the tragic can be formulated.

Even for the theater, man is tragic, because the war with the gods is lost. In ancient tragedy the heroes wrestle with the gods and men were invulnerable. Now the war is lost, the gods have won. The contemporary gods, all those conventional things which we see, all those grotesque figures and images have strangled man. Contemporary god has won. In this sense we live during the dark ages, a period like the Middle Ages, and a period of ashes. This is the world.

We have imprisoned the authentic gods. Their place has been taken by other gods. We have them. The gods weep. And they seek food. Because food is the conflict of man who tries to reach god and god who gives him advice. This conflict has been lost. The utopia of

Classical Greece is lost forever. And we all try to seize a minute glimpse of that utopia. The world through the eye of Müller—now I perceive it: catastrophe, namely all these dynamics, all this is a dynamic. Perhaps in the twenty-first century men will laugh at the mistakes which the men of the twentieth century commit, the last humanists. And they will be laughing with us as well; perhaps they will view us as people of the Middle Ages, without God. Perhaps they will discover some gods—not that we'll have a refuge in those gods—but that they may remember, may communicate and come into conflict with the gods and from within that fermentation and conflict the world advances. "God is a house with many windows." Now no windows exist. The houses are shut up.

Truth remains inside all, but emerges in only a few people. There is a little fire but it will be extinguished, and then if this fire is extinguished where will Prometheus be found? Where will the jar of Pandora be found?

Myself, what I do is very small, it is small, it is small. It is the effort of some people who communicate in order to offer truth. Life consists of cells. You, five others; we, my group, another twenty, another fifty others. That is, there exist some people somewhere who communicate and they form a dynamic on a world-wide scale. These are the hope of the world; these people are the hope. There exists no other hope. I am a bit of a pessimist, perhaps, but a realist, I would say. And this gives me some strength: the fact that I see things in motion gives me some strength.

XI

Thomas Murphy's *The Sanctuary Lamp*: The Light at the End of the Night

THOMAS MURPHY culls threads from Aeschylus' *Oresteia* and weaves his own tapestry, his crimson rug, to trap the Church, and possibly Ireland itself, into trampling the precious weave as they are caught in its subtle and beautiful mesh. *The Sanctuary Lamp* met with harsh criticism in Ireland, particularly from the Church, but also praise from those who understood the bittersweet message. It has been ranked "in the first three of the great plays at the Abbey Theatre" along with J. M. Synge's *Playboy of the Western World* and Sean O'Casey's *Juno and the Paycock*.[1]

Ireland in modern times has faced the well-known crisis of a traditional society that is being suddenly industrialized; this began in earnest around 1960.[2] Earlier, the continual financial crises—due to scarcity, poverty of land and crop failures—had led to massive emigration. Murphy has woven these crises into a web of words, which like incantations evoke a freedom that seems threatened by the dual evils of an infantilizing tradition from church and family on the one hand, and a prostituting slavery from industrialization by outsiders, on the other (or in some cases forced emigration to a similar situation, with even fewer prospects for escape).

The Sanctuary Lamp deals with the theme of survival in a corrupt world in which performances of varied kinds seem to offer the easiest income. This is also a play that criticizes, resents, and shows the tragedy of a priest-ridden society that stifles more than it encourages; yet the play offers hope, a hope found in man that is based on defiance. Part of the hope comes through mutual forgiveness. A commemoration of defiance may be found in Greek tragedy, mostly in Sophocles with his imperfect sacred monsters (Ajax, Philoctetes, Hercules), but also in Euripides with his less noble and more disturbed characters; these are still admirable in their fallibility, in contrast to perverse gods or more traditional heroes (e.g. Hercules, Hippolytus, Medea, Iphigenia). This belief in man, who in spite of his frailty can achieve something noble, is a common theme in other plays by Murphy (such as *The Gigli Concert*).

The location of *The Sanctuary Lamp* is not stated (the play describes the setting simply as "A church in a city"), but Murphy had England in mind, and the character Maudie speaks in an accent from the Midlands. This is a story of three people who come together in a church at night: Harry, an Englishman and a Jew, who was a circus strongman, meets Maudie, who has run away from home and anguishes about her lost child; they are joined by Francisco, an Irishman, educated by the Jesuits, who had earlier seduced Harry's wife, Olga.[3] Harry was complicit in winking at her "shared sexuality," as long as there was some financial benefit for him. However, they lost a child, Teresa, through mutual neglect, it seems. She represents an Iphigenia sacrificed for dreams of power.

At the beginning of the play Harry is hired by a priest (the Monsignor) to guard the church and to keep the fire burning in a sanctuary lamp. It is the beginning of evening. As the night progresses—and it is a long night in its labored journey toward day— Francisco peels layer after layer off Harry's psychological defenses to make him face his own responsibility for what has happened, and to come to terms with his guilt. The trio of Francisco, Maudie and Harry are themselves an unholy family reminiscent both of Agamemnon's family in the *Oresteia* and of Joseph, Mary, and Jesus. Harry's final act of lifting the pulpit provides a catharsis for his anger and gradually guilt passes, too, at least for a while. Through their mutual forgiveness, Orestes is temporarily acquitted.

The ending of this play finds hope in Francisco's defiance of the Jesuits; he forgets the prayer asking for forgiveness: "Oh my God I am heartily sorry for having offended thee and I . . . See? I can't remember. I've beaten them. Goodnight, Har." And Harry says, after a pause, "Y'know!" The introductory notes to the play tell us that this is said with "an affectation in his sound ('y'know?' 'old boy' etc.—British officer type), but it started a long time ago and is now part of his personality" (p. 9). Now it seems in its own way to sum up the play, and in another to signal its continuation. As in Aeschylus' *Oresteia*, man learns from his pain: "Zeus, whoever he may be . . . who showed the way of wisdom to man / and determined he would learn through suffering. / Drip, drip in the heart, during sleep, comes the pain of a remembered past, / and even the unwilling learns to be wise, / the grace of the gods which comes by force / as they sit high on their holy thrones" (*Ag.* 174–83). The theme that man must learn from suffering is a leit-motiv of the *Oresteia*, and it reappears in the "Y'know" of Harry, who along with Francisco has learned through experience (one manifestation of which was the violent grace of the Jesuits). Harry claims, "You never feel your soul when you're happy" (p. 15). It seems that Harry has often felt his soul.

This incompatibility of feeling one's soul along with happiness is a theme in Murphy's plays. We can trace it to the notion in *The Gigli Concert*: "Happiness and beauty are not meant to mate" (which derives from Goethe's *Faust*, "Happiness and Beauty are not mated long)."[4] Feeling one's soul has a religious connotation as well as a sense of beauty. Religion permeates Murphy's plays in much the same way that it permeates Frederico Fellini's films. The criticism is side by side with the language of the believer. Guido in Fellini's *8 1/2* (1963) complains to the Cardinal that he is not happy. The Cardinal says happiness is not what is important, but salvation, and there is no salvation outside of the Church. All these examples are variations on a theme, that somehow happiness blurs one's perception of true values—a notion that goes back to the Greeks, who warn against a happiness that might lead to *hybris*, either through the envy of the gods or man's own blindness.[5]

One finds in the philosophers, such as Plato and Aristotle, that happiness is the goal of man, but it is a happiness based on goodness, which is the only true and lasting kind. In Murphy (and Fellini), one senses that goodness is impossible according to the rules that the Catholic Church has set up, so man is bound to sin and feel guilt— and perhaps feel his soul in the process. But one senses also the need to go beyond tragedy and beyond the Church to invent a new set of rules.

The ending of *The Sanctuary Lamp* is escape through defiance and a vote for humankind, rather like the ending of *The Gigli Concert:* "Do not mind the pig-sty, Benimillo . . . Mankind still has a delicate ear . . . that's it . . . that's it . . . sing on forever . . . that's it" (p. 75). And for Francisco and Harry their life is their song, and it will go on in spite of the pigsty.

How does the *Oresteia* reappear in *Sanctuary Lamp?* Fintan O'Toole has dealt with some of the parallels in *The Politics of Magic,* but I would like to go into greater detail, and also from a different perspective.[6] Murphy says that he had Aeschylus in mind in a general way.

The Oresteia begins with a watchman looking for the light that will signal that Troy is taken and his master will return. In some ways this light can be the sanctuary lamp, and the king an absent god who vanished when the Church made him into an institution: "Evaporated himself. When they painted his toe-nails and turned him into a church he lost his ambition, gave up learning, stagnated for a while, then gave up even that, said fuck it, forget it, and became a vague pain in his own and everybody else's arse."[7] This is Francisco's insight, the doctrinally oversaturated disbeliever.

The believers in *The Sanctuary Lamp* seem to be a disappointed monsignor, frustrated in his hopes for advancement and a wandering Jew, Harry "Sol'min," the outsider, who represents more of the inside than the insider Francisco, who rejects it (cf. Bloom versus Stephen in Joyce's *Ulysses*). The monsignor claims the lamp signifies "the constant Presence," and still needs personal attention: the candle must be changed every twenty-four hours (p. 13). This is part of the job that the priest offers Harry. Harry becomes a watchman, like the one at the beginning of *Agamemnon,* watching a flame that is more than a flame. He addresses it in the play as something, someone, watching him, capable of resentment, and for whom/

which he will work, and from time to time calls it Jesus: "Supposing in exchange for the accommodation I engage to make good conversation—break the back of night for you?" (pp. 14–15). Harry, like Job, has a dialogue with God. He also has had to endure what seem to be unfair losses.

Along with Francisco and Maudie, Harry robs the sanctuary of its wine and plans to leave in the morning, but he still dutifully replaces the light at 3:00 A.M. He does this just as he delivers a parable of hope: when you die your soul is like a silhouette, and if it has something missing or damaged it is fixed by "loved ones . . . one is implanted on the other. And the merging—y'know? Merging?— merging of the silhouettes is true union. Union forever of loved ones, actually" (p. 53). This light seems to be the hope provided by man to man, a merging through love, perhaps only in death, perhaps only in the mind, but still an illuminating hope.

Francisco also speaks of his thoughts about passions: "all the passions of the passions, in heaps higher than all the cathedrals, burning in a constant flame. And my own heart, the fuse, keeping things burning" (p. 32). This is the anti-sanctuary lamp, the lamp of man's heart. As Yeats says, "All that flames upon the night, man's own resinous heart has fed."

There is also negative light: the lamp that Maudie climbed to show off, in her theatrical way, which led to her pregnancy and the subsequent loss of her child (and the guilt that came from that). But the most negative light in this play is the vacuum/absence of light (a clerical black hole) which comes from the priests. According to Francisco, "Those coonics! They're like black candles, not giving, but each one drawing a little more light out of the world"; and Christianity itself is seen as a "poxy con," a light that misleads: "All those predators that have been mass-produced out of the loneliness and isolation of people, with standard collars stamped on!" (p. 49). Francisco is the Apollo who dispels these furies with his passionate light, but he is also a Mephistopheles with creative fire.

Light is also the fame of performance, the spotlight they all crave: "The showman must go on. Right Har? This senseless desire that some of us had to please. And be liked" (p. 41). Even the Monsignor had sought this in seeking his advancement; he realizes he lost his humility, which he calls "a cunning way of dealing with God" (p. 28). The showman is more honest. Maudie would climb her lamp-post, she would attract her audience, then she would go into the house and continue the performance: "I'd've took off my clothes, and stick my bottom out at them" (p. 24).

There were other occasions for performances. Olga, Francisco and a dwarf named Sam, all act in the same circus as Harry, but also occasionally hire out their services and perform at private parties. One such occasion was at a party given by "a mighty man who writes only for the most important papers and who even has his own television show." The host also provides the seduction of fame: "Why it was said of this man that he could turn an artist into a cult" (p. 44). Olga, Harry's wife, decided to give her own private performance, on a "Sir Basil Wedgwood kitchen table," an act observed by "Madame Standby," the wife of the man who had initiated the table performance. It is when the public performances become private, and randomly private, that disaster follows. The hired performers are abruptly asked to leave the party. Olga turns out to be a sort of prostitute, and Francisco a type of pimp, and along with the dwarf, the third member of their performing troupe, they were all selling their services (and stealing when they could). Even so, they were more exploited than exploiting.

The Sanctuary Lamp contains Murphy's usual sociological commentary: the circus players may be corrupt, but their exploiters are worse. The thought that these decadent ones will suffer the consequences of their exploitive acts in the afterlife provides a satisfying fantasy for Francisco: "But the pattern of man's sins will be the pattern of his punishment. See the depraved ones, who so loved their own pleasures, now bathing in black, hot, bubbling pitch and reeking sulphur! See the gluttonous pigs, now parched and hungry!" (p. 42). Freedom in this play, as well as in many others by Murphy, is obtained through dreams and alcohol. Madness is also nostalgically regarded as an escape.

Lost children are another theme of this play, and when they are gone "there's no one to bless you. And, worse, there's no one to curse you" (p. 52). All the protagonists in this play have been performers, and their lives have a theatrical quality. And these actors have all suffered losses, of children and audiences.

Harry has been a circus strongman; and his heroic feat in this play is to lift the pulpit from which Francisco is sermonizing (Harry tries this earlier in the play but does not succeed). When he finally does succeed, he is panting, and doubled up after his effort, but proud of his achievement, and Francisco bestows the coveted "Bravo!" upon him. This is almost comparable to God's incarnation, or when the host becomes God in the Mass and it is displayed to all. O'Toole sees Harry as a type of Samson, or the giant in the folktale (who has lost his strength through sadness), who regains his strength before our very eyes.[8] Harry's performance carries on in the final word, "Y'know," that affected phrase that is so much of Harry's personality. Without the "You" (the audience, to whom God proffers knowledge), life would be meaningless, but the light makes the performance possible.

But violence, physical or verbal, is never far beneath the surface in any of Murphy's plays. Harry the strongman may be able to lift a pulpit, but Francisco the juggler is also an adept juggler of words. What the strongman can do physically, Francisco does intellectually, defying the Church while also systematically stripping Harry of his last illusions (before allowing these to be replaced with some life-enhancing new ones).

In the play, the figure of the crucified Jesus is also the final audience, hinting at the resurrected Jesus, the real audience, as in Yeats' "The Fiddler of Dooney." Here, whom did St. Peter welcome? Not the priest, but the fiddler:

> I passed my brother and cousin:
> They read in their books of prayers;
> I read in my book of songs
> I bought at the Sligo fair.
>
> When we come at the end of time,
> To Peter sitting in state,
> He will smile on the three old spirits,
> But call me first through the gate
>
> For the good are always the merry,
> Save by an evil chance,
> And the merry love to fiddle
> And the merry love to dance.[9]

So also, in *The Sanctuary Lamp*, Jesus is not the one described by the Jesuits: "And they insist—Insist!—that Jesus, total man, life-enhancing man, Jesus!—should be the only killer of life! Die to self? I doze father, I doze!" (p. 50). But instead Francisco dreams:

"The day is coming, the second coming, the final judgment, the not-too-distant future, before that simple light of man: when Jesus, Man, total man, will call to his side the goats—'Come ye blessed!' Yea, call to his side all those rakish, dissolute, suicidal, fornicating goats, taken in adultery and what-have-you. And proclaim to the coonics, blush for shame, you blackguards, be off with you, you wretches, depart from me ye accursed complicated affliction! And that, my dear brother and sister, is my dream, my hope, my vision and my belief" (p. 50). This is the conclusion of Francisco's sermon, which began with the account of the disastrous "final performance" at the party. This dream, this belief, is the "light of man," the "vision" that gives hope, like the sanctuary lamp. Francisco's sermon is also a performance, a performance showing belief that man might choose his own role, rather than one designated by a Jesuit: "What's a Jesuit? It is a distortion of a Jesus with sex in the head and tendencies towards violence" (p. 36). Francisco can no longer remember what the Jesuits taught, and Harry chooses his own role and his own words, "y'know."

This bittersweet ending simply reaffirms that the path will continue, much like Synge's Christy faces when he says, "Ten thousand blessings upon all that's here, for you've turned me a likely gaffer in the end of all, the way I'll go romancing through a romping lifetime from this hour to the dawning of the judgment day."[10] Neither for Christy, nor for Harry or Francisco is life such a romp, but the optimism is there, in the dream of what life can be in the light of a sanctuary lamp. Day will follow. Even as Ireland itself is still an isle of dreams dreamt by its artists, though troubled by the occasional nightmare, day will follow.

The Sanctuary Lamp is also a play about loss and guilt. Again we return to the *Oresteia*, to which is added the later idea of original sin. Also we find here the notion that there is "always a kind of melancholy attaching to the glory we attain in this world" (p. 43). No performance is unmixed. The great gap between "a gallous story and a dirty deed" often leads to guilt and depression.[11]

In the *Oresteia* guilt is manifold: Agamemnon's for slaying Iphigenia and bringing Cassandra home, Clytemnestra's for Agamemnon's death and her adultery with Aegisthus, Orestes' for killing his mother. There is acquittal for Orestes, a symbolic forgiveness (which also seems justified since he had been following Apollo's command). That the guilty will pay is a repeated maxim as much as the one involving learning through suffering, and the interrelationship is obvious. In *The Sanctuary Lamp* everyone is guilty, even the gods, and as Francisco says, "Who's to forgive the gods? . . . There's no such thing as forgiveness" (pp. 30–31). And perhaps there is none for God and his representatives. Guilt seems endless. Francisco is guilty for stealing Harry's wife (he is Aegisthus); Harry is guilty for his daughter's death (although he did not cause it) as well as for not killing the adulterous lovers, "But I do not want to be like them, I believe in life!" (p. 17), and ultimately he is guilty for abandoning them, thus in some strange way being responsible for his wife's (Olga's) death from an overdose following her last disastrous performance (Olga as Clytemnestra, killed by proxy).[12] Maudie feels guilty for giving up her baby, who died shortly after its birth; she sees him as she saw her dead mother. She has been told forgiveness will stop the visions, and it is forgiveness that she seeks. Forgiveness is needed in life, since we all feel guilty at some point, and forgiving each other is superior to the ritualistic absolution of priests.

We see that Harry, in his imagined contribution to his daughter's death, is like Agamemnon, and also by his being spiritually slain by Olga/Clytemnestra and cuckolded by Francisco/Aegisthus. He is also Orestes with a mission to kill Aegisthus, but resembles Hamlet more in his weak vacillations and morbid guilt, or then again Euripides' Orestes, rather than Aeschylus' or Sophocles.' Harry's prayer to the Lord of Death resembles Orestes' at the beginning of the *Choephoroi*, but now it appears in a new ironic context, given Harry's incapacity for action. Part of his tragedy seems to be that he cannot even commit sin. Maudie also resembles Orestes in her visions of the dead which are exorcised by forgiveness (acquittal), through the vanishing of her mother's ghost. All three make their confessions throughout the night; all three are tried in absentia by the furies (priests) and give up their illusions, and finally through the symbolism of a confessional turned on its side for a bed, they achieve an undisturbed sleep, the sleep of forgiveness.

The use of ghosts is interesting too. Religion and superstition seem to be weapons for controlling oppressed people, along with alcohol "for crowd control." The gifted American playwright Au-

gust Wilson routinely uses ghosts as powerful foils to his protagonists, often as opponents, for self-definition, as he does in *The Piano
Lesson.*

The acquittal at the end of the *Eumenides* is a legalistic one, and
the suspicion remains that the Eumenides will be tucked away in
their caves only temporarily and artificially. As Thomas Rosenmeyer has said of the end of the *Eumenides:* "The dissonances are
by no means suppressed. But in the festive clamor of the final scenes
they are set aside as if they no longer mattered. The tragedy is
completed, and transcended; the festival carries the day."[13] And the
day dawns.

Murphy identifies the priests with the furies, thus also realizing
their usurped psychological power in playing on man's guilt. He
then transcends the tragedy through dreams and fantasies and the
vision of the sanctuary lamp, but the new heroism is one man's own
lifting of the pulpit in a grandiose gesture, and the other's rejection
of a debilitating myth, the myth of forgiveness, which is impossible,
at least in a permanent way, as long as one is alive. Francisco has
reclaimed himself, the self the Jesuits stole: "Give me a child until
he is seven they say, and then you can have him back!" (p. 35). God
was also trapped that way; Harry talks about His presence. Maudie
asked if it were Jesus. He answers, "Not quite. Well, it's his spirit
actually. They nabbed his spirit and they've got it here. . . . Personally, I think they should let him go but, there you are" (p. 19). By
the end of the play we realize that God is as free as man, and when
the three leave the church in the morning, one has the sense that
God will be with them—but not the God of the Jesuits. In this play,
God has come off better than the capitalists. The sanctuary lamp, a
church, and a priest have provided more of a refuge than the party
at the "mansion of a mighty man."

The priest in the opening of *The Sanctuary Lamp* (who wants
more time to read Hesse) resembles the priestess who watches the
temple at the beginning of the *Eumenides.* The lamp itself is a
synthesis of both Athena and Apollo, and the reconciliation at the
end of the *Eumenides* is Francisco's and Maudie's and Harry's reconciliation with their dreams of a god free from the "black" clergy
who in this case are not part of the celebration.

O'Toole points out that many characters need to be merged in
Murphy's works to obtain what might be considered a balanced

personality. An example would be Joe and Frank in *On the Outside;* as O'Toole notes, "The two halves of a whole personality must be joined before salvation becomes possible."[14] So also Francisco and Harry, in planning to leave together achieve a symbolic mingling, even though much of their relationship has been rivalry. They both have shared Harry's wife, but what begins as a desire for vengeance ends with them sharing their sorrow for her death. Thus all three plays of the *Oresteia* have been combined. From the *Agamemnon,* the messenger looks for the light, and the memory of past misdeeds is revived in the monologues by Harry and Francisco and Maudie. The *Choephoroi* is represented in the invocation by Francisco, reminiscent of Orestes' invocation, a plea for strength. Then Orestes confronts Aegisthus (in the clash of our two protagonists), Francisco and Harry circling each other with their impromptu weapons. There is also imagery reminiscent of the *Choephoroi*, e.g., Teresa snuggling under her father's arm "like a little bird nestling," like Electra and Orestes calling themselves their father's nestlings ("the orphaned offspring of a father eagle"; *Choephoroi* 247). Possibly Maudie evokes Electra (in her alliance with Harry/Orestes), but she also brings to mind Clytemnestra, not only because (like Olga), Francisco/Aegisthus tries to seduce her, but also in her complex relationship to her dead child.

O'Toole sees *The Sanctuary Lamp* as most reminiscent of the *Eumenides:* the opening scene takes place in a church as it did in a temple, and finally there is a reconciliation between rivals who realize that ultimately guilt can never be eliminated or expiated, only accepted (with the holes patched over by loved ones in an afterlife).[15] What in the *Oresteia* was physically acted out is here psychologically experienced. The myth of the past has become the ghost of the present, not so much with the excruciating exactness that we find in Eugene O'Neill's *Mourning Becomes Electra,* but in a more general sense in that *The Sanctuary Lamp* deals with the guilt of the human race as foisted upon individuals by the dogma of original sin as promulgated by the Jesuits. The Church is shown to be more interested in its own power than in humanity's suffering.

The Sanctuary Lamp also differs from T.S. Eliot's *Murder in the Cathedral* (Eliot's nod to *Agamemnon*) or *The Family Reunion* (his *Choephoroi, Eumenides*) in many ways, not the least of which is its use of the Irish vernacular; though both Orestes-figures are called

Harry, they come from opposite ends of the social spectrum. One also feels there is a ritualistic rather than an emotional resolution in Eliot's plays, unlike Murphy's. Further, in Eliot there is an obvious acceptance of conventional religion, with a distinct distrust of man. Guilt and retribution figure prominently in the work of Eliot and Murphy, but in Eliot life is one long expiation to rid oneself of conscience, or "the cancer that eats away the self."[16] Eliot's Harry has "wakened to the nightmare" of everyday life, and his furies haunt him (p. 234). *The Family Reunion* ends with an incantation to lay the dead to rest ("May they rest in peace"), a return to the Christian liturgy, with the women circling a table clockwise and incorporating magic in their chant "round and round the circle completing the charm" (p. 293). These actions, by what could be called a coven of witches, seem to parody the Mass. *The Sanctuary Lamp* ends similarly with Francisco wishing Harry a goodnight (a secular "Rest in Peace"). The *Oresteia* ends with the Eumenides being accompanied to their cave; peace is invoked as a "joyful cry in response to song." In Eliot and Aeschylus women complete the ritual; in Murphy the men bid each other goodnight. The furies in Eliot and Aeschylus are women; in Murphy, they are men.

An untroubled sleep is also a kind of forgiveness. In *The Sanctuary Lamp*, Murphy uses introductory and bridging music from Tchaikovsky's *Sleeping Beauty*; the fantasy and the refuge of the sanctuary is further conveyed through the music. As in *The Gigli Concert*, music and magic go closely together.

Both Eliot and Murphy borrow freely from the Catholic Mass as much as they borrow from Aeschylus. In both plays, wine is consumed along with bread, sins are confessed, forgiveness sought; in these ways one finds parodies of all the parts of the Mass throughout —the Introit, Sermon, Agnus Dei, Communion, to the final Dismissal: in one play, to sleep before a new day ("Goodnight") and in the other as a Requiem ("May they rest in peace"). Murphy has optimism in despair; Eliot despair in optimism.

In many Irish works (e.g., *Playboy of the Western World, Ulysses*) and in other plays by Murphy (e.g., *Whistle in the Dark*), a father has to be overcome.[17] In *The Sanctuary Lamp* it is the Fathers, the priests, who must be overcome so that all men can be free, not simply one son. Orestes as a class will be acquitted and freed.

What is only cold satire in Eliot becomes warm humor in Murphy. His Harry displays delightful pretensions, such as when he introduces himself to Maudie: "I'm the clerk. Assistant Monsignor, y'know. Silly sort of title really but, there you are" (p. 20). Harry provides philosophical commentary: "Mary. It was a good idea alright: holy family—y'know—the three of them. But see that expression of hers? I know someone like that. And she was a Catholic too. But of course it was all a front to conceal a very highly-strung neurotic nymphomaniac" (p. 20). Or consider Francisco's irreverent comments: "Do you sleep with women, my son? I doze, father, I doze" (p. 36). Part of the humor consists in conscious blasphemy, such as the description of Olga, the dwarf, and Francisco as "a right Holy Family" or the more secular humor of Francisco calling the wine "Bourgeois" rather than Beaujolais.[18] Even the names Olga and Francisco are humorous variants, the first of Winifred and the second of something probably like Sean.

In an ironic way, Maudie and Francisco and Harry seem to be the real Holy Family (Maudie, the virgin mother, attended by nuns; Harry, a Joseph to his Olga; and Francisco the anti-Christ, with his apocalyptic sermon). Besides having additional religious connotations, the number three is also the usual number of actors in ancient tragedy. Moreover, in this play violence, when it occurs, is described rather than seen, another way that Murphy is faithful to his ancient source.

The Sanctuary Lamp differs from Jean-Paul Sartre's *The Flies* in that it is more religious and sociologically oriented than philosophical. Both plays deal with the question of guilt, and both defy the authority of a traditional religion, but differently. Sartre sees religion as offering peace (Zeus: "I am forgetfulness, I am peace"), but Murphy sees it as providing endless guilt (contrast Sartre's Orestes: "The most cowardly of murderers is he who feels remorse").[19] Both plays put faith in man (Orestes: "For I, Zeus, am a man, and everyman must find out his own way"; pp. 122–23), but whereas Sartre speaks of a freedom and a human life beginning on the "far side of despair," Murphy still seems to believe in dreams, visions, ghosts, and human relationships as well as a potential for happiness instead of such an austere freedom. His Harry even keeps madness "as a standby in case all else fails" (p. 15), and this contrasts with the clear vision that contributes to the despair-filled freedom of the existentialist. As Sartre's Zeus says, "You will tear from their eyes the veils I had laid on them, and they will see their lives as they are, foul and futile, a barren boon" (p. 126), which is enough for his Orestes as long as he is free (Orestes: "I AM my freedom. . . . I am doomed to have no other law but mine"; pp. 121–22).

Murphy's *Sanctuary Lamp* affirms man in a quest for survival; we learn something similar from his *Famine* in John's concluding speech: "Cause—I—will—live!"[20] This survival will also be one with dignity, free from a priestly imprimatur. Francisco wishes that he had died before he'd been baptized, because then he could stay in Limbo, an earthly paradise without the God described by the Jesuits: "The only thing that babies feared was the hand of God, that could hold your little baby body in his fist, before dipping you into the red hot coals of hell. Then take you out again and hold you up before his unshaved and slobbering chin, before dipping you again, this time into the damp black heat of purgatory. Experimenting. Playing with Himself. Wondering what type of heat to cook you on" (p. 54).

Francisco's Limbo without God is a paradise almost anyone could want ("With just enough light rain to keep the place lush green, the sunshine and red flowers, and the thousands and thousands of other fat babies sitting under the trees, gurgling and laughing and eating bananas"; p. 54), a combination of Ireland and Tahiti, untroubled by God. As Seamus Deane has noted, Murphy's conception of freedom is Dionysiac; his conception of repression is totalitarian.[21]

But Francisco did survive and was baptized, and so must take the responsibility and guilt for not following the rules. A forgotten catechism in this play is therefore liberating, and there is comfort in man's relation with his fellow man. O'Toole noted the relation between James in *The Morning After Optimism* and Francisco: "His [Francisco's] problem is that in a world where God is a burst balloon, there is no sin and without sin he cannot get himself properly damned. . . . With salvation not an option, and damnation unachievable, James' only option is to live in a world and face it."[22]

At the end of *The Sanctuary Lamp* the idealism of the outsider Harry must merge with the realism of Francisco, the insider who chooses to be an outsider. The rationalism of the one balances the idealism of the other (as Harry accuses Francisco, "You believe in nothing. . . . I always believed in things"; p. 40). We find this duality also in Murphy's *The Orphans*, in the opposition between Roddy and Dan; as O'Toole says, it is England versus Ireland, with Ireland identified as instinct and England as reason.[23] One needs both instinct and reason, the physical and the mental to survive in a coherent way. Harry, who abandoned his wife and Francisco when his values were violated, and who has taken the job protecting a sanctuary lamp in a religion that is not his own, will go on the road with Francisco and seek survival in the real world. Heart will join with head. As Francisco says, acknowledging their union, "We'll go together, right? It's quite an adventure though. It isn't half bad down here" (p. 54). Francisco is already like the babies in purgatory, content because he knows nothing better.

The Catholic liturgy and the *Oresteia*, along with the problems created by industrialization and urbanization, inform the entire work. The *Oresteia* ended by wresting power from the gods and putting it in human hands (creating the court of the Areopagus to decide in matters of homicide, rather than leaving it to vengeful gods). The ending of *The Sanctuary Lamp* also shows a resolution. The Mass has become an evening of conversation, and wine the facilitator. Man has become all the God he needs, and survival with camaraderie enough of a goal. Francisco, Harry and Maudie will go on, as Ireland will go on, without their former illusions, but still with a faith in the exchanged or simply witnessed word ("Y'know"). The Church will yield to the world and the sanctuary lamp to the sun, after a sleep that shows our characters forgiven for being human. The sanctuary lamp will go out, but the sun will rise.

XII

Thomas Murphy's Interview

OUR CONVERSATION began with a discussion of *The Sanctuary Lamp*, and some of the religious themes that appear in it:

MURPHY: Perhaps one of the things that was influencing me is that great book by William James, *Varieties of Religious Experience*. William James was invited to give a series of lectures, I think at Edinburgh University, round about the turn of the century, and decided to do a section on personal religion and institutionalized religion, and he got so caught up in personal religion that he would have nothing to do with the institutionalized religion, other than his denial of it in writing the book. His insistence about religion is to do with feeling and the apprehension of the spirit, about something being bigger, man being bigger than himself, if you like. But there was a phrase of his which he said apropos of the liturgy, particularly to do with Catholicism. He said, "The menu is not the dinner." His style of writing is wonderful. I was perhaps influenced by this when I have Francisco talk about "all the passions of the passions, in heaps higher than all the cathedrals." He is rejecting, and denying, the edifices and the whole idea of religion and the liturgy, in sections like that. You know I'm thinking about the passions of the passions, burning in a constant flame, all about feeling and emotion, and apprehension rather than comprehension.

Francisco describes the absence of God, and he represents many people when he says, "There's no one to bless you. And, worse, there's no one to curse you." He sees that it is a godless world. I think that you elaborated on this point: if there is a God there to curse you, that, of course, is better than this vacuum. Francisco is screaming for answers, "Speak up, speak up, Lord, I cannot hear"— you know, he's shouting in the church, "speak up, speak up Lord, your servant is listening"—but there's no master involved and the gods are in the people.

It would be a help, if there were somebody to curse you, but we're on our own. There is no deus ex machina, there is no God; we are moving toward this achieving of forgiveness through people rather than through gods. Francisco's guilt seems endless. Francisco is guilty for stealing Harry's wife, etc. Francisco feels guilty about everything.

MCDONALD: Not all of these things are valid sources of guilt per se. This guilt seems to be a composite, something like weltschmerz. It's as if original sin consisted in being born, and the guilt continues because one is alive.

MURPHY: Well, that's a good example. And then Francisco regrets he hadn't died, and he talks of Limbo. Why? Alright, he was terrified of damnation but he has been damned to life, so that's another reason for the childish dream emerging about Limbo, which he sees as tropical.

MCDONALD: You know the translation by Yeats from Sophocles' *Oedipus at Colonus*:

> Never to have lived is best, ancient writers say;
> Never to have drawn the breath of life, never to have looked
>   into the eye of day;
> The second best's a gay goodnight and quickly turn away.

Those ideas are typical of a type of Greek pessimism. You find comparable ideas in Theognis and others. One might say it is all rather obvious.

MURPHY: Well, the greatest profundities are usually the obvious ones, aren't they? You mention that Maudie feels guilty for giving up her baby, who died shortly after birth. She's told that forgiveness will stop everything and she seeks forgiveness. That's all true, but another thing that would be very operative, and that was operative in my mind writing it, was that the explanation of life given to Maudie is forgiveness. This is how life was explained to her.

MCDONALD: By the vision of her mother?

MURPHY: Well, the grandmother told her, and then after the experience when her mother came along, she needed to change and so she's saying: "But then mam got up . . . and went out . . . the door opened again and my mam were standing there. . . . She said, 'Oh, by the way, Maudie, I'm very happy now. . . . ' And I were so grateful. And then I told my gran, whether it were dreaming or not, it were all over." And Harry asks, "And what did your gran say?" Maud answers, "She said it were forgiveness." This is the explanation of life, to be forgiven, and it complements the theme that I'm moving on to about forgiving each other.

MCDONALD: That's crucial.

MURPHY: You mention Harry contributing to his daughter's death. It's maybe repressed, but Harry is just as responsible for his daughter's death as anybody else, as her mother, as Francisco. Francisco keeps taking layers of stuff off Harry to make Harry face himself. Francisco says, "And what of the tardy-footed giants who did not lift a finger?" Harry is the "tardy-footed giant." He continues, "The ones who didn't lift a finger—but who now claim they know better."

They are masters of sorrow, and Harry is the master of sorrow. Harry is the one, he knew that his wife was being screwed on the top of a Wedgwood table. He knew this, alright. Harry contributed. He tells his bit about the two of them in the dark, eyes open, in the night, through the night, every night, and nothing but his little girl's cough which he mimics. But yes, he did that, but Olga did something for the child, as well, and Francisco—when Harry tells his side of things, by inference Francisco is saying, "Others did things too, but if she died through neglect, you were just as responsible"—which he was. Harry refuses to get the message, and Francisco is essentially talking about Olga's death when he tells the story of the last engagement that they had.

Francisco's lines are very, very loaded, but rightly so. He's very sharp; he's a very intelligent man. His rage grows through that long song that he does, and he's quite prepared to be killed at the end of it. Harry asks, "Would you die for your belief?" Francisco retorts, "Would you kill for yours?" Practically everything he says, when directed at Harry, is about "that poor, unhappy, lost, unfaithful wife." Harry, the master of sorrow, tells Jesus that he believes in life and so he does. But what about the other side of things? He was the one—in the sub-text of the lines—he was the one who knew his wife was getting screwed in the kitchen, but as long as he could have his ten-year-old "Napoleon," the "VSOP Cognac," and so on . . . Francisco calls Harry a celebrity and says, "Oh, the great man knew your name, Har, and of your erstwhile fame, and many were the regrets expressed at your inability to be among us." This guy was a celebrity.

I call it "The Jack Doyle Syndrome." There's this Irish guy I met on a few occasions in Notting Hill. He was the one with the affected voice, which I stored away in the back of my head. It was a combination of Jack Doyle's sound and this California Irish priest, Father Peyton, the Rosary priest of "The family that prays together stays together." I heard him being interviewed on the radio one day. I was driving with the radio on, and this friend of mine was interviewing this priest and he talked about going to California as a kid—fourteen, fifteen years of age. His uncle was a priest in some parish in California, and gave him a job sweeping up the church and locking it at night and he talked about the mold. Before closing the door, he'd always have a last peek into the sanctuary. And the unlikely combination of Jack Doyle and Father Peyton gave me the trigger action for me to start writing because something had my spirit by the short hairs for a few years.

Three uncles of mine had died in the space of six months. I had always considered them as mere ballast, people I would pay a duty call on occasion. Now that they'd died, I found that my isolation was increasing, because they were some sort of support, and I had some sort of peculiar imagery that they were like legs that were supporting me and that they were disappearing away into space.

In my hometown, which was very small, the mortality rate was twice the national average: freak accidents, guys coming home from dances, running into horses, a car would come along where another car would have stopped, and three fellows got out and were mowed down. Something like twenty-six youngish men were killed. Now this was a holocaust of death. A brother-in-law of mine died of cancer. He was thirty-two, a painter, young painter. He had just had his first painting accepted by the Royal Academy. One of my closest friends got killed in his car. I remember walking in Connemara, and feeling resentment of the hills and that poignancy of death in such numbers, and I wondered if it would stop. I remember discussing it with my wife and she said, "I don't think it will. You know we're both arriving at the age." But as it happened, death in those sort of numbers did stop. The freak things, that sort of thing stopped. But all of this is to point you toward the sort of mood I was in. It was "Poor Tom," and the self-pity was incredible. I'm prone to suffering from depression, really wallowing in it. The next vacant chair at the table would obviously be my own.

And I'll tell you about a poem I wrote. I've only written one or two, and this one comes back to me as I usually use it in the talk I give on *The Sanctuary Lamp* as another indication of what I call the incubation period of a play, and all the different forces that come in that one isn't even conscious of. I had already started the play two years before the actual writing, but I didn't know about it. For instance, I used this Father Peyton whom I don't particularly like or respect. I find most of those guys suspect—and him, when he talked about having the peek in at the sanctuary lamp. I remembered myself as a child, I used to have to lock up the hens at night—always singing a song for them, you know, because they were being locked up for the night and it was in a childish way. Harry is quite childlike in his apprehension of the spirit and tends to pictorialize a lot.

We were talking about the sleeping giant, and that kind of thing. The idea of the lamp—snap of the fingers—it was nearly as dramatic as that. I started to go into churches occasionally, just to look at these lamps, and I thought, "It was man who lit that lamp, not the Church, and whatever degrees of grief I was going through, no matter what isolation—feelings of isolation exist within people—that glimmer of light in the heart cannot be extinguished." This is the faint music in the soul. *The Gigli Concert*, which came seven years after, speaks of the music in the soul, and in that play, the Irishman sold his soul. He wants it back, and still there's a glimmer of light. It's like a candle in the window in the distance, the light of a bonfire in the distance, that faint music, and man, that is the light that will always, I feel, be there, and it has nothing to do with institutions or churches. It is to do with the spirit, and I think that it is your business to move from the light to the sun, which is one of the things I really liked in your commentary and analysis.

But keeping it with man, it's like the song of Apollo; that man's saying I'm in my small corner and you are in yours, but whether it's the sun or not, there is that faint light which cannot be extinguished. I recognized that I got some sort of breakthrough that had to do with *The Sanctuary Lamp*. As usual a process of the play was discovering the play in the process of doing it, rather than my using some formal outline, as one would use a coat hanger to put one's coat on.

MCDONALD: You mentioned that there was a poem.

MURPHY: There's a poem, the only one I've ever had published. It explains to me my personality, my state and attitude at the time. It shows the emasculated man, and the emasculated God, and the play shows that too. I now realize that I took up some of the images in this poem and elaborated on them two years later in the play. It goes something like this:

> Where are the angry mountains,
> The winds that whispered with revengeful solace,
> Long ago in Catholic childhood,
> When I could quench my pain
> In the burning fires of Hell,
> When fear was food to my existence,
> Was mystery, and was meaning to my soul.
> Now, to quench this dark, monotonous despair,
> I shut my eyes,
> And the poor evaporated God
> That was found now
> Is but a sad, slow-moving mist
> In the vacuum of space.
> Now in the darkness,
> To recharge my soul
> With wonder, power, astonishment and awe,
> I explore the possibilities
> Of murder and of love,
> Or further in perversity,
> Try to heat my vapid senses
> With induced insanity,

But fail.
And find it all, incredulity,
All mundane response.

And that is the theme of the play.

MCDONALD: And insanity is the last refuge, as Harry says, "Do you think madness must at least be warm? . . . I keep it as a standby in case all else fails."

MURPHY: Yes. And Francisco is evil. Like Harry, he is predominantly an emasculated man, the emasculated god, "The sad, slow-moving mist in the vacuum of space," the man who is from the mountain, gods being mountains: "But where the winds that whisper with revengeful solace, nobody to curse you. Long ago in Catholic childhood when I could quench my pain in the burning fires of Hell, when fear was food to my existence. . . ."

MCDONALD: Later you have to live with it. But there's also a different type of fear that's touched on, when the evaporated god becomes a mist, you're rid of that fear too, a particular fear. But then you get a worse one, not just the existential fear that the "other" is hell, but the awful discovery that there may be no other and that we are all condemned to monadic isolation. Our fears are only ours, and we die alone.

MURPHY: Well, you're given a sort of format, a framework, if you like, within which you can deal with life, but then when your own intelligence removes that, or it is removed from you, what do you do? I mean, you've just got the guilt, which has nowhere to go. It can't be absolved, because you can't deal with it. Now part of the odyssey of this play consists of Harry's wanderings. Harry declares that it is a homeless land, and a savage people, and most of us feel similar to Harry. There's nobody to bless you, nobody to curse you.

MCDONALD: But isn't part of the guilt something that was put on you by the Church?

MURPHY: Certainly, and I would have been much more forceful in saying it, stronger certainly, but you did remind me that the Greeks, in 500 B.C., go on and on and on about the guilt, and looking for forgiveness, and so on.

MCDONALD: They're talking about death, not forgiveness, suffering, not guilt, when they say that the best thing is not to be born. The Christians introduced the idea of an original sin, something that must be forgiven; in fact there wasn't a word for sin in ancient

Greek. They spoke of *hamartia*, which meant "mistake, missing the mark." But there was not this idea of absolute guilt. When you have someone like Orestes seeking forgiveness, he's not seeking forgiveness from any god, for being human, so much as expiation for a specific crime. The *Oresteia* deals in part with a socially organized trial by jury, which is a rather controlled framework, and it either condemns or acquits. There is not the sense of absolute guilt that you get with Catholicism. Orestes speaks of guilt as a disease of the mind in Euripides, but this is an acquired disease. Even the guilt of the Stoics is different from the absolute guilt of Christianity which is always already there.

MURPHY: Well, is there an equivalent of the Adam and Eve thing?

MCDONALD: Hesiod tells us Prometheus took clay and water and made man in the shape of the gods and Athena gave him the breath of life. Woman came later and was the source of evil, of all man's troubles: Pandora and her box. There is also the story, which is rather like the story of Noah, that the earth was flooded to destroy the evil which had come to exist, and only one pious couple survived, Deucalion and Pyrrha, who recreated the human race by throwing stones behind them, and Ovid suggests that's why we're a "hard" race. So they were our second ancestors, and far from committing a sin, they were the good ones spared to re-create the race.

MURPHY: Perhaps the original sin was the self-consciousness of thinking, and obviously, the Greeks thought . . .

MCDONALD: The Greeks certainly equated thinking with existence, far before Descartes. Aristotle says in the *Nicomachean Ethics*, "It seems that life consists mainly in perception and thought" (9.1170.a). Existence is to be able to perceive and to think, and the word for thought is used in a semimoral way. So also, Plato said that the unexamined life is not worth living. This is perhaps the opposite of your claim about original sin as self-conscious thought. The Greeks considered thought as mainly beneficial for their lives, although it may be a source of pain. Cadmus tells Agave that she would be better off if she could remain ignorant of the fact that she has killed her son in the *Bacchae*. So also the chorus in this play make the claim that knowledge is not wisdom, nor collected facts valid philosophy.

MURPHY: Perhaps perception of a higher code also allows for breaking it. The knowledge that came with eating the apple in the Garden of Eden and knowledge, there, was used as temptation—it might make one equal to God.

MCDONALD: Adam and Eve may have gained knowledge, and lost paradise, but then it was a fool's paradise wasn't it? Prometheus gave man fire, which led to his mastery of technology and ultimately the arts. It made man in some ways equal to the gods, and it angered Zeus that man had this power, rather like the story of the forbidden apple. The gods can be jealous. The Greeks glorify man more, and create the gods in man's image. In the Old and New Testament man is seen as inherently sinful. The Greeks offer happiness more as a reward for good works rather than think about punishment for wrongdoing. Also praise was very important in the Greek tradition. Aristotle says that if one fails, it is natural to be criticized, but to succeed, and have no one praise you, that is unbearable. The reward is in this life and in other people's eyes, and man is not born evil, or guilty. One of the main messages of the *Oresteia* was that man learned through suffering. One's mistakes were one's teachers. So there really is a profound difference, I think, between Greek thinking and the Catholic idea that man is born with original sin.

MURPHY: I wonder if this is such an evolutionary process. Does man really learn? Perhaps the Greeks were mistaken to talk about man as if he were a rational or reasonable human being.

MCDONALD: Aristotle did claim that. He says that thought and the capacity for speech distinguished man from the animals.

MURPHY: If Aristotle can state what the course of life should be, why doesn't man follow it?

MCDONALD: It's a capacity, not an inevitability. More honored in the breach.

MURPHY: OK, OK, then that qualification is essential to it, because I'm not sure about the evolutionary process. I may not make the same mistakes; I just make others now. I thought that because the tractor had taken over the horse that we were learning, but we're not, not at all. And it is the natural course of life that flesh of flesh remains the flesh of flesh, but we disown each other, we insult each other, we offend against each other, in tiny ways, in major ways. Christ allegedly said that we were all brothers. I doubt that he was that foolish. You know, if he had said, "We're not brothers but we should be," then you stand a chance.

MCDONALD: Exactly. Euripides said the same thing: *Philia*, or "the love of man for man" is a weapon used to protect man against the gods, or to fill their absence. If there is anything to be counted on, it is man, not the gods.

MURPHY: The gods, and art, we might as well talk about our police force or look at the church parish priest or the curate: here's the deus ex machina who comes in to solve everybody's problems at the end. And, of course, that isn't possible at all, or feasible. But on the thing of guilt, take something that we were talking about last year. You know the line in *Medea*, "Happy the man who has no children." I think it is essential as far as the play is concerned. Do you think that when Medea kills her children perhaps Jason thinks that it was a deserved recompense? If you have a divorce today, no matter who is at fault, no matter what insults and slights are cast, there is always the question, "What did I do wrong?" One really suffers guilt because of an action even though the action is natural. I suppose ultimately what I'm saying is that the mind would appear to be the unnatural thing. That is the difference between us and the rest of the animal kingdom.

I often watch dogs, you know, when they're sleeping, and when they have dreams. They obviously have some sort of a mind, a brain, and ours is a little bit greater, but the dog I think can feel guilty. You've heard the phrase "hangdog." The phrase is derived from the way a dog looks. I had two dogs up there on the top step last Saturday morning. The rubbish was there, the refuse, and I heard—there are usually a few bottles—some bottles rolling around the place, and there's this team of two hobos, two dogs outside, and one is a lovely old gentleman, you know; had all the marks of life about him; the other one is more cunning; he stays at the bottom of the step and doesn't look, though he knows what's going on. Well, I told this dog to get out; and the dog went down a few steps and then stopped at the gate and looked back and thought about it, then "Woof!" [barking and snarling] "What do you mean, you prick?" Or whatever. "You've got a warm house and you throw out food and I'm not allowed to eat it?" And then he had a little bit of anger there, you know, life is very unfair. And the other dog, the little sidekick, you know, he was just keeping his mind to himself since this other dog was feeding him. Very, very similar to human behavior.

MCDONALD: And if it were your own dog he'd look guilty.

MURPHY: Yes. Hangdog. And it seems to be exacerbated throughout the Western world, by institutions like the Church, by teachers trying to teach a moral code. It is intensified. But I think it's there.

MCDONALD: They provide a theoretical framework for dealing with some of the guilt, but then they also set up some of the problems that wouldn't be there but for them. So it's sort of like a political organization. I think that's how the Catholic Church succeeded. It was the same way that the Romans rose to such comprehensive power, because of their political organization. Divide and conquer, and if you can have guilt working for you, you are all the more powerful.

MURPHY: Well, in a way that's what Francisco says in *The Sanctuary Lamp:* "All these predators, that have been mass-produced out of the loneliness and isolation of people. They deal with poverty by saying, 'The poor will have their just rewards in the next life.' " Now the people who thought out those things originally knew what the human mind was capable of in terms of wishful thinking, in terms of grief, and how do you capitalize on that? How do you exploit it? How do you keep a populace together? What are the propensities that man has? How do you keep him in tow? How do you keep him in subjection?

MCDONALD: I found the two sermons I've heard most often are on how guilty you should be, and "We happen to be building our church now, and how much are you going to contribute?" and they both are related. Contributions helped absolution. Priests washed away your sins for a fee. Obviously there are a few good priests, and a few understand and convey a sincerely beneficial message, the ones who genuinely try to help assuage human suffering, rather than use that suffering as a weapon to control the "flock" they are busy "fleecing," and the emotional "fleecing" is the worst.

MURPHY: Mommo says in *Bailegangaire,* "There's nothin' like money t'make the clergy devout." I'm not knocking the Church for it; it happens to be a fact of life, that they get very devout around money.

MCDONALD: Do you think that man has an innate religious instinct? If so, do you think it can be satisfied by some translation into ideals and goals in purely human terms?

MURPHY: I think it needs some sort of structure, but it's been so defiled by institutions to date, as we know them. I'm still trying to work it out, and I don't sit here all day trying to work these things out; they only cross my mind when I'm trying to write a speech or something for somebody. I would have thought that man's imagination is so vast that it's enough, that without creating, falsifying, the archetypes which are there in myths, for us to look at and say that's a constant that runs through life, but when they start to talk about it, and in such a way that they pictorialize it. . . .

For instance, "In my father's house there are many mansions," and whether Jesus said those things or not, the words are really selling something, you know. You talk about a mansion, and there are many mansions, and yours is Number 15. I would have thought that the imagination in man is sufficient, but maybe it has to be channeled in some way, and the Church used to have a stabilizing effect. Now there seems to be an emergence of a much more hysterical form of religion, particularly in the States, the evangelical movement, but for a while it was a stabilizing force. It did present people with a set of codes and morals, even the obvious superficial ones like observing the Sabbath, which is terrific for man, that he/she can say Sunday is a day of rest. That helps; that sort of thing helps.

MCDONALD: For reunion with the family, if nothing else. The Greeks, on the other hand, more consistently celebrate man.

MURPHY: I see the celebration by the Greeks of man manifested particularly in their sculpture. The Greeks also wanted to see what was going to happen next, and how is it going to happen again, and again, in the same repeating pattern, which is life. You make the same mistakes and have the same joys that your mother had, and the same way with your children: they too will repeat those things.

This idea can be attacked. I know, in the last few days, I was attacked, being accused yet again of a romantic attitude, but to me, a romantic attitude is a big collar, but a factual attitude doesn't give a creative artist much leeway to explore or isolate those aspects of character that one is interested in. I'm interested in outsiders, like Harry, in *The Sanctuary Lamp*, who is an ex-strongman from the circus. I couldn't have dealt with a solicitor or a teacher or a housewife. I needed somebody whose spirit was also caught by the short hairs, within whom I could isolate those aspects of man that interest me. There's a guy who's trying to feign insanity or induce insanity, which really means that he is crazier than he knows, because if a human being says, "I keep insanity as a standby," well, he's crazy. I show his character in broad strokes.

MCDONALD: So the outside can make the inside more visible.

MURPHY: Yeah. Yeah, that's a good way of putting it.

MCDONALD: Does *The Sanctuary Lamp* take place in England?

MURPHY: I don't say where it is set. It was set in a Dublin church, and the actors played it in Irish accents.

MCDONALD: So it's really basically, then, Dublin; well, but you don't say.

MURPHY: I simply say it's a city. I wrote it here when I'd come back to live here, but before I left England I had seen in the late sixties a sign "For Sale" on a church and I thought good, they're disintegrating.

MCDONALD: There's still a God in the world.

MURPHY: Yeah, so that rather pleased me, but that church was for sale in London, and other churches are for sale. I see some of them are already converted into office blocks and that now, and because a very important period of my life was spent in London, and because, outside of Dublin, London is the city I know best, so I probably had London in mind without saying it. What has been delightfully misinterpreted is when Maudie gets her tenses mixed up: "When I went to bed last night, my mam were there and I were so tired," and "She were sitting reading the paper . . . " The verbs are wrong, but that's common to the Midlands, in England. Other people have interpreted it as a mistake a child makes. Some people, the more sensitive ones, saw it as a childlike attitude. I would like to think that I had covered that as well when I wrote it, but I hadn't.

MCDONALD: Well, it's there.

MURPHY: It's there; there is an innocence that I found through this by way of trying to establish where on earth the play is set.

MCDONALD: And Harry's Jewishness makes him maybe an outsider, but also one who represents the ones who talk to gods, with the Old Testament merging into the New Testament.

MURPHY: Yeah, yeah, I found that; I find it very difficult.

MCDONALD: And the strongman, do you think of him as Samson?

MURPHY: Yeah, I thought about Samson and also the *Oresteia*. I find that in writing a play, I come to the numerous full stops which are also areas of great despair. I feel, you know, I can't go on. I think, "This is ridiculous, this means nothing to me, and what could it possibly mean to anybody else?" And then I start to look for some sort of precedent in mythology on which I can hang it to make it work, and I usually reject that and say, well, am I trying to make this play work? Or am I trying to write some mood, feeling, attitude, that I feel within myself? I don't comprehend it, but I feel it within myself.

MCDONALD: This sounds like the obscure process of retention, re-creation and creation we all do. So this is our end and we're back at the beginning.

OUR PAST has shaped our present, and our present reshapes our past. Modern reworkings of ancient drama help inform the present. We have looked at Medusa, and we have not been turned to stone. We can see the horrors of our age in the reflection of the past, and by reflecting ourselves, leave the theatre with more understanding.

Each playwright and /or director discussed in this book has used Greek tragedy, and one the Greek satyr play—to convey his own message. Suzuki Tadashi has rewritten Japanese theatre and revised Western theater to evolve a new type of "Holy Theater," which is critical at the same time that it enchants. American devastation, whether in the form of Hiroshima or an imposed market mentality, is unveiled and exorcised by enacting ancient tragedy.

Peter Sellars is clearly critical of the political atmosphere in which he lives. He has taken the ancient values and shown modern times coming up short. He shows us an ancient hero who was no longer valued in his own time for those heroic qualities that are also derogated in modern times. He is critical as well of the manipulation of the media to shape opinion, and he uses Sophocles' *Ajax* as an example from antiquity to elucidate the power of the Pentagon. Sellars shows the illusion of heroism and virtue as created by headlines and the power brokers of mass communication. His footlights show us the truth behind the headlines.

Tony Harrison is a poet of the theatre, but he is a poet who is wounded by his own time and lets his blood flow on the page and stage. We also hear the heartbeat of the pleading rhythms, and our own echo in response. Through the ancient satyr play, he mixes the tragic with the comic, high and low art, and explodes the categories. In *The Trackers*, a fascist Apollo tries to segregate art, but the Dionysian satyrs show that if power is not shared, it will be destroyed. The satyrs, whose rhythm contributed to Apollo's melody, end by trampling the set and setting it on fire. Harrison's *Medea: A Sex War Opera*, also ends in the destruction that comes from opposition without understanding. But the opposition also creates definition—and good theater.

Heiner Müller attacks us through his images. The words of antiquity assault us in our present. He shows us corpses and mutilates them; we are forced to gaze on a necropolis. We are not even invited to enter, yet we know we shall fall into the same heap. The pyres have been extinguished; Müller shows us only ashes. Theodoros Terzopoulos inscribes Müller's message on our bodies. Together they show us the devastation of modern war and industrial abuse. Müller compares the ecological devastation of our planet to Jason's use of Medea. Benefits are taken and the husk abandoned, with no concern for mutual dependency, whose neglect can be fatal.

Thomas Murphy is a playwright of living, loving, sinning people who forgive each other for living. Modern Ireland joins ancient Greece in a reaffirmation of life through the mutual support of man for man.

War (of various kinds) and power (its illusions and its effects) are constant themes. Each postmodern play discussed here has a historical framework and setting that provides its own commentary. The past informs the present: the ancient themes form and are formed by the present. Japan, America, Britain, and Germany have conducted their own wars (and sometimes continue to do so), as did Greece long ago; these postmodern productions present us with new variations on everlasting human themes. Thomas Murphy's war is with the Church; he wins. The ancient Greeks define issues and cordon off the territory.

Suzuki and Harrison criticize the past and the present, whereas Müller simply uses both as weapons in his arsenal for attack. Sellars tries to reshape the present with information as a tool for change, and Murphy provides an incantation or prayer, as poetical music to evoke a better future. The presentations are also rituals with each aimed at the modern audience in a way calculated to seduce, alienate, or in some way shatter everyday complacency. I would suggest that these efforts gain force by using the missiles of ancient texts to sabotage the memory.

Each reworked play can be rated on a scale of hope. The bleakest by far is Heiner Müller's vision, where man becomes the latest addition to the detritus of civilization. The individual heroic death is over; now we have "body counts." Ajax's "the noble man must with live with honor or die with honor" (ll. 479–80) is a quaint concept in Heiner Müller's scheme. So even death is deprived of gestural significance, and is seen as merely another accident in a technological age in which man happens to be the tool of nature. Man is not even the ultimate accident.

Suzuki's composite drama is more dialectical. The confrontations raise questions, and even though past resolutions have been disastrous, the questions must still be asked. There is at least some implication that an answer may yet be possible (rather than irrelevant, as Müller seems to suggest).

Sellars' *Ajax* deals in particular with the issue of *who* is allowed to ask questions. The victory of the dead Ajax (he is finally buried and recognized as a hero) carries on the qualified hope of the original Sophoclean play. Odysseus is forced to admit Ajax's value, as we are forced to see that our classics have shaped us, although we may disagree with their particular theses.

Harrison's tragic vision makes hope possible. He shows us that death is essential for appreciating the value of life, shocking us into the realization of the preciousness and precariousness of life as we know it now. The past also enhances, adding a richness and savor to the present moment. Harrison celebrates the human condition in its totality. He also sees tragedy and satyr plays as parts of another whole, showing the different faces of life and death. Since the human race is one, so also there should be no preference accorded to "high" art, while "low" art is scorned. As he says, "In honour of that ancient wholeness we performed our piece, and we became *Ichneutai,* 'Trackers', seeking in fragments of our past and present a common wholeness, a common illumination, a common commitment to survival." This mélange of "high" and "low" beside past and present (and threatened future) makes this play an elegant postmodern celebration.

Most optimistic of all is Murphy, who carries on the image of light and the greeting of a new day as man's resurrection. In *The Sanctuary Lamp* the priests are seen as "black candles, not giving, but each one drawing a little more light out of the world." Murphy restores that light in the heart of man, in the image of the dawning of a new day. Even the soul is defined in terms of light. The soul is "like a silhouette" that "moves out from the world to take its place in the silent outer wall of eternity." At the end of this play man turns away from the sanctuary lamp and moves into the light of the sun. Francisco and Harry leave the church to face the day with the warmth of mutual friendship. Man in the fullness of this world basks in the sunlight. Orestes finds his earthly paradise.

Each of the writers and/or directors discussed in this book has, in his own way, used the classic texts of the past to define or comment upon our present crisis. Through their genius we are invited to know our present in terms of the past so that we may have a future. But whatever interpretive course these creative artists have taken toward these ancient works, the alarums have been sounded. The result is that we are awakened; we can face our day with new eyes of understanding, and perhaps even some joy.

NOTES

Prologue

1. See his monograph, *To Reclaim a Legacy: A Report on the Humanities in Higher Education,* (National Endowment for the Humanities: 1984).

2. "Orientalism Reconsidered," *Race and Class,* XXVII.2(1985).

3. "The Politics of Misogyny: Myth and Mythmaking in the *Oresteia,*" *Arethusa,* 11.1,2 (1978), 149–184.

4. I shall follow the Japanese order for proper names, the family name followed by the given name (i.e., Suzuki Tadashi), except in the case of titles or quotations from other people who follow the Western order, and especially well-known names, such as Akira Kurosawa.

5. Jean-Paul Sartre, "Why the Trojan Women," trans. Jeffrey Mehlman, Introduction to Sartre's adaptation of *The Trojan Women* (Paris: Éditions Gallimard, 1965) reprint in *Euripides: A Collection of Critical Essays,* ed. Erich Segal (Englewood Cliffs, N.J.: Prentice-Hall, Inc. 1968), p. 131.

6. "Shakespeare and the Stoicism of Seneca," in *Selected Essays,* new ed. (1950; reprint, New York: Harcourt Brace Jovanovich, 1964), p. 115.

7. *Cromwell* (1983: reprint, Newcastle upon Tyne: Bloodaxe Books Ltd, 1987), p.127.

8. In a paper delivered at a Symposium, *The Classics in Contemporary Theatre* (University of California, San Diego, 1990).

9. *Antigones* (Oxford: Oxford University Press, 1984), p. 131.

10. *Antigones,* p. 303.

11. "That is the moment at which pastiche appears and parody has become impossible. Pastiche is, like parody, the imitation of a peculiar or unique style, the wearing of a stylistic mask, speech in a dead language: but it is a neutral practice of such mimicry, without parody's ulterior motive, without the satirical impulse, without laughter, without that still latent feeling that there exists something normal compared to which what is being imitated is rather comic." "Postmodernism and Consumer Society," in *The Anti-Aesthetic: Essays on Postmodern Culture,* ed. with an introduction by Hal Foster (1983; reprint, Seattle, Washington: Bay Press, 1989), p. 114.

12. Benda suggests "the causes for this change in the 'clerks': The imposition of political interests on all men without any exception; the growth of consistency in matters apt to feed realist passions; the desire and the possibility for men of letters to play a political part; the need in the interests of their own fame for them to play the game of a class which is daily becoming more anxious; the increasing tendency of the 'clerks' to become bourgeois and to take on the vanities of that class; the perfection of their Romanticism; the decline of their knowledge of antiquity and of their intellectual discipline, *"The Treason of the Intellectuals,* trans. Richard Aldington (1928; reprint, New York : W.W. Norton & Company, 1969), p. 176. So the classics might even save the integrity of the "clerks"!

13. Takeo Doi, *The Anatomy of Dependence,* trans. John Bester (1973, Tokyo; reprint, New York and San Francisco: Kodansha International, 1978).

14. Martin Bernal, *Black Athena: The Afroasiatic Roots of Classical Civilization,* I: *The Fabrication of Ancient Greece 1785–1985* (London: Free Association Books, 1987).

15. This is my translation of a fragment by the famous fifth-century sophist, Gorgias (a frequent character in Plato's dialogues), and it is cited in Hermann Diels and Walther Kranz, *Die Fragmente der Vorsokratiker* II(1907; reprint Zurich: Weidmann, 1969), pp. 305–6. Gorgias is quoted by Plutarch as saying this in reference to Greek tragedy.

16. Frank Kermode, *The Classic: Literary Images of Permanence and Change* (1975; reprint Cambridge, Massachusetts: Harvard University Press, 1983), p. 141.

1. *Suzuki Tadashi's* The Trojan Women

1. There are many histories of the development of drama in Japan. Leonard C. Pronko gives a useful bibliography in his *Guide to Japanese Drama* (Boston: G. K. Hall, 1973); also useful is his *Theater East & West: Perspectives Toward a Total Theater* (1967; reprint, Berkeley: University of California Press, 1974). See also Peter Arnott, *The Theatres of Japan* (New York: St. Martin's, 1969); and J. Thomas Rimer, *Toward a Modern Japanese Theatre: Kishida Kunio* (Princeton: Princeton University Press, 1974).

For particular information about Suzuki Tadashi I have consulted various articles, his program for the Waseda Sho-Gekijo, *SCOT: Suzuki Company of Toga* (hereafter cited as *SCOT* Program) (Tokyo: The Japan Performing Arts Center, 1985), and Tadashi Suzuki, *The Way of Acting: The Theatre Writings of Tadashi Suzuki,* trans. J. Thomas Rimer (New York: Theatre Communications Group, Inc., 1986).

2. *SCOT* Program, p. 20.

3. *SCOT* Program, p. 21.

4. Ryusaku Tsunoda, Wm. Theodore de Bary, and Donald Keene, eds., *Sources of Japanese Tradition* (New York: Columbia University Press, 1964), I. 246.

5. *SCOT* Program, p. 17.

6. Article by Roderick Mason Faber in *SCOT* Program, p. 18.

7. *U.S. News and World Report*, (Dec. 28, 1987/Jan.4, 1988) 98.

8. *SCOT* Program, p. 17. Hereafter cited in text.

9. H.D.F. Kitto, *Greek Tragedy: A Literary Study*, 3d ed.(1961; reprint London: Methuen, p. 212.

10. Michael Cacoyannis, "Translators' Introduction," *Euripides: The Bacchae* (New York: New American Library, Mentor Books, 1982), p. xi.

11. *SCOT* Program, p. 2.

12. Edith Hamilton, *Three Greek Plays: Prometheus Bound, Agamemnon, The Trojan Women* (1937; reprint, New York: Norton, 1965), p. 86.

13. Cacoyannis, "Introduction," *The Bacchae*, p. xi.

14. *Ibid.*, p. xiii.

15. Yamanouchi Hisaaki, *The Search for Authenticity in Modern Japanese Literature* (Cambridge: Cambridge University Press, 1978), p. 152.

16. This type of theater is the "Holy Theater" that Peter Brook speaks of when he describes the work of Antoine Artaud: "A Holy Theatre in which the blazing centre speaks through those forms closest to it. A theater working like the plague, by intoxication, by infection, by analogy, by magic; a theatre in which the play, the event itself, stands in place of a text." *The Empty Space* (1968; reprint, London: Penguin Books, 1988), p. 55.

2. *Suzuki Tadashi's* Clytemnestra

1. Ruth Benedict classified the Japanese as members of a shame culture: "In anthropological studies of different cultures the distinction between those which rely heavily on shame and those that rely heavily on guilt is an important one. True shame cultures rely on external sanctions for good behavior, not, as true guilt cultures do, on an internalized conviction of sin." *The Chrysanthemum and the Sword: Patterns of Japanese Culture* (1946; reprint New York and Scarborough, Ont.: New American Library, Meridian Books, 1974), pp. 222–23.

2. *SCOT* Program, p. 23. Suzuki's drama is much like James L. Calderwood's "metadrama" ("in which the boundaries between the play as a work of self-contained art and life are dissolved,"). Calderwood, *Shakespearean Metadrama* (Minneapolis: University of Minnesota Press, 1971), p. 4; quoted in Charles Segal, *Dionysiac Poetics and Euripides' Bacchae* (Princeton: Princeton University Press, 1982), p. 216. This description could also be applied to Japanese Noh drama.

3. Gilbert Murray, "Introduction to *Electra*" in *The Plays of Euripides*, 2 vols. (London: George Allen, 1914) 2:vi.

4. Philip E. Slater, *The Glory of Hera: Greek Mythology and the Greek Family* (Boston: Beacon Press, 1971), p. 186.

5. Slater, *Glory of Hera*, p. 180.

6. Slater, *Glory of Hera*, p. 314 and passim.

7. For example, Melanie Klein, and Joan Riviere, *Love, Hate, and Reparation* (New York: Norton, 1964). See also Melanie Klein, *Envy and Gratitude and Other Works 1941–1963* (London: Hogarth Press, 1975), particularly her chapter "Some Reflections on *The Oresteia*," pp. 275–99; also M. Mahler, *On Human Symbiosis and the Vicissitudes of Individuation* (New York: International Universities Press, 1968); and H. Kohut, *The Restoration of the Self* (1977; reprint Madison, Conn.: International Universities Press, 1986).

8. For a concise discussion of "le stade du miroir," see Jacques Lacan, *Écrits*, trans. Alan Sheridan (New York: Norton), pp. 1–7.

9. Lacan, *Écrits*, p. 6.

10. Terry Eagleton, *Literary Theory: An Introduction* (Minneapolis: University of Minnesota Press, 1983), p. 164.

11. Takeo Doi, *The Anatomy of Dependence*, trans. John Bester (1973, Tokyo; reprint New York and San Francisco: Kodansha International, 1978).

12. Chie Nakane, *Japanese Society* (Berkeley and Los Angeles: University of California Press, 1970), p. 128.

13. Keigo Okonogi, "Depression and Psychosomatic Illness in View of the Ajase Complex," *Dynamic Psychiatry* (1980), 13:116–30.

14. Okonogi, "Depression," p. 126.

15. Joseph L. Anderson and Donald Richie, *The Japanese Film: Art and Industry* (1959; reprint Princeton: Princeton University Press, 1982), p. 188.

16. Anderson and Richie, *The Japanese Film*, p. 262.

17. See pp. 48–49, and passim, in Takie Sugiyama Lebra, *Japanese Women: Constraint and Fulfillment* (Honolulu: University of Hawaii Press, 1984).

18. See Helene Foley, "The Conception of Women in Athenian Drama," in Foley, ed. *Perspectives on Women in Ancient Greece* (New York, London, Paris: Gordon and Breach, 1981), pp. 127–68; Michael Shaw, "The Female Intruder: Women in Fifth-Century Drama," *CP* (1975) 70(4): 255–66; and Helene Foley, "The 'Female Intruder' Reconsidered: Women in Aristophanes' *Lysistrata* and *Ecclesiazusae*," *CP* (1982) 77(1): 1–21.

19. Cf. Sherry Ortner, "Is Female to Male as Nature Is to Culture?" in M. Rosaldo and L. Lamphere, eds., *Women, Culture, and Society* (1974; reprint Stanford: Stanford University Press, 1983), pp. 68–88, and first essay in this collection.

20. Foley, "Conception of Women," in *Perspectives*, p. 148.

21. This has also been translated "man-hearted"; see Thomas Rosenmeyer, *The Art of Aeschylus* (Berkeley: University of California Press, 1982), p. 239. Rosenmeyer adds that Sophocles and Euripides had the notion of "women who are both feminine and heroic," but "Aeschylus plays on the perception that the natural woman is not of heroic dimensions. Hence the emphasis on unnatural masculine elements in Clytemnestra's constitution" (pp. 262–63). Foley "Conception of Women," in *Perspectives*, p. 151, sees the masculine attribution as more ominous: Clytemnestra is seen as invading the masculine sphere, leaving the *oikos* and invading the *polis*, "playing a male to Aegisthus' female." This inversion carries a penalty: "Violators of the cultural norm are generally punished, and women are often returned to silence, death or suicide, and the domestic interior where they 'belong' " (p. 153).

22. The notion of patriarchy conquering matriarchy in the *Oresteia* has been noted by many. For instance, Simone de Beauvoir said, "The *Eumenides* represents the triumph of the patriarchate over the matriarchate." Quoted in Simon Goldhill, *Reading Greek Tragedy* (Cambridge: Cambridge University Press, 1986) p. 53.

We have earlier instances of this claim. E. Cantarella says, "Friedrich Engels . . . in the preface to the fourth edition of *The Origin of the Family: Private Property and the State*, cited Bachofen's interpretation of the *Oresteia* of Aeschylus as a description of the struggle between matriarchal and patriarchal law and the victory of the second over the first." *Pandora's Daughters* (Baltimore: Johns Hopkins University Press, 1987), p. 4. The whole idea of matriarchy preceding patriarchy, however, has yet to be definitively established. Nevertheless, the notion seems still popular: Gunther Grass has a fish advise that matriarchy cede to patriarchy in *The Flounder*.

23. Rosenmeyer, *Art of Aeschylus*, p. 365.

24. Klein, "Some Reflections on the *Oresteia*," in *Envy and Gratitude*, p. 298. Hereafter cited in text.

25. Tadashi Suzuki, *The Way of Acting: The Theatre Writings of Tadashi Suzuki*, trans. J. Thomas Rimer (New York: Theatre Communications Group, 1986), pp. 121–23. See also J. P.Sullivan, "Literature and the Cinema: Film-making as Creative Translation," (Lecture, 1959) and "Fellini's *Satyricon* and the Myth of Eternal Rome," (unpublished paper delivered in 1979 at an *APA* panel called "On the Cinema and the Classics" in Boston). Here also in Fellini's film an ancient work is used in a creative way to provide commentary on contemporary society.

26. *International Herald Tribune*, June 9, 1986, p. 8.

27. There are many works that deal with Japanese "group-think," and the loss of individuality. See Arthur Kimball, *Crisis in Identity and Contemporary Japanese Novels* (Rutland, Vt., and Tokyo: Charles E. Tuttle, 1973); Takie Sugiyama Lebra and William P. Lebra, eds., *Japanese Culture and Behavior: Selected Readings*, (Honolulu: University of Hawaii Press, 1974), and, for men's conflicted relations with women, Ian Buruma, *Behind the Mask: On Sexual Demons, Sacred Mothers, Transvestites, Gangsters and Other Japanese Cultural Heroes* (New York: Pantheon, 1984).

28. Emile Durkheim, *Les Formes élémentaires de la vie religieuse* (Paris: Presses Universitaires de France, 1968); Walter Burkert, "Greek Tragedy and Sacrificial Ritual," *GRBS* (1966), 7:87–121; *Greek Religion*, trans. John Raffan (Cambridge: Harvard University Press, 1985); and René Girard, *Violence and the Sacred*, trans. Patrick Gregory (Baltimore: Johns Hopkins University Press, 1977).

29. Roland Barthes, *Empire of Signs*, trans. Richard Howard (New York: Hill and Wang, 1982), pp. 4–5.

30. Suzuki, *The Way of Acting*, p. 110.

31. Suzuki, *SCOT* Program, p. 32.

32. As Suzuki says, "I hold that nothing, if not the fiercely sober, existentialist spirit, will ever enable men to work as an ensemble in order to create something of lasting value" (*The Way of Acting*, p. 110).

33. Professor Avrum Stroll quotes Marx in a lively speech (University of California, La Jolla. Oct. 1986) on *The Great Gatsby:* "All our invention and progress seem to result in endowing material forces with intellectual life, and in stultifying human life into a material force." Karl Marx, "Speech at the Anniversary of the People's Paper," in *Selected Works* (London: Lawrence and Wishart, 1942), 2: 428. Suzuki reasserts human values through the medium of drama. See also Fritz Lang's film *Metropolis* (Germany, 1926) as a cinematic protest against people being used simply as tools.

34. These quotations from Rilke and Heidegger are in Simon Goldhill's *Language, Sexuality, Narrative: The Oresteia* (Cambridge: Cambridge University Press, 1984), pp. 99 and 121n32. This is a close reading of the text which reinterprets the *Oresteia* in the context of recent criticism, especially deconstruction, concentrating on the defining clash of the sexes with ambiguous resolution: "The *telos* of closure is resisted in the continuing play of difference. The final meaning remains undetermined" (p. 283).

35. "The Japanese language has no tense system, but aspects. That seems to mean that sequentiality is left ambiguous because of the mixture of the complete and incomplete aspects (which are often misunderstood to be the present and past 'tenses')." Miyoshi Masao, "Authority, Authorship, and the Narrative Forms in the First World and the Third," p. 12 (unpublished paper delivered in 1986 at the

University of California, San Diego). Miyoshi later showed how this tense system helps distinguish the *shosetsu* from the Western novel with its godlike preterit: "Now the Japanese language, which lacks a past tense and depends for temporal notation on the perfect and imperfect aspects, provides a possibility for art in a clearly different fashion . . . Unlike Barthes's—and Aristotle's—model, the *shosetsu* rejects the interpretive beginning, middle, and end"; Miyoshi, "Against the Native Grain: The Japanese Novel and the 'Postmodern' West" in a special issue of the South Atlantic Quarterly on the theme of "Postmodernism and Japan," ed. Miyoshi Masao and H.D. Harootunian (Summer 1988), 87(3):536. Later published in book form as *Postmodernism and Japan* (Durham: Duke University Press, 1989).

36. Jonathan Saville, *Reader*, "Hoarse Opera" (May 15, 1986): 15(19):30–32.

37. Said comments: "My contention is that Orientalism is fundamentally a political doctrine willed over the Orient because the Orient was weaker than the West, which elided the Orient's difference with its weakness." Edward Said, *Orientalism* (1978; reprint New York: Vintage, 1979), p. 204. This remark follows a marvelous quotation from Nietzsche, "Truths are illusions about which one has forgotten that this is what they are" (p. 203). These "truths" obviously lead to the cultural imperialism of applying Western standards to Eastern art. For Miyoshi's article, see note 35 above.

38. Miyoshi, "Against the Native Grain," in *Postmodernism and Japan*, p. 536.

3. Suzuki Tadashi's Bacchae

1. Barthes says of Tokyo, "One of the two most powerful cities of modernity is thereby built around an opaque ring of walls, streams, roofs, and trees whose own center is no more than an evaporated notion, subsisting here, not in order to irradiate power, but to give to the entire urban movement the support of a central emptiness, forcing the traffic to make a perpetual detour. . . . In this manner we are told, the system of the imaginary is spread circularly, by detours and returns the length of an empty subject," Roland Barthes, *Empire of Signs*, trans. Richard Howard (New York: Hill and Wang, 1982). p. 32.

2. Isozaki Arata, "Of City, Nation, and Style," in Masao Miyoshi and H. D. Harootunian, eds., *Postmodernism and Japan*, (Durham: Duke University Press, 1989), p. 58.

3. Karatani Kojin, "One Spirit, Two Nineteenth Centuries," in *Postmodernism and Japan*, p. 271.

4. Suzuki Tadashi is quoted in the *SCOT* Program, p. 13.

5. Michael Cacoyannis, "Translator's Introduction," *Euripides: The Bacchae* (New York: New American Library, Mentor Books, 1982), p. xii.

6. I develop this idea in "'Vengeance is Mine,' ll. 877–81: *Philia* Gone Awry in the Chorus of Euripides' *Bacchae*," *Proceedings of the Third International Meeting of Ancient Greek Drama*, Delphi, June 24–28, 1987 (Athens: European Cultural Centre of Delphi, 1989), pp. 41–49. The chorus, as the god Dionysus, goes to extremes. Although the chorus spouts the equivalent of Delphic platitudes (such as "nothing in excess") it goes too far. Democracy and moderation may be the text, but murder is the message, and we "are left with the image of revenge in practice, the opposite of *philia*" (p. 48). This is typical of many revolutions and all civil wars, particularly the civil war Euripides himself knew (if I may be allowed to characterize the Peloponnesian War as a civil war).

7. See Edward Said, *Orientalism* (1978; reprint, New York: Vintage, 1979) who concludes, "I hope to have shown my reader that the answer to Orientalism is not

Occidentalism. . . . If the knowledge of Orientalism has any meaning, it is in being a reminder of the seductive degradation of knowledge, of any knowledge, anywhere, at any time" (p. 328).

8. Karel Van Wolferen, *The Enigma of Japanese Power* (New York: Knopf, 1989), p. 9.

9. For an interesting treatment of the major oppositions see Charles Segal *Dionysiac Poetics and Euripides' Bacchae* (Princeton: Princeton University Press, 1982). He sees an ultimate merging of oppositions in the ecstatic experience: "The figure of the king, focus of world order, social stability, emotional coherence, becomes a field for the systematic reversal of ritual, domestic, and civic order and heroic values. Through the shifts from active to passive, the king also becomes the field for the confusion of the basic syntax not only of language but of all reality, that system of logical correspondences through which we find, or make, coherence in our world and in our ever-changing selves. In these reversals the role of the god becomes no less ambiguous than that of the mortal hero" (p. 346).

Coherence, if there is any, Segal sees in the organizational and creative ability of the artist—e.g., Euripides, who "has given this play a highly formalized, traditional structure, marked by careful articulation of the parts, striking beauty of language, intricate strength and deliberate orderliness of design," a counterbalance to "the random creativeness, and destructiveness, of the smiling god" (p. 347). Suzuki subverts this orderliness. Has "the smiling god" won in the end?

10. Although I disagree with many of Van Wolferen's generalizations, perhaps the way he summarizes political control in Japan is appropriate here: "The administrators of post-war Japan have been able to create a world in which socio-political disorder threatening their security and peace of mind is kept to a minimum. Japan's political culture, shaped by a succession of political arrangements in which the cult of submission has been a major common denominator, helps them to do this. This tradition discourages individual growth and fosters dependency. The Japanese accept a high degree of organization and restrictions; they tolerate the ways that officials meddle in their lives, and do not question their permanent political tutelage. Very few can conceive of civil disobedience as legitimate political action" (*Enigma of Japanese Power*, p. 366). This conformity extends even to the arts: "The 'perfect' way of doing anything is comparable to the rigid expectations in communal behavior; the performer must, as it were, live up to the model. According to Japanese learning methods, the skill or art has an authoritative and predetermined existence demanding subservience. There is no room for idiosyncratic variation to suit the practitioner's individual aptitude or taste" (p. 379). One might even apply this to the Suzuki method, which demands rigid compliance.

11. Thomas Rosenmeyer describes Pentheus as coming full circle: he has assumed Dionysus' identity; he has become what he tried to suppress and destroy: "He is woman and child and beast, an amorphous organism susceptible to all influences and realizing itself in a life of instinct and unthinking sense. The victory of Dionysus is complete; the king is dead, and the man has been found out, in the god's image." "*Bacchae* and *Ion*: Tragedy and Religion," in *The Masks of Tragedy* (New York: Gordian Press, 1971), p. 149.

12. Leonard C. Pronko, *Theater East and West: Perspectives Toward a Total Theater* (1967; reprint Berkeley: University of California Press, 1974), p. 145.

13. Masao Miyoshi, "Against the Native Grain: The Japanese Novel and the 'postmodern' West," in Masao Miyoshi and H. D. Harootunian, eds., *Postmodernism and Japan* (Durham: Duke University Press, 1989), p. 148.

14. R. P. Winnington-Ingram, *Euripides and Dionysus* (Amsterdam: Hakkert,

1969), p. 179. G. M. A. Grube claims that both schools ("recantation of an aging atheist" versus "another attack upon religion, another exposure of a god, another work by Euripides the rationalist") are wrong, because "they put the poet himself in front of the play instead of behind it." *The Drama of Euripides* (1941; reprint with corrections, London: Methuen, 1973), pp. 398–99.

15. See Edward S. Herman and Noam Chomsky, *Manufacturing Consent: The Political Economy of the Mass Media* (New York: Pantheon, 1988).

16. John Dower, *War Without Mercy: Race and Power in the Pacific War* (New York: Pantheon, 1986).

4. *Peter Sellars* Ajax

1. For example, "Medea is presented to the audience in the unmistakable style and language of the Sophoclean hero." Bernard Knox, "The *Medea* of Euripides," in *Greek Tragedy*, Yale Classical Studies, 25(Cambridge: Cambridge University Press, 1977), p. 198. See also Marianne McDonald, "Cacoyannis and Euripides' *Iphigenia at Aulis*: A New Heroism," in *Euripides in Cinema: The Heart Made Visible* (Philadelphia: Centrum, 1983), pp. 129–91.

2. Much work has been done on the notion of *philia*, and in particular *philia* in Euripides. See Marianne McDonald, "Iphigenia's *Philia*: Motivation in Euripides' *Iphigenia at Aulis*," *Quaderni Urbinati di Cultura Classica* (1990) Nuova Serie 34(1):69–84. Schein says, "*philoi* and *philia* provide some consolation and compassion, which makes the suffering not understandable, for Euripides rarely allows that, but endurable." Seth Schein, "Mythical Illusion and Historical Reality in Euripides' *Orestes*," *Wiener Studien* (1975)9:50–66. So also we have Ute Schmidt-Berger, "Philia: Typologie der Freundschaft und Verwandtschaft bei Euripides" (Ph.D.: Diss., Eberhard-Karls-Universität, Tübingen, 1975); James Tyler, "*Philia* and *Echthra* in Euripides" (Ph.D.: Diss., Cornell University, 1969); and Samuel Edward Scully, "*Philia* and *Charis* in Euripidean Tragedy" (Ph.D.: Diss., University of Toronto, 1973).

General studies of *philia* include Jean-Claude Fraisse, *Philia: La notion d'amitié dans la philosophie antique* (Paris: Librairie Philosophique J. Vrin, 1974); L. Dugas, *L'amitié antique d'après les moeurs populaires et les théories des philosophes* (Paris: Felix Alcan, 1894); Horst Hutter, *Politics as Friendship: The Origins of Classical Notions of Politics in the Theory and Practice of Friendship* (Toronto, Canada: Wilfrid Laurier University Press, 1978); and Ronald A. Sharp, *Friendship and Literature: Spirit and Form* (Durham: Duke University Press, 1986). See also David Konstan, "*Philia* in Euripides' *Electra*," *Philologus* (1985), 129(2):176–85; and A. W. H. Adkins, "'Friendship' and 'Self-Sufficiency' in Homer and Aristotle," *CQ* (1963), 13:30–46.

3. There is a great debate on what is dominant in Greek tragedy, particularly whether character or plot, and then again what constitutes character. Tycho von Wilamowitz-Moellendorff, for instance, reacted violently to earlier psychologically oriented interpretations of character, *Die dramatische Technik des Sophokles* (Berlin, 1917); see the discussion in R. P. Winnington-Ingram, *Sophocles: An Interpretation* (Cambridge: Cambridge University Press, 1980), pp. 6–8. Thomas Rosenmeyer, in abstracting the reason that Greek tragedy is revived, says, "The appeal must have something to do with the characters or rather with the desires and the refusals of those characters, with what Aristotle calls their *ēthē*," *Proceedings of the Second International Meeting of Ancient Greek Drama*, Delphi, June 15–20, 1986 (Athens: European Cultural Centre of Delphi, 1989), p. 23.

4. For a discussion of Ajax in the epic tradition, and also the suggestion that it was Sophocles' addition that Ajax offended Athena, see Sir Richard C. Jebb, *Sophocles: The Plays and Fragments with Critical Notes, Commentary, and Translation*, vol. 7: *The Ajax* (Cambridge: Cambridge University Press, 1907; reprint, Amsterdam: Hakkert, 1967), "Introduction," 7:ix–liv.

5. Thomas Rosenmeyer, *The Masks of Tragedy* (New York: Gordian Press, 1971), pp. 168 and 170.

6. Rosenmeyer, *The Masks of Tragedy*, p. 198.

7. Bernard Knox, *The Heroic Temper* (Berkeley: University of California Press, 1966), p. 42.

8. Knox, *Heroic Temper*, p. 36.

9. Charles Segal, *Tragedy and Civilization: An Interpretation of Sophocles* (Cambridge: Harvard University Press, 1981), p. 110.

10. Georgios Anagnostopoulos discussed wars now fought by machines instead of humans in his course on "Philosophy and Technology," taught at The University of California, San Diego in spring 1984.

11. This quotation and the ones that will be cited from the play are from the unpublished script by Robert Auletta, "Sophocles' Ajax: A Modern Version by Robert Auletta" (1986).

12. For the phrase and dynamics of textual "molestation and power," see Edward Said, *Beginnings: Intention and Method* (1978; reprint Baltimore and London: Johns Hopkins University Press, 1975), p. 137 and passim.

13. In the 1986 production, Tecmessa was played by Lauren Tom.

14. Karl Reinhardt, *Sophocles*, trans. Hazel Harvey and David Harvey (New York: Barnes and Noble, 1979), p. 130.

15. Jebb, *Sophocles: The Plays and Fragments*, 7:xxxii. M. Sicherl agrees in his "Die Tragik des Aias," *Hermes* (1970), 98:14–37, as does R. P. Winnington-Ingram, who has two chapters dealing with the first and second part of the *Ajax*, calling the first, "The Mind of Ajax," and the second, "The Burial of Ajax," in *Sophocles: An Interpretation*.

16. Reinhardt, *Sophocles*, p. 130.

17. See Edward S. Herman and Noam Chomsky, *Manufacturing Consent: The Political Economy of the Mass Media*, (New York: Pantheon, 1988).

18. Some interesting questions about this play asked by Albert Liu: "Are we—precious humanity that must be saved—only a repository for the remembrance of heroes? Does the disappearance of heroes signify an obliteration of our collective memory? Do we demand this death in order to constitute our memory, to make *us*? In that case, it's no longer a question of 'them or us,' but a much more complex, integrated reciprocity governing the relationship between the hero and the polis."

19. Physical deafness reflects the breakdown in communication between Ajax and his contemporaries, as various commentators have noted. In reference to Tecmessa and Ajax, Reinhardt says, "in the epic they speak to each other, in the tragedy they speak without communicating with each other for each speaks his own language to which the other does not listen. The words of the wife die away without a syllable having reached her husband's ears, and vice versa." *Sophocles*, p. 21.

20. Joseph Conrad once commented, "Say what you like, man lives in his eccentricities (so called) alone. They give vigour to his personality which mere consistency can never do" (November 11, 1901). Gerard Jean-Aubry, *Joseph Conrad: Life and Letters* (Garden City, N.Y.: Doubleday, 1927), 1:301; quoted in Said, *Beginnings*, p. 125.

6. Tony Harrison's The Trackers

1. Rainer Maria Rilke, "Orpheus.Eurydike.Hermes," in *New Poems [1907]*, trans. Edward Snow (San Francisco: North Point Press, 1984), p.172. This translation is my own.

2. The iambic trimeter of the satyr play is more flexible than in tragedy; we find, for example, violations of Porson's Law and anapests appearing in the iambics outside of the first foot. There are rare words and often words ending in *-ma*, besides a certain colloquial usage (although A. C. Pearson notes that the *Ichneutai* is less colloquial than the *Cyclops*). There is an excellent discussion of the satyr play in general and the *Ichneutai* in particular with acute linguistic and metrical observations by R. G. Ussher, "Sophocles' *Ichneutai* as a Satyr Play," *Hermathena* (1974), 118: 130–38. Pearson's remark about the *Cyclops* being more colloquial than the *Ichneutai* is found in his introduction to *The Fragments of Sophocles*, 3 vols. (Cambridge: Cambridge University Press, 1917), 1:229. See also his "Notes on Sophocles' *Ichneutae* and *Eurypylus*," CR 26 (1912): 26:209–12.

3. David Konstan has written an insightful article discussing the satyr's relation to man and also the Cyclops, so that the satyr is a type of mediating figure: "The triplet of man, Cyclops, and satyr is structured by the logic of exchange in such a way that the two hybrid types, who blur the boundary between man and beast, appear as two modes of negation. With respect to each other they are at once similar and contrary, while the human community appears as the positive realization of social relations." "An Anthropology of Euripides' *Cyclops*," *Ramus* (1981), 1(1):100.

In the *Ichneutai* there are no humans, or monsters, to help form one typical triad found in satyr plays. Satyrs are somehow to be valued as between man and monster, hardly, as Dana F. Sutton claims that, "Although he is less than human, he embodies a kind of wisdom: he represents what man can and should be." *The Greek Satyr Play* (Meisenheim am Glan: Verlag Anton Hain, 1980), p. 179. Man can certainly learn from the satyr, but one might question the satyr as an all-encompassing role model. Sutton is perhaps making the point that the satyr is not neurotic, civilized man is, so man can learn from the satyr: "The satyr can be and, as we shall see in the final chapter of this book, has been pressed into service as a symbol of man in his ideal state, living according to Nature, uncorrupted by civilization and its discontents, not neurotic" (pp. 178–79). This claim seems rather simplistic, besides naive, and in this resembles most "back to nature" theories in which "nature" is a utopia. In contrast to Sutton, Harrison exploits the symbolic complexities of the satyr.

4. A useful discussion of the origin of the satyr play can be found in the introduction in D. M. Simmonds and R. R. Timberlake, eds., *Euripides' The Cyclops* (Cambridge: Cambridge University Press, 1963), pp. ix–xiv. Richard Seaford also gives useful information in his introduction to Euripides' *Cyclops* (Oxford: Clarendon Press, 1984). Pratinas, from Phlius in the Peloponnesus, was said to be the originator of the satyr play. It is likely that the fragments that we have are from a later Pratinas, perhaps from the later fifth century. I owe the suggestion of a later Pratinas to Thomas Rosenmeyer, who in turn said that Hugh Lloyd-Jones convinced him of this. The arguments in the fragments have a similarity to Aristophanes, and therefore support a later date.

5. That tragedy popularized earlier aristocratic art forms is a commonplace: see the "Introduction" by J. Peter Euben, *Greek Tragedy and Political Theory* (Berkeley and Los Angeles: University of California Press, 1986). Much, of course, has been written on the topic of tragedy and comedy in their social context and, for some of

the latest theories, see John J. Winkler and Froma I. Zeitlin, eds., *Nothing to Do with Dionysus: Athenian Drama in Its Social Context* (Princeton: Princeton University Press, 1990). For some interesting suggestions on the relation between tragedy and comedy see Bernard Knox, "Euripidean Comedy" in *Word and Action* (1979; reprint Baltimore: Johns Hopkins University Press, 1986), pp. 250–74.

6. Dana F. Sutton, "The Relation Between Tragedies and Fourth Place Plays in Three Instances," *Arethusa* (1971), 4:55–72. In particular, Apollo's search for the thief who has stolen his cattle in *Ichneutai* recalls Odysseus' search for the killer of the cattle in *Ajax*. There are also double choruses in both. Sutton further notes linguistic and structural parallels. He also makes a case for Euripides' *Andromeda* being followed by *Helen*, and the *Cyclops* following *Hecuba*.

7. Jane Harrison, "Sophocles' *Ichneutai* Col. ix 1–7 and the *dromenon* of Kyllene and the Satyrs," in *Essays and Studies Presented to William Ridgeway* (Cambridge: Cambridge University Press, 1914), p. 147.

8. See the article by Dana F. Sutton on the satyr play in *The Cambridge History of Classical Literature* (Cambridge: Cambridge University Press, 1985), 1:353; see also Sutton, *The Greek Satyr Play*.

9. In a talk given at the University of California, San Diego, in April, 1988; see also Shirley Strum's book, *Almost Human* (New York: Random House, 1987).

10. Igor Stravinsky, *The Poetics of Music in the Form of Six Lessons* (Cambridge: Harvard University Press, Massachusetts, 1947), p. 65, quoted in Tony Harrison, "The *Oresteia* in the Making," *Omnibus*, JACT Jubilee Issue (July 1987), p. 52.

11. These words are from Plotinus, quoted in Jacques Derrida's *Speech and Phenomena*, trans. David B. Allison (Evanston, Ill.: Northwestern University Press, 1973), p. 107. The trace is a vestige of truth left behind when immanence (or the god) vanished. The word is then the trace of the thing that is desired; it simultaneously marks the thing *and* its absence.

12. See the introduction to William Arrowsmith's translation of the *Cyclops* in *Euripides*, Grene and Lattimore, eds. (Chicago: University of Chicago Press, 1956): "He [Cyclops] speaks exactly the language of Plato's Thrasymachus and Callicles, a straightforward egoism resting on an appeal to Nature for the disregard of morality" (2:8).

13. Ussher, "Sophocles' *Ichneutai*," p.137.

14. Harrison quotes Lion Feuchtwanger at the beginning of his *Dramatic Verse, 1973–1985* (Newcastle upon Tyne: Bloodaxe Books, 1985):

I, for instance, sometimes write
Adaptations. Or some people prefer the phrase
"Based on," and this is how it is: I use
Old material to make a new play, then
Put under the title
The name of the dead writer who is extremely
Famous and quite unknown, and before
The name of the dead writer I put the little word
"After"
Then one group will write that I am
Very respectful and others that I am nothing of the
sort and all
The dead writer's failures
Will be ascribed

To me and all my successes
To the dead writer who is extremely
Famous and quite unknown, and of whom
Nobody knows whether he himself
Was the writer or maybe the
Adaptor.

With *The Trackers,* Harrison has indeed made a new play while reviving the ancient text.

15. Harrison, *Dramatic Verse,* p. 201.

16. The ancient texts are filters for modern ideas. A modern can only see the past from his own perspective; he can never know the past as one who was of that past time. Adkins, Snell, and others have tried to reconstruct value systems of antiquity, tracing a development and progress from Homer to the fifth century, which other scholars have refined or refuted (e.g., Lloyd-Jones, Rosenmeyer, Long, and Gagarin). Although such an attempt is admirable, ancient values seem as difficult to determine as ancient pronunciation, and often tend to serve more as a Rorschach test for the interpreter.

See Arthur W. H. Adkins, *Merit and Responsibility* (Oxford:Oxford University Press, 1960), Bruno Snell, *Die Entdeckung des Geistes,* 4th revised edition (Göttingen: Vandenhoeck & Ruprecht, 1975), *The Discovery of the Mind,* trans. Thomas Rosenmeyer into English (Oxford: Oxford University Press, 1953), Hugh Lloyd-Jones, *The Justice of Zeus* (Berkeley: University of California Press, 1971). Snell's idea of choice in Homer has been further revised and refined by Thomas Rosenmeyer, who shows how limited choice actually is in tragedy, whereas there was a relative freedom in Homer, in "Wahlakt und Entscheidungsprozess in der antiken Tragödie," *Poetica* (1978) vol.10, no.1. There is a fascinating answer by Long to Adkins: A. A. Long, "Morals and Values in Homer," *JHS* (1970), 90(4):121–39. The discussion goes on: Michael Gagarin, "Morality in Homer," *CP* (1987), 82(4):285–306, and Hugh Lloyd-Jones, "A Note on Homeric Morality," in the same issue, pp. 307–10 and finally, A. W. H. Adkins, "Gagarin and the 'Morality' of Homer," also in the same issue, pp. 311–22.

17. Tony Harrison, "Them & [uz]," I and II in *Selected Poems* (1984; reprint, Middlesex: Penguin), pp. 122–23.

18. For the translations and recreations of Martial see *Tony Harrison, U.S. Martial* (Newcastle upon Tyne: Bloodaxe Books, 1981); for Palladas see Tony Harrison, *Palladas: Poems,* 2d ed. (London: Anvil Press, 1984).

19. Tony Harrison, V. (Newcastle upon Tyne: Bloodaxe Books, 1985).

20. Harrison, "Durham," in *Selected Poems,* p. 70.

21. Harrison, *Dramatic Verse,* p. 87.

22. Following an interview with Tony Harrison, Rosemary Burton says, "As it stands the production of the *Oresteia* is not quite as he would have liked. The trilogy as presented seems to end with the arrival of democracy, the surrender of the Furies. Harrison believes that the whole work is about the historical defeat of women. 'You should feel that, like [the villainous] "Jaws" in the James Bond film, the Furies will be back, and that there is only a specious resolution.' " Rosemary Burton, "Tony Harrison," *Quarto* (May 1982), 28:7. Harrison said in a letter to Peter Hall about the *Oresteia,* "My own feeling is that the feminist movement is the next thing to make us reassess our lives and societies. Our futures depend on it." Harrison, "The Oresteia," *Omnibus,* p. 52. And R. B. Parker quotes from Harrison's notes in the program to the *Oresteia:* "Though it is a fact that men played all the parts of the

Oresteia in 458 B.C., that in itself is not of course sufficient justification for our wish to have an all-male company. The victory of father-right over mother-right is the social pendulum of the trilogy. To have women play in our production would have seemed as if we in the twentieth century were smugly assuming that the sex war was over and that the oppressiveness of the patriarchal code existed only in past times. The maleness of the piece is like a vacuum-sealed container keeping this ancient issue fresh." "The National Theatre's *Oresteia*, 1981–82." In Martin Cropp, Elaine Fantham, S. E. Scully eds., *Greek Tragedy and its Legacy: Essays Presented to D. J. Conacher* (Calgary, Alta: University of Calgary Press, 1986), p. 353. In *The Big H* both males and females head the Herodic Prel ("pro rege et lege"; read also "regina" for "rege") death squads.

23. Harrison in Burton's interview said, "There's a certain amount of relief in translating. It's not that the work has been done for you, but it comes from not having to face a destructive and hostile milieu alone," Burton, "Tony Harrison," *Quarto*, p. 7.

24. I disagree with Sutton's claim that "The essential business of tragedy is to proclaim that there is a natural order of things, a determinative world-order against which one transgresses at his peril" (*The Greek Satyr Play*, p. 158). Even if this were remotely true of Aeschylus' plays, it could not possibly be true of Euripides'. Does Euripides' *Orestes*, or his *Heracles*, or his *Medea* show us "a determinative world-order against which one transgresses at his peril?" Or his *Heracles*? Or his *Medea*?

25. Harrison, "A Kumquat for John Keats," in *Selected Poems*, p. 182.

26. See Stefan Radt's text, *Tragicorum Graecorum Fragmenta*, vol. 4 (Göttingen: Vandenhoeck & Ruprecht, 1977). Also useful is E. V. Maltese, *Sofocle Ichneutae, Papyrologica Florentina*, vol. 10 (Florence: Edizioni Gonnelli, 1982).

27. Harrison, "A Kumquat for John Keats," in *Selected Poems*, p. 184.

28. "Irony, with intuitive double vision, can see where God is to be found in a world abandoned by God . . . the highest freedom that can be achieved in a world without God." Georg Lukács, *Theory of the Novel*, trans. Anna Bostock (1971; reprint Cambridge: Harvard University Press, 1985), pp. 92–93. See also Paul de Man, *Blindness and Insight* (1971, reprint Minneapolis: University of Minnesota Press, 1983), p. 56: " . . . irony [in Lukacs] as the positive power of an absence." Are we back to the ambiguous trace as the form of the formless?

29. I owe some of these connections to Fredric Jameson's talk on Adorno's theory of art at the University of California, San Diego, in April 1988. There is also an interesting chapter on Adorno in Jameson, *Marxism and Form* (Princeton: Princeton University Press, 1971), pp. 3–59.

7. *Tony Harrison's* Medea: A Sex-War Opera

1. Tony Harrison, *Dramatic Verse: 1973–1985* (Newcastle Upon Tyne: Bloodaxe Books, 1985), pp. 363–448.

2. See B. M. W. Knox: . . . Medea is presented to the audience in the unmistakable style and language of the Sophoclean hero." He sees the "energy she had wasted on Jason . . . tempered to a deadly instrument to destroy him. It became a *theos*, a relentless merciless force, the unspeakable violence of the oppressed and betrayed which, because it has been so long pent up, carries everything before it to destruction, even if it destroys also what it loves most." "The *Medea* of Euripides," *YCS* 25 (1977), 25:193–225.

Elizabeth Bongie also saw Medea as a hero: " Euripides gives another portrait of a woman and a wife, one whose character and principles, however, have their closest affinities, not with Alcestis and women of her kind, but rather with the great male heroes of Greek literature such as the Homeric Achilles and the Sophoclean Ajax." "Heroic Elements in the *Medea* of Euripides," *TAPA* (1977), 107: 27–56. Cf. the earlier and more general comment by D. J. Conacher: "Jason plays the sophist to a heroic Medea." *Euripidean Drama* (Toronto, Canada: University of Toronto Press, 1967), p. 189.

3. For Knox, see note 2. According to Denys L. Page: "Because she was a witch she could escape in a magic chariot," *Euripides Medea* (1938; reprint Oxford: Oxford University Press, 1967), p. xxi. For Medea as primarily woman and mother, see Kawashima Shigenari, "Literary Criticism in Euripides' *Medea*" (Delphi Festival, 1989); and also "Man and Beyond in Euripides' *Medea*: Another Interpretation of 1062–63 and 1078–80," *Proceedings of the International Christian University* (1987), 4(B):79–101.

4. See Philip E. Slater, *The Glory of Hera: Greek Mythology and the Greek Family* (Boston: Beacon Press, 1968). But the monster mother seems preferred to the monster wife, and it is for this reason that Medea goes free and Clytemnestra is punished. "Medea . . . slaughters her brother, her children, two kings, and a princess, and attempts the life of Athens' most famous hero. Does the murder of one's husband, then, outweigh all of these crimes? The answer is, of course, that it did. The marital bond was the weakest point in the Greek family, and the murderous hatred of a wife for her husband was felt to be the greatest potential danger and had therefore to be guarded against with the most rigid care and punished with the most compulsive severity" (Slater, p. 164). Mother as monster now reappears in the modern mythology of horror films and science fiction thrillers; see Lynda K. Buntzen, "Monstrous Mothers: Medusa, Grendel, and now Alien," *Film Quarterly* (1987), 40(3):11–17.

5. Bruno Snell, *The Discovery of the Mind*, trans. Thomas Rosenmeyer (New York: Harper & Row, 1960); see also his *Scenes from Greek Drama* (Berkeley: University of California Press, 1967), p. 60: "For these words of Socrates, directed against the assertion that a man could have insight and yet lack self-control, we need only presuppose Euripides' Medea, who knows so exactly where her path is leading her."

6. Many have dealt with the interpretation of this passage, and the general inconsistencies of this monologue—from questions concerning the presence of the children to those concerning Medea's motivations and changes thereof, see, for example, Hans Diller, "*Thumos de Kreissōn tōn emōn Bouleumatōn*," *Hermes* (1966), 94:267–75; G. A. Seeck, "Euripides, *Medea* 1059–68: A Problem of Interpretation," *GRBS* (1968), 9:291–307; M. D. Reeve, "Euripides, *Medea* 1021–80," *CQ* (1972), 65:51–61.

The power of *thumos*, whether anger or passion, is unquestioned, and Knox sees Medea at the end of the play as deified *thumos* (see note 2). James Diggle has eliminated this passage from his edition. Another interesting discussion is Bernd Seidensticker, "Euripides, *Medea* 1056–1080, An Interpolation," in Mark Griffith and Donald Mastronarde, eds., *Cabinet of the Muses: Essays on Classical and Comparative Literature in Honor of Thomas G. Rosenmeyer* (Atlanta: Scholars Press, 1990), pp. 89–102. He accepts these lines as authentic, meaning her *thumos* is "stronger than the considerations of her motherly love" (Seidensticker, *Cabinet of the Muses*, p. 98).

7. "Medea herself is really the only one capable of resisting Medea," *Euripidean Drama*, p. 195.

8. This immortal fame is the "kleos aphthiton" of Achilles (*Il*.9.413), which is most important to Medea as pointed out by Jason; this is what he gave her by bringing her from Colchis to Greece (*Med*. 541: "doxan eches . . ."). He says that if she had stayed on that far-flung shore (Colchis), then she would not be spoken of: "Would I have neither gold in my house, nor sing a song sweeter than Orpheus' if my fortune did not have fame." And Medea wants to be known for helping her friends and harming her enemies (cf. *Od*. 6.184–85 and passim). As she says, "The life with the fairest fame is concerned with this: being a threat to one's enemies and kind to one's friends" (*Med*. 809–10). In lines 404–6 she says specifically that what she has suffered should not provide material for laughter to the sons of Sisyphus, her in-laws by Jason, she who is a child of the royal father Helios; in line 797 she says more generally, "Friends, it would be unbearable to be laughed at by one's enemies." And one of her final taunts to Jason, in response to his saying that she shares his sorrow, is that her "pain has profit as long as he cannot laugh" (1361–62). Euripides' Phaedra also takes the terrible vengeance that she does for the sake of the public perception of her honor (cf. *Hipp*. 715 ff.); her death will ensure that she leave her children a life of fair fame.

See also Bennett Simon, *Tragic Drama and the Family: Psycholanalytic Studies from Aeschylus to Beckett* (New Haven: Yale University Press, 1988). He points out "the extreme frequency of 'my' and 'mine' in the play [*Medea*] and the rarity of 'us' and 'our,' " citing Marianne McDonald, *A Semilemmatized Concordance to Euripides' Medea*, (Irvine, Calif.: TLG Publications, 1978). This self-centering in the *Medea* suggests epic values that are oriented towards self-validation more than the social conscience so needed by the *polis*. Thomas MacCary, for instance, cites the "famous speech of Sarpedon to Glaukos" as "a clear statement of the necessity for the hero to risk his life to prove his existence." *Childlike Achilles* (New York: Columbia University Press, 1982), p. 115. He fights not for any political purpose, but rather to prove himself to himself.

9. See note 8; also Medea's speech *Med*. 465ff.: she has sacrificed all for Jason and bore him children. Because of her crimes on his behalf, she has no place to which she can return. As she says, she was more "devoted than wise" (485). She harnessed all her wisdom to his service. Now the man who was everything to her has betrayed her (228–29). Jules Dassin in his *Dream of Passion* (Greece, 1978), another modern reworking of the Medea myth, quotes these lines several times throughout the film. Dassin does not focus so much on Medea's crimes, but rather on what could motivate her to commit them.

10. Harrison, *Dramatic Verse*, p. 432.

11. Erich Neumann, *The Great Mother: An Analysis of the Archetype*, trans. Ralph Manheim, Bollingen Series 47 (1963; reprint Princeton: Princeton University Press, 1972), p. 288. Harrison also quotes Joseph Campbell: "In the older mother myths and rites the light and darker aspects of the mixed thing that is life had been honored equally and together, whereas in the later, male-oriented patriarchal myths, all that is good and noble was attributed to the new, heroic master gods, leaving to the native nature powers the character only of darkness—to which also a negative moral judgement now was added," *The Masks of God: Occidental Mythology* (1964; reprint New York: Penguin, 1976), p. 21.

12. Cf. what Medea says in a modern version by Carol Sorgenfrei: "Nurse: 'You did what no normal woman would care to do,' Medea: 'I did what all normal women wish to do,' " *A Noh Cycle based on the Greek Myth* (Toronto: Samuel French, 1975), p. 15.

13. Bachofen, *Myth, Religion and Mother Right: Selected Writings of J. J.*

Bachofen, trans. Ralph Manheim, Bollingen Series 84 (Princeton: Princeton University Press, 1973), p. 176; originally, *Johann Jakob Bachofen: Mutterrecht und Urreligion* (Stuttgart: Kroners Taschenausgabe, Vol. 52, 1954).

14. Harrison, *Dramatic Verse*, p. 434.

15. Harrison, *Dramatic Verse*, p. 438.

16. Harrison, *Dramatic Verse*, p. 433. As corroboration of this thesis, see the feminist unmasking of the women masked by men in modern opera, in Catherine Clément, *Opera, or the Undoing of Women*, trans. Betsy Wing, with a foreword by usan McClary (Minneapolis: University of Minnesota Press, 1988).

17. Edward Said, *Orientalism* (1978; reprint, New York: Vintage, 1979), p. 328. Cf. also the attack on the religion of "Freudianism" by Gilles Deleuze and Felix Guattari, *Anti-Oedipus: Capitalism and Schizophrenia*, trans. Robert Hurley, Mark Seem and Helen R. Lane, (1977; reprint Minneapolis: University of Minnesota Press, 1983); originally, *L'Anti-Oedipe* (Paris: Les Editions de Minuit, 1972).

18. There are many studies that show the reworking of the drama of *Medea*, e.g., Wolf-Harmut Friedrich, "Medeas Rache" (1960; reprinted in Ernst-Richard Schwinge, ed. *Euripides* (Darmstadt: Wissenschaftliche Buchgesellschaft, 1968), pp. 177–237; *Medeia: Mélanges Interdisciplinaires sur la figure de Medée*, in *Cahiers du Gita* (October 1986), 2:1–168; Joachim Schondorff, ed. *Medea: Euripides, Seneca, Corneille, Cherubini, Grillparzer, Jahnn, Anouilh, Jeffers, Braun* (Munich and Vienna: Theater der Jahrhunderte, 1963).

19. Bachofen, quoted in Neumann, *The Great Mother*, p. 265.

20. This quotation from Sophocles' *Tereus* prefaces a chapter called "Bearing Children, Watching the House," in Eva Keuls, *The Reign of the Phallus* (New York: Harper and Row, 1985), pp. 98–128. This book is a powerful documentation of the abuse of women in antiquity, but according to Keuls, "Compared to his modern equivalent . . . the Athenian Greek was an amateur in the exploitation of the women of his own class for his material comfort" (p.99). She also has a chapter called "Brides of Death, in More Ways than One," which includes a section on "The Bride as Symbolic Victim" (pp. 130–132) . See also Helene P. Foley for her interpretation of Iphigenia's sacrifice as a perverted marriage ritual, in *Ritual Irony: Poetry and Sacrifice in Euripides* (Ithaca: Cornell University Press, 1985); and R. A. S. Seaford's illuminating article, "The Tragic Wedding," *JHS* (1987) 107:106–130.

21. Harrison, *Dramatic Verse*, p. 385.

22. Tony Harrison, "A Kumquat for John Keats, in *Selected Poems* (1984; reprint Middlesex, England: Penguin, 1986), p. 182.

23. Harrison, *Dramatic Verse*, pp. 401–2.

24. This quotation, and the three that follow are from Tony Harrison's *The Fire Gap* (Newcastle upon Tyne: Bloodaxe Books, 1985).

9. Theodoros Terzopoulos' Production of Heiner Müller's Medeamaterial: *Myth as Matter*

1. Manfred Kraus, "Heiner Müller und die griechische Tragödie," *Poetica* (1985) 17(3–4):299–339.

2. See the interview at the end of Heiner Müller, *Hamletmachine and Other Texts for the Stage*, ed. and trans. Carl Weber (New York: Performing Arts Journal Publications, 1984), p. 137. This text contains the English text for *Verkommenes Ufer Madeamaterial Landschaft mit Argonauten* (*Despoiled Shore Medeamaterial Landscape with Argonauts*). The German text to which we refer is in *Theater heute* (1983) 6:36–38.

3. Müller, *Hamletmachine*, p. 139.

4. "The novel is the epic of a world abandoned by God." Georg Lukács, The Theory of the Novel, trans. Anna Bostock (Cambridge, Mass.: MIT Press, 1971), p.88; originally, Die Theorie des Romans: Ein Geschichtsphilosophischer Versuch über die Formen der grossen Epik (Berlin: P. Cassirer, 1920).

5. Müller, *Hamletmachine*, p. 45.

6. Heiner Müller, in "Ein finsteres Stück," *Theater heute*, (1968), 8:28–31.

7. Müller, *Hamletmachine*, p. 122.

8. *Theater heute* (1983), 6:37.

9. *Verkommenes Ufer*, p. 38.

10. Müller, *Hamletmachine*, p. 122. Note also the close connection between man and nature. We find much the same in Gilles Deleuze and Feliz Guattari: "There is no such thing as either man or nature now, only a process. . . . We make no distinction between man and nature." *Anti-Oedipus: Capitalism and Schizophrenia*, trans. Robert Hurley, Mark Seem, and Helen R. Lane (Minneapolis: University of Minnesota Press, 1983), p. 2 and 4. In this book, as in Müller's play, man is seen not only as a machine that has needs in order to function, but also as one that produces: man the machine absorbs and excretes. Will the earth ultimately absorb and excrete man?

11. Müller, *Hamletmachine*, p. 120.

12. Quoted in Kraus, "Heiner Müller," p. 313.

13. Kraus, "Heiner Müller," p. 325.

14. Müller, *Verkommenes Ufer*, p. 36.

15. Müller, *Hamletmachine*, p. 58.

16. Müller, *Verkommenes Ufer*, p. 37.

17. H. Rischbieter, ed. *Theater 1980: Jahrbuch der Zeitschrift Theater heute* (Velber bei Hannover: Friedrich, 1980), p. 135.

18. Quoted in Kraus, "Heiner Müller," p. 312.

19. Kraus, "Heiner Müller," p. 338.

11. Thomas Murphy's The Sanctuary Lamp

1. According to "the then President of Ireland, the late Cearbhall O' Dalaigh," quoted in Fintan O'Toole, *The Politics of Magic* (Dublin: Raven Arts Press, 1987), p. 13.

2. "American multinational industries began to establish themselves in Ireland: Hallmark Cards in 1958, Burlington Textiles in 1960, General Electric in 1962, until, by 1983, foreign firms had invested nearly six billion pounds in the Republic of Ireland, four and a half billion pounds of which came from America," O'Toole, *The Politics of Magic*, p. 29.

3. Thomas Murphy, *The Sanctuary Lamp* (1976; reprinted and revised, Dublin: Gallery Books, 1984), p. 8. All quotations and references to this play are from this edition.

4. Thomas Murphy, *The Gigli Concert* (1984; reprint, Dublin: Gallery Books, 1988), p. 48. All quotations and references to this play are from this edition. Johann Wolfgang von Goethe, *Faust*, Part II, trans. Philip Wayne (1933; reprint, Middlesex: Penguin Books, 1986), p. 209 (a translation of Helen's words to Faust: Ein altes Wort bewährt sich leider auch an mir: dass Gluck und Schönheit dauerhaft sich nicht vereint," lines 9939–40).

5. Cf. the chorus on happiness in Sophocles' *Oedipus Rex*: "Oh, race of man . . . I consider your happiness a mere seeming, and once seen, to disappear. . . . With your example, Oedipus, I count no man happy" (1186–95); or even more

appropriate here, Cassandra's words, "Oh, affairs of man, when they go well a shadow can overturn them, when they go badly, a wet sponge erases the trace" (*Ag.* 1327–29).

6. O'Toole's *The Politics of Magic* is filled with useful insights, and also informative background. There are some minor errors. For instance, in describing parallels with the *Oresteia* he says, "In the first place, it uses, as he does, the image of a family torn apart, the doomed House of Atreus in which father kills daughter, mother kills husband, and son kills father [sic], as the embodiment of the terrible turmoil in the relationship of man and God" (p. 146). The son, Orestes, kills the MOTHER (Clytemnestra), who had killed his father (Agamemnon). So also, O'Toole refers to "the Orestes of Euripides' *Iphigenia in Aulis,* who has, as Gilbert Murray puts it, 'the shadow of madness and guilt hanging over' him . . . ," but it is the Orestes of Euripides' *Iphigenia in Tauris* that O'Toole means, and he correctly cites this play in the notes. Euripides' Orestes of the play *Orestes* shows madness and guilt even more. I also differ with O'Toole's generalizations about Greek tragedy, namely, "Tragedy, for the Greeks, is the realization that man has outgrown the gods, that human anguish is no longer contained within the bounds of their moral imperatives," and also "The vision of absurdity implicit in Greek tragedy is one which has returned in the twentieth century theatre" (p. 145). Both of these statements might in some ways apply to plays by Euripides, but not to plays by either Aeschylus or Sophocles. Gods and men clash, to the detriment of both, and so do their imperatives. Greek tragedy presents us with dilemmas and paradoxes, so that somehow both the gods and man are responsible. The image of the gods and the image of man, particularly the "tragic hero," changes with each tragedian, so it is difficult to generalize in the way that O'Toole does. I also disagree with O'Toole's saying, "In this fundamental form, Christianity is in line with the Greek and Roman mythologies, where the past is represented as an everlasting foundation. . . . Conventional Christian thinking is bound together with Greek thought which is oriented to a static, all-embracing notion of 'being' and which is profoundly anti-historical in the sense of not being open to change and development" (p. 172).

This is again a simplistic generalization applied to both Christian and Greek thought. One can find a school that embraces this notion in each tradition, and one that does not. One might see a "static, all-embracing notion of 'being' " in Parmenides, and possibly Plato, but certainly not Heraclitus ("Everything flows") or Aristotle, who had quite sophisticated notions of "becoming." Protagoras' notion that "man was the measure of all things" led to the sophistic school, which advocated relativity even in moral issues; and Aristotle saw the good as a mean, hardly the static form envisioned by Plato.

7. Murphy, *The Sanctuary Lamp,* p. 30.

8. O' Toole, *The Politics of Magic,* p. 160.

9. W. B. Yeats, "The Fiddler of Dooney," in *The Celtic Twilight and a Selection of Early Poems* (New York: Signet, 1962), p. 193.

10. J. M. Synge, *The Playboy of the Western World,* in *Plays,* ed. Ann Saddlemyer (1968; reprint, Oxford: University Press, 1980), p. 163.

11. Synge, *Playboy of the Western World,* in *Plays,* p. 161. As Aeneas says on seeing the events of Troy depicted on Dido's walls, "Sunt lacrimae rerum et mentem mortalia tangunt" (Vergil, *Aeneid* ll. 461–62): "There are tears for things, and mortal affairs touch the mind," perhaps an echo of "Many events call for tears and touch the heart" (*Med.* 1221). See Marianne McDonald, *"Sunt Lacrimae Rerum,"* *Classical Journal,* (1972/3), 68:180–81. There is glory and fame in the performance, but tears for the losses. We recall Andromache laughing through her tears with

pride at Hector, but knowledge of what attends fame and his particular performance (*Il.* 6.484). See also the laughing contest based on the most sorrowful memories in Thomas Murphy's *Bailegangaire* (Dublin: Gallery Books, 1986), pp. 68–73.

12. Murphy, *The Sanctuary Lamp*, p. 17.

13. Thomas Rosenmeyer, *The Art of Aeschylus* (Berkeley: University of California Press, 1982), p. 376.

14. O'Toole, *The Politics of Magic*, p. 38.

15. O'Toole, *The Politics of Magic*, p. 149.

16. T. S. Eliot, *The Family Reunion* in *The Complete Poems and Plays, 1909–1950* (1930; reprint, New York: Harcourt Brace Jovanovich, 1980), p. 236. All quotations and references to this play are from this edition.

17. On the theme of a father who must be overcome in Irish literature in general and Murphy's plays in particular, see O'Toole, *The Politics of Magic*, pp. 54–56.

18. Murphy, *The Sanctuary Lamp*, pp. 49 and 39. Francisco's speech in general shows less education than Harry's (another possible contrast between the Irish Catholic and English Jew?).

19. Jean-Paul Sartre, *No Exit and Three Other Plays*, trans. Stuart Gilbert and Lionel Abel (1945; reprint, New York: Vintage Books, 1949), pp. 122 and 119. All quotations and references to Sartre's *The Flies* are from this edition.

20. Thomas Murphy, *Famine* (1977; reprint, Dublin: Gallery Books, 1984), p. 81.

21. Deane, in his brilliant and sensitive study of the Irish literary tradition, also pointed out that in *The Gigli Concert*, "Murphy had an indisputable triumph. Here he finds a means of demonstrating the subtle accord between actuality and fantasy and, in doing so, reminding us of the alliance between the drama and the Irish novel." *A Short History of Irish Literature* (Notre Dame, Ind.: University of Notre Dame Press, 1986), p. 247.

22. O'Toole, *The Politics of Magic*, p. 85.

23. O'Toole, *The Politics of Magic*, p. 108.

phenomenon, 59; spying on bacchants, 64-65, 70; subduing Dionysus, 68; as tyrant, 42-43, 62, 63
Perception, 194
Performance theater, 72
Persians, victories against, 78
Persians (Aeschylus), 129
Phaedra Britannica (Harrison), 108
Phaedriades, 100-101, 134
Pheres, 137
Philia (benevolent love), 18, 54, 75, 195-96
Philoctetes, 13, 76
Philoktet (Müller), 147, 150, 151-52
Pindar, 104, 106
Pinter, Harold, 113
Plato, 194; hero concept, 5; *methexis* concept, 4
Platonic tradition, 66
Play, as mirror of reality, 17
Play-within-a-play, Suzuki's *Bacchae* and, 61
Playwright, as clever liar, 17
Plutarch, 77, 119
Poetry, film and, 134
Poets: Harrison's *The Trackers* and, 111; language and, 133
Police actions, 84
Political abuse, of the "other," 109
Political commentary, 15-16, 29
Political suppression, Japan and, 66
Politicians: creating public opinion, 84; "truth" and, 80
Politics, women in, 146
Politikon zoon (political animal), 87
Polyphemus, 155
Polyxena, 35-36, 37
Poor, repression of, 197
Poseidon, 40
Postmodern audience, conscience of, 73
Postmodernism, 6, 148
Potential, innate, 5
Power, 202; abuse of, 14, 15-16, 105; democratic sharing of, 132; military's abuse of, 15-16; nonverbal, 69; progress harnessed to pursuit of, 62; sacrifices for, 172; satyrs' protest against abuses of, 105; words as, 16
Praise, Greeks and, 195
Presence, absence versus, 61

Priam, King of Troy, 35, 46
Priests: furies and, 179, 180; overcoming, 182; sins and, 197; *see also* Catholic Church
Prisoners, satyrs and, 101
Prisons, U.S. budget for, 90
Production, misuse of means of, 150, 151
Productions: failure of, 12-13; settings for, 16
Prometheus, 139-40, 194, 195
Prometheus Bound (Aeschylus), 60
Pronko, Leonard, 69
Protagonists, emotional commentary and, 8
Public passivity, 92
Pyrrha, 194

Quartett (Terzopoulos), 164, 165, 166, 168
Questioning, 13

Race, of actors, to express conflict, 16
Racial lines, division of roles along, 65-66
Racism: Japan and, 67; rape of Athena and, 77
Ran, 24
Rashomon, 70
Rationality, unconscious as weapon to destroy, 18
Reagan, Ronald, 89-90
Reality: play as mirror of, 17; versions of, 141
Reason, 12, 185
Refinement, culture and, 131-33
Regime, expressing discontent with, 9
Relatives, duty-bound, 47
Religion: controlling oppressed people and, 179; evangelical, 198; guilt and, 183, 193, 197; instinct for, 197; peace and, 183; personal, 187; state government versus, 66; *see also* Catholic Church; Priests
Religious settings, 16
Repressive force, 63
Revenge: ghosts in Noh drama and, 15; Suzuki's *Clytemnestra* and, 51; women and, 149-50
Reynolds, Roger, 60
Rhythm, Harrison's *The Trackers* and, 104

(continued from front flap)

Sophocles' *Ichneutae*) and with Murphy about *Sanctuary Lamp* (based on the *Oresteia*). Brief talks given by Sellars in response to McDonald's remarks about his production of *Ajax*, and a talk by the Greek director Theodoros Terzopoulos about his production of Müller's *Medeamaterial* are also included.

MARIANNE MCDONALD teaches in the Department of Theatre at the University of California, San Diego. Her books include, *Euripides in Cinema: The Heart Made Visible* and *Terms for Happiness in Euripides*. A forthcoming book will address Ancient Greek drama as opera.

STOMP! WHOMP!

YOWL! GROWL!

WHAM! SMASH!

STOMP! WHOMP!

Copyright © 2020 by Vince Cleghorne.
All rights reserved. Published in the United States
By Puppy Dogs & Ice Cream, Inc.

ISBN: 978-1-953177-64-3
Edition: October 2020

For all inquiries, please contact us at:
info@puppysmiles.org

To see more of our books, visit us at:
www.PuppyDogsAndIceCream.com

For the Children and Staff of
Christ Church Primary School.

One day while Owl was taking a nap....

HOO'S THERE?

Is it loud claps of thunder?
A backfiring car gone kaput?
A wind goblin blowing with gusto
The door that I left open shut?

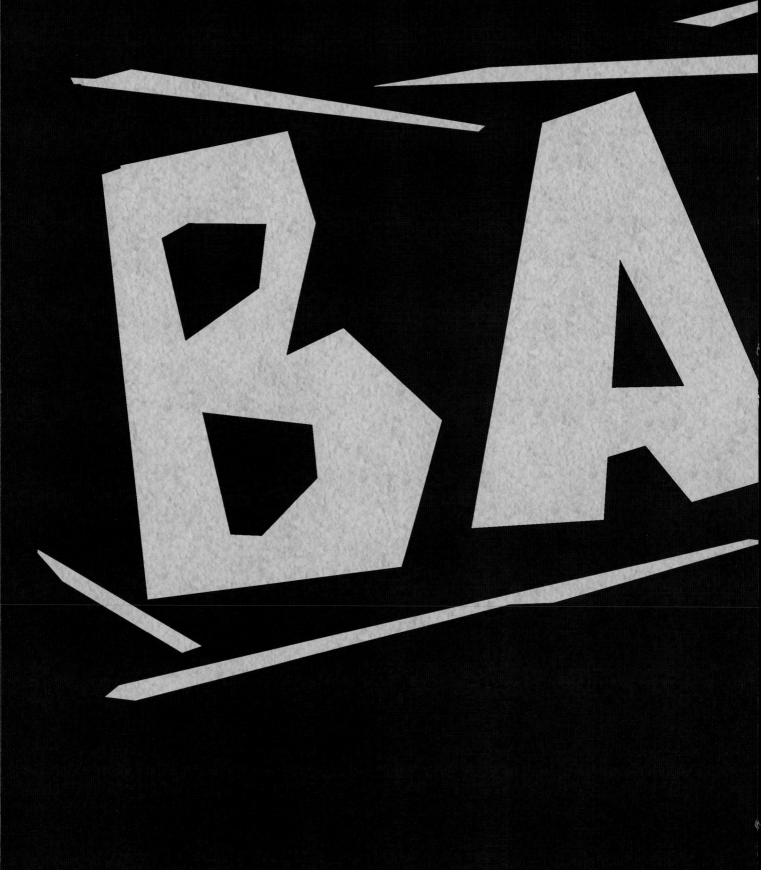

HOO'S THERE?
Are ghost carolers calling
Who failed to call last Christmas time?
Or noisy rock witches ascending
A wall that they've chosen to climb?

HOO'S THERE?
Could it be nasty ogres,
A troll, or a scary bog beast?
A bug creature from a dark forest
Who fancies a juicy owl feast?

But then...

SMA

HOO'S THERE?

Are there zombie street dancers
All turning their music up high?
Or bags of earwax being tossed from
An air balloon high in the sky?

HOO'S THERE?

Are there fiends with pick axes
All digging up ghouls from a bog?
Or clamorous croaks coming out of
The mouth of the world's biggest frog?

CRA

HOO'S THERE?
Are there bones being crunched on
By teeth that are massive and sharp?
Or claws hacking through wooden floorboards
From under a slimy brown tarp?

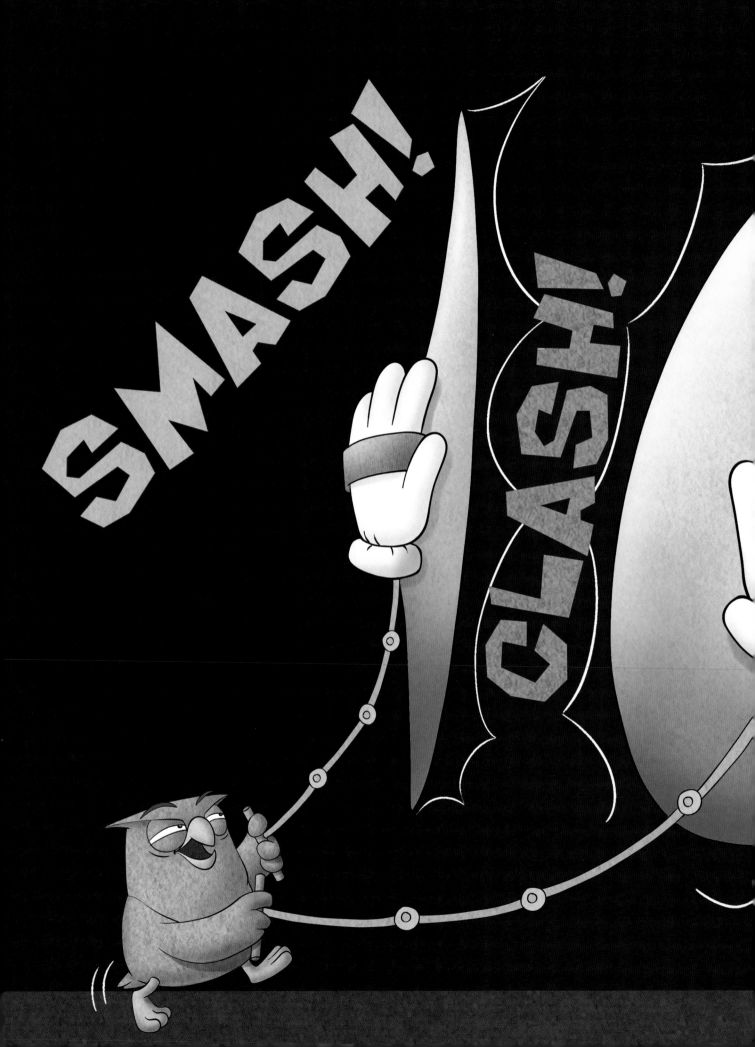

But then...

HOO'S THERE?

Are two boogeymen neighbours
Both prodding the ceiling with poles?
Or maybe a massive mole creature
Is filling the garden with holes?

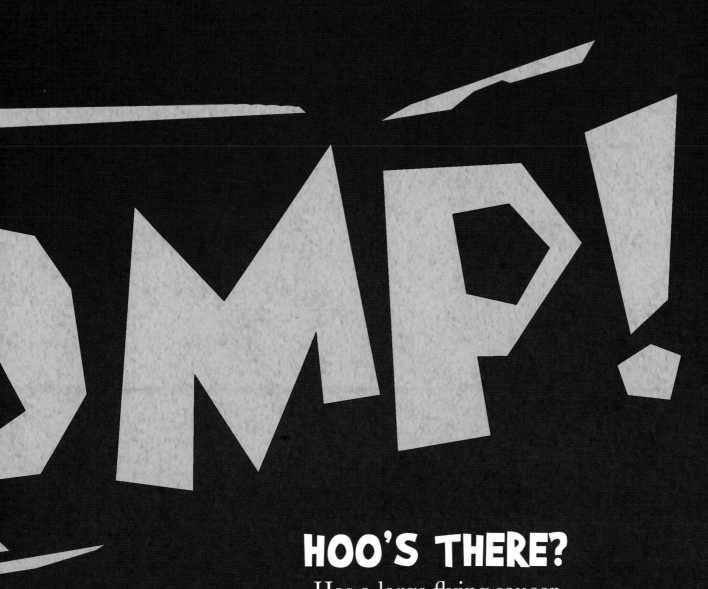

HOO'S THERE?
Has a large flying saucer
Just crash-landed onto my shed,
Ejecting an angry space mutant
Who's now creeping under my bed?

HOO'S THERE?

While you lurk in the shadows,
Creating a terrible din,
We really have only one question:
"Just how did you ever get in?"

Sometime later...

Howl as much as you want to,
We're not going to play anymore.
The game was at first very scary,
But now it's becoming a bore!

Sometime much later...

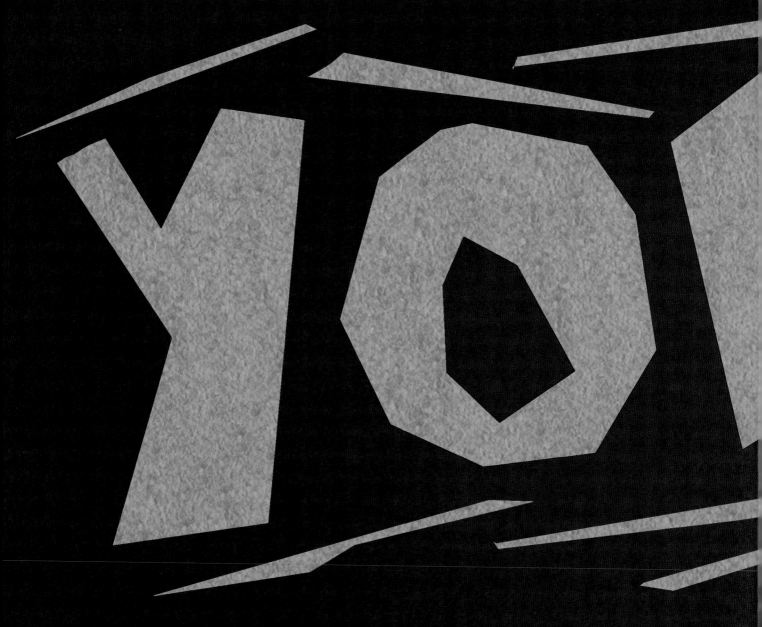

Really it's quite annoying,
You Yowling in that silly way.
We told you it's no longer scary;
We've found a brand new game to play...

"SNAP!"

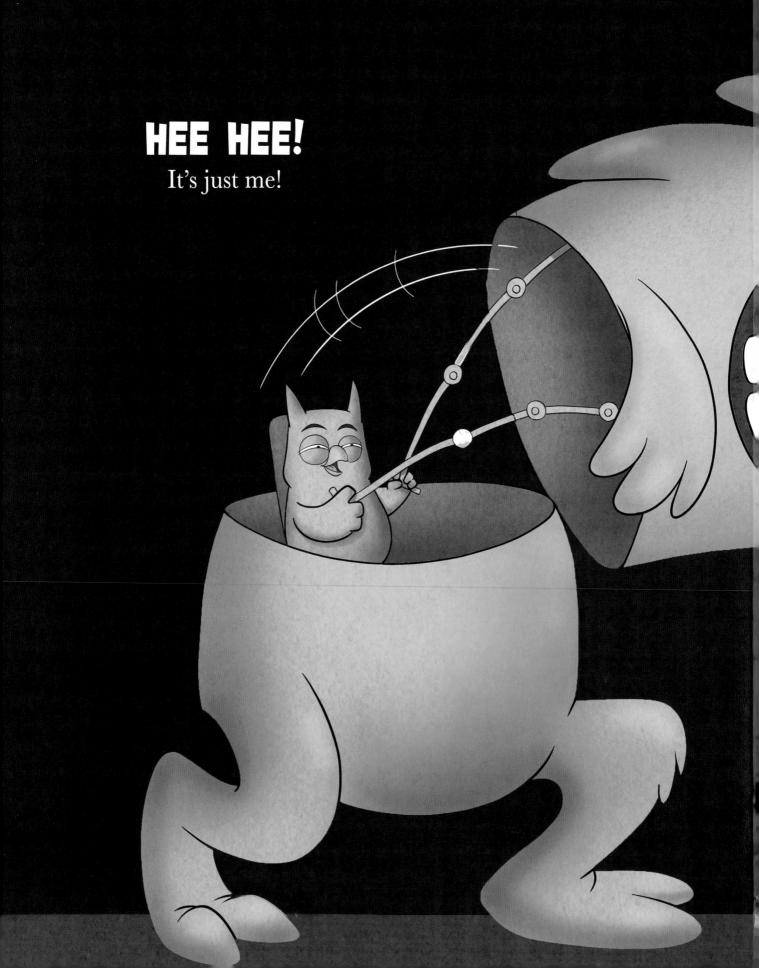

HEE HEE!

It's just me!

Claim Your FREE Gift!

Visit ➡ PDICBooks.Com/Gift

Thank you for Purchasing, Hoo's There?
and Welcome to the PUPPY Dogs & ICe Cream family.

We're Certain you're going to love the little gift we've
Prepared for you at the WeBsite aBove.

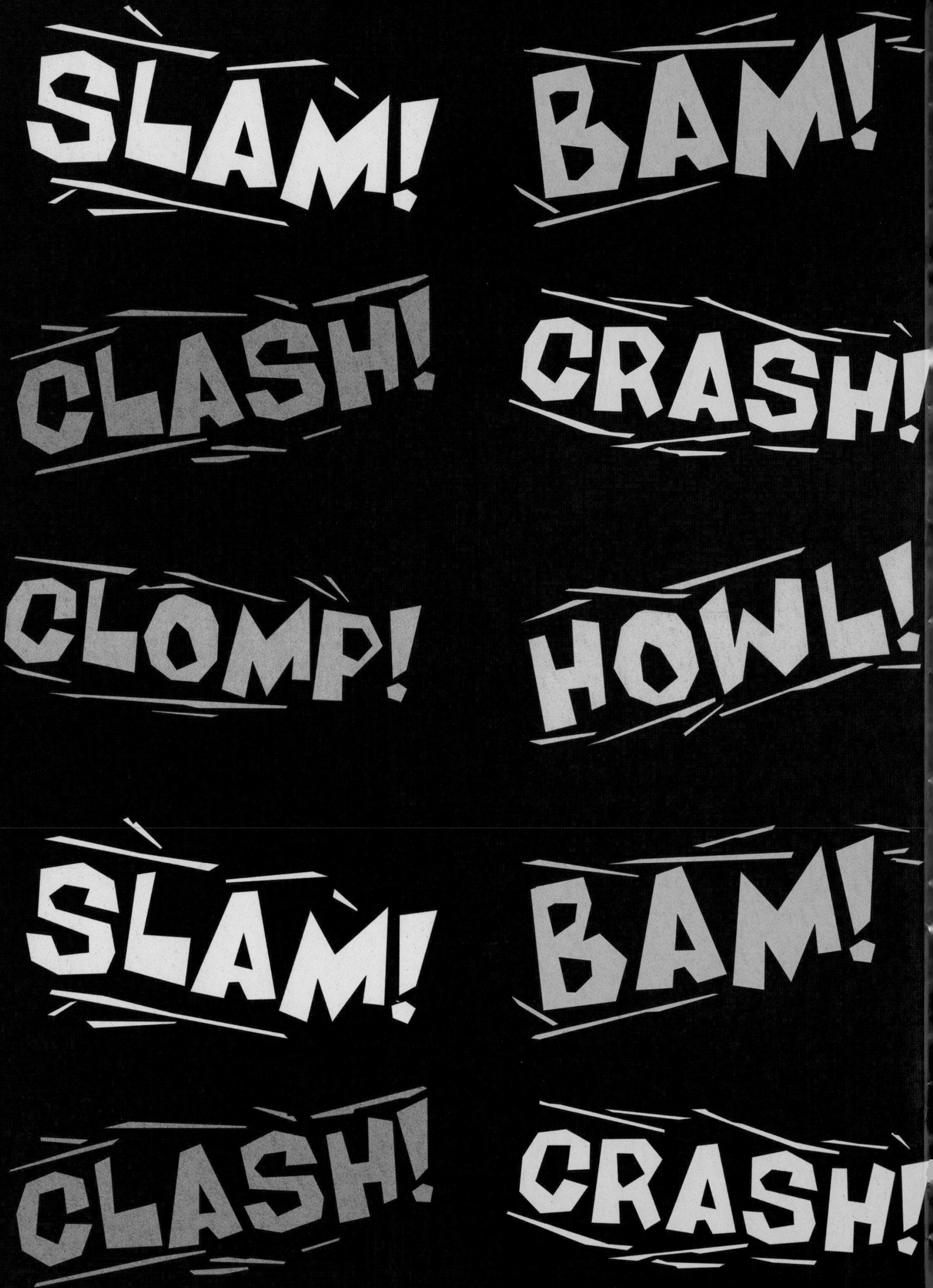
SLAM!
BAM!
CLASH!
CRASH!
CLOMP!
HOWL!
SLAM!
BAM!
CLASH!
CRASH!